Share the Fire
Parables for Sunday Scriptures

Francis Patrick Sullivan

Sheed & Ward

All Bible passages are from *The Jerusalem Bible* or *The Grail Psalter*.

Sheed & Ward™ is a service of National Catholic Reporter Publishing Company, Inc.

Library of Congress Catalogue Card Number: 89-61222

ISBN: 1-55612-305-1

Published by: Sheed & Ward
115 E. Armour Blvd. P.O. Box 419492
Kansas City, MO 64141-6492

To order, call: (800) 333-7373

For Margaret
Who Listened

Contents

Ordinary Time

Legions

*For love of my brethren and friends
I say: "Peace upon you!" For love of the
house of the Lord I will ask for your good.*
—Psalm 122:8-9

A young man was talking to an old man. They were on a bench on a small hill overlooking the bend of a river. Not much of a river, thirty yards, forty yards wide, but flowing through flats between hills, making an L-shaped turn below the men, then passing under a nice concrete bridge to go on through further flats for many miles. There was a nursing home behind them, a hospital behind that, and in the hospital the Doctor's office where the young man had just heard he had some cancer, how much, not certain. Tests would tell. He had walked to the lookout over the river to let some weeping go on inside him. The weeping fooled him for a while, he thought it was self-pity. But then he spotted it was the same feeling he used for other people when they were in danger. So he let it lick him. Like a cat, he thought. He favored cats. He saw two beautiful Angoras in harness one day. And a couple with them. Near the exercise logs on a running trail. He had been jogging, but stopped for the cats and to say how beautiful they were. The couple was surprised and pleased.

The old man had been clipping his nails when the young man came to the lookout point over the river. His clipping stopped after a few minutes. He said, "Come sit," to the young man. Who was surprised that an old man would speak to anybody. So the young man went over and sat.

"This sure is pretty when you first see it," the old man said. "But then it gets dull until you live its rhythm and not your own. Then it gets pretty again. So what have you got?" "Cancer," the young man said, "some. Don't know how much." "It's not your fault," the old man said. And he put his hand on the young man's thigh and stroked it a minute. "My wife

1

thought it was her fault, she said to me she was sorry, and I nearly choked trying to tell her no. But she thought I'd feel better after. She just couldn't hear me on some things. More than fifty years."

"So, she was old too," the young man said.

"Yes," the old man said. "And it was time. But it's not time for you." And he started to weep. His hand was stroking the young man's shoulder now, as one would stroke an athlete. "Well, it's not your fault either," said the young man. "And it's too soon to panic. I feel awfully good physically." The old man had forgotten his handkerchief. So the young man reached him his. "It's clean," he said.

"Thanks," the old man said. "I sit here and watch the sun. But funny, when it gets down in those trees and near that hilltop, I go in. I know why. But I also like to watch birds fly up into it or across it. I only see a blur for a bird. And I like to watch the beavers when they swim across the water down there, the long V they leave. And some days late, twenty or so Canada geese will land. It's a thrashing and splashing, then they're home as if they never flew. And I know why I watch them."

"You like life to work right," the young man said. "And you don't want to go out before it's time."

"You ever see a baby born?" the old man said.

"Yes," said the young man. "Out in the villages. The firefights would scare some of the women. I saw a baby born off the end of my rifle sights. I had a dead aim on the woman. I thought she was a tunnel in the bushes with a gun port, I'm not kidding. Then this baby comes out in a kind of rush and she grabs it and starts to push herself on her back away from us. I never saw her face."

"So you got your cancer there," the old man said. "I read about it."

"Yes," the young man said. "But I remember how that woman worked. I couldn't shoot anything for days. Then I couldn't shoot anything. So they sent me home before I caused any trouble."

"Well, I watch the sun come up," the old man said. "Everybody's usually still snoring away. It's like my babies. I saw them, though I wasn't supposed to in those days. So she's the river here for me. And she's the trees.

And she lands twenty or thirty at a time. And I shouldn't be here anymore. You should."

"O, old man, I should be dead twenty or thirty times myself," the young man said. "I guess life happens in a minute. Or doesn't in a hundred years."

"But when someone goes," the old man said, "they really pull you after them."

"I can see," the young man said. And he put his hand on the old man's thigh. There was very little there. Some knots of flesh that felt strangely familiar. "You've been shot too," the young man said.

"Yes," the old man said. "In the everlasting war. Are you ready to go?"

"No," the young man said. "I haven't anybody over there to pull me yet."

"Maybe all of this is over there," the old man said. "Anyway, I feel like pulling it after me. Except I want someone else to love it."

"I have to go, old man," the young man said. "Thanks."

"I just bent you some more, I'm afraid," the old man said.

"The sun's gone," the young man said. "You stayed. Want me to walk you back?"

"No," the old man said. "I didn't notice. I'll stay some more. Watch things land while I can. I've been neglecting them. I hope you are all right."

"I am not afraid of it," the young man said. "So don't you be. Good night."

"Good night," the old man said.

The Spoils

The wolf lives with the lamb,
the panther lies down with the kid,
calf and lion cub feed together...
   —Isaiah 11:6

A stewardess was checking seats for clutter during a stop-over. Some people had stayed on, some had deplaned and left "Occupied" cards, a lot had left newspapers every which way. She had to stoop to get some. That's how she noticed a white bundle under a window seat. It was a baby. Wrapped tight. Only its face showed. It's eyes were open but dullened and passive. As if it were drugged. The stewardess got down on her knees, crawled in and pulled the bundle from under. Then she raised it and sat herself back in a seat and looked at this creature whose glazed eyes saw nothing. "Weighs a ton," she thought to herself in amazement. Then she froze. "The baby's a bomb," she thought. The horror of it, the pity of it, struck her like a fist. "It's drugged to keep it quiet. And it's the way they got the bomb on board. And if I move it . . ." She had already moved it and nothing had gone off.

The back ramp of the plane was near. So she raised her voice, "I want everyone out of this cabin by the front door!" No one moved, but the few people looked up. "Move out of this cabin if you want to stay alive," she shouted. "Tell the Captain." People did move, they sensed a panic in her voice even though they didn't know what about. The Captain came down the aisle part way toward her but she shouted, "Stop! This baby is a bomb. I don't know how or why. Clear the plane. I'm going to walk it down the back ramp and out onto the taxiway as far as I can go. When you clear the plane, lower the ramp and get the fire trucks."

"Just put it down," the Captain said, "and slide free. We'll have people come in."

"No, no," she said. "There's a clock. I'm going to get up, go down the ramp and as far out as I can. Right now."

The Captain returned quickly to the cockpit, cleared it, got on to the tower and gave the info while watching back through the door as the stewardess stood up slowly and walked the few yards to the back ramp. The Captain hit the button and the ramp lowered.

The stewardess freed one hand from holding the baby, opened the bulkhead, and walked down the steps. She was wearing flats so she was steady. And she was holding the baby into herself so its forehead was against her cheek and she could feel it had a fever. It seemed to be trying to burrow into her. She walked quickly away from the plane toward the grass between the taxiway and the runway.

Meantime the alarm had been given. She could hear the crazed hootings of the fire trucks and the sirens of the police cars which started to clear the space around her. It was like cowboys driving cattle. The wind was chilly and cut through her uniform so her flesh quivered from more than fear. She could now sense the clock through the baby's wrappings. And she could feel the plastic explosives. "My God," she thought, "we'll be specks!" She was almost running, without joggling anything. And airport security kept making a huge circle of emptiness around her.

And a megaphone voice said, "Keep going, keep going, see if you can get across the second runway. Everything's on hold."

She noticed an airplane abort its landing, hit the power and zoom up. There was grass under her feet, ground harder to stay balanced on. But she kept going. The baby began to whimper a bit as the cold air cut into its drugged numbness. She took a quick glance at it and saw it was looking at her and its mouth was moving for food. So she pressed its whole face against her own and could feel it start to suck. She was breathing hard now as she crossed runway one, but knew her body could keep this up for a long time. She crossed another grass divider then over runway two and headed toward the chain link fence several hundred yards away.

And all around her at very respectable distances were fire trucks and police and airport cars and the one megaphone in command that said, "Okay, okay, now stop. Put the baby down. And come out of there as quick as you can."

The baby was wet on her cheek. And beginning to struggle inside the bundle of plastic explosive. The stewardess felt herself almost locked to the baby. The two stood in the center of a frenzy of lights and sounds and the megaphone voice saying as if to a crook, "Put the baby down. Come out of there as quick as you can. We will defuse the bomb." But something didn't sound right to her. So she made a decision. She freed a hand and waved in whoever it was would come. And despite the megaphone she kept waving someone in. Finally a man left an armored vehicle and jogged in towards her. He was padded head to foot and had a tool kit.

When he reached her, he said, "Now place the baby on the ground and leave. God only knows if this is an amateur device."

"No," the stewardess said. "We unwrap this and I take the baby."

"I get paid to get killed," the man said. "You don't. So let's not argue. Down with that baby. And let me see. And you go as fast as you can."

The stewardess lowered the baby to the ground. She knelt down to do it. The bomb expert had moved behind her in case the bomb went off. A move she understood. She would stop some of the blast from hitting him. So then she stood up and started away. He moved in and she moved behind him into the same protected stance he had used. And did not move any further. "This is as far as I go," she said. "You work."

"It's dumb, lady," the man said.

"Work," she said, "or I will."

He could feel the passion in her voice. He turned and scrutinized the bundle. Then he slid a zipper open, very slowly but very surely. And there were the plastic packages in against the body of the baby. With plugs in them connected to the clock. Which was tucked between the baby's legs and covered with waste from the baby who must have let go sometime between the plane and the fence. But the man could see what kind of device it was. And now he looked for tricks. He saw the trick and made a jump back, grabbed the stewardess and started to run. It was a temperature change trigger he had spotted. Some yards out he pulled her to the ground. But nothing happened. So the trick didn't work. He crawled then toward the baby and the stewardess crawled right behind him. He reached in and started to undo the clock. Because he saw that the baby's waste had jammed the mechanism, kept the contacts from being made. He removed the clock. Unplugged the plastic bags, laid the bared baby on the grass, made another quick check for any other possibilities. The stewardess was out of her jacket in a second and had it around the baby who was now shivering and beginning to cry. The drugs were wearing off and the baby was slightly convulsive as it fixed its eyes on her. She ran with it then toward the rim of the circle, toward the ambulance whose lights were spinnning. Medics ran in toward her. They picked her up with the baby and ran her into the safe zone. The explosives truck drove in to where the defusing had taken place and the plastic was put in the steel safe on the back of it and driven off in a convoy of lights and wild sounds. The bomb expert walked to the ambulance and looked in at the stewardess. The baby had been treated and was now wrapped in non-lethal clothing.

"You okay?" he asked.

"No," she said.

Then he said further, "I've never seen something like this. You should have left when I told you."

"No," she said. "You would have blown that baby up if I let you."

He said nothing. He climbed into the ambulance and looked at the baby in the basket where they had put it. The ambulance was ready to go and he was holding it back. He was still in his protective gear.

"Shit," he said, "saved by shit."

Factual Account

*The spirit of the Lord has been
given to me. He has sent me to
bring good news to the poor.*
—Isaiah 61:1

There was a woman who filled her retirement writing letters to people about issues. She had mastered many styles so she could seem more expert than she was. But she was expert in several things. She had been a nutritionist all her life when that expertise was not too well respected. She had never married. Most of the men she knew were red meat, potatoes, scotch and water men. Not that she was a fanatic. She could sit at banquets and talk about baseball with the best of them. She was fanatic about baseball. About athletics. That's how she had gotten to plan training tables. For small colleges first, then big ones, then pros, though not for baseball players, football, food to go with the red meat. She had studied homeopathy, even gotten into the study of primitive cures, those done by shamans and witch doctors. And that had gotten her into music and music therapy. And into ecology. There were some exhilarating days when she had worn a face mask on city streets to protest smog. Or a rubber rat onto buses, a rat she could make run up and down her arm. But she always wore a protest headband when she carried the rat. It said: "THIS rat is a fake. Not THAT one." She had to turn in circles so people could read the whole sign.

Well, it came time to retire. She was civil service the last twenty years, in charge of a VA hospital cafeteria. She had fed presidents and heroes and secretaries and the driftwood, years later, of foreign wars. Now she was writing letters. In every style she had learned. To the President first.

"Dear Mr. President. Do you know that American toilet paper is contaminated by nuclear radiation? Several factories that make it and several

8

forest areas are near nuclear power plants or nuclear waste dumps. Do you realize the havoc irradiated bowels could work on American life? Pretty soon everyone will be wearing bags. Sincerely." And she signed her name with an official flourish.

Then: "Dear Mr. Secretary. Do you realize that Asian fruit fly eggs come into the country on chinese silks, T-shirts, pajamas, slips, etc. When they are washed, the eggs are fed with an ingredient in ordinary detergent, instead of being killed. They multiply in treatment plants and are then let into the watersheds. When they surface, they become flies, head for the orchards and begin their damage. In a few years we will have no fruit. Sincerely." And she signed her name with a shaky hand, a lab hand. She saw the consequences of everything. It was the result of all her reading over the years.

One day she got a letter back from a Secretary. It said: "Madame. You're nuts. Nature doesn't work logically. It loves poisons. Which is what human beings are. And some pens. So read novels, not journals. And write pen-pal letters. You will be happier. Sincerely." It was a big Secretary who signed it.

Then she got one back from the President. It said: "Dear Madame. Our paper money is not made from the fiber of the marijuana plant. So people who rub or kiss money do not become addicted to money for that reason. And when old money is burned, the air around the plant is not hallucinogenic. There are economic causes for the social unrest in those areas. It would be better if you studied those economic causes. Sincerely." And it looked as if he actually signed it.

But such letters only increased her mania. She saw the condom ads on TV leading to forms of them like body stockings so no human flesh ever came in contact with human flesh. She saw special breast ones for nursing mothers. She saw ones for cold weather joggers to keep men from frost bite. She saw hand ones, head ones, then just lip ones for kissing, like the mouthpieces ballplayers have attached to their helmets. All communicable diseases would stop for sure, but there might be a failure in bodies to build up immunities to other bodies. She saw bras as directly related to breast cancer and panty hose to infertility in women and impotency in the stevedores in the Northeast ports who wore them on bitter winter days.

She wrote and wrote about these things. Most of her social security check went to pay for stationery and stamps.

One day she got a letter back. It was from her congresswoman. It said: "Dear Madame. Can't you do something better with your imagination? There is electricity in our bodies. If we cancel electric power we will die. Whale oil goes only so far. And wood and steam are limited quantities. And there are many windless and sunless days in our district. Why don't you write fiction? Your style is gripping. Then people seated by their electric lamps can imagine what a pollution free world would be like. You would be fooling them, but doing them a favor at the same time. That's politics. And why I'm in Congress. Sincerely."

So the woman wrote a fiction. She thought she could control it to make the points her letters had made. But nothing of the kind. It began with someone going into a bathroom in a hotel and seeing the toilet paper roll glowing like a radium treated dial on a watch. But the glow was in patterns. And the patterns were words. Foreign words. Then the phone rang in the room and it was the desk saying she had been given the wrong one and would she please not touch anything until the bellhop came to take her to the right one. She had discovered a secret drop, her heroine, so she replaced the glowing roll with another, quickly wrapped the first around her waist like a cummerbund, put on her coat and waited for the bellhop. He appeared with two foreign gentlemen at the door who sort of blocked her exit while one sped to the bathroom to look, found the glowing roll not there, returned, gave a signal to the other. The other found an excuse to get the bellhop into the bathroom while the first man pulled open the woman's coat, not knowing where to look on her. He saw the toilet paper, pushed her against the wall, took a knife and cut the roll as you cut a rubber band, put both into the deep pocket of his trench coat, and said, "No one will believe you, so go!" The bellhop came out and took the woman to her correct room. There she noticed some burns on her silk dress. The message from the roll was burned into the chinese silk. Heavily burned into the delicate fabric. In fact as she got out of her dress she noticed further burns on her skin. She called the FBI. They came and between the burns on the dress and burns on the skin discovered that a crucial American secret, fusion fission, was being communicated in a foreign tongue to a foreign power. The message was to have been copied and then flushed. The sewage treatment plants would have diffused the radiation. The message was made by a radiation gun that was the result of the secret process and was proof to the foreigners that the process existed. The FBI caught the spies and the secret. The woman then found she was to die from too much radiation. But someone at the VA hospital discovered a special diet that would keep the cancer at bay. It was a rare moss that only grew on old limestone buildings in big cities. The moss was caused by a reaction between the stone and smog. The end.

The woman was intensely happy when she finished. She sold the story soon, after she had spiced it with more gory details and some soft sex at the suggestion of the editors. And she got letters from her readers telling her how bold and courageous her heroine had been and the nutritionist who found the diet to stave off death. Life was so different for them now. Life could win. Her congresswoman wrote: "Loved the story. Made the time fly between here and the west coast. Gave the best talk I ever gave." The Secretary wrote: "From now on I will require that you check elements in your story with the Defense Department. You have come close to revealing classified material. You are to say nothing more on the subject and you are to destroy this letter. Sincerely." And then she received a letter from the President. "Dear Madame. I have wanted someone for a long time to represent realism on the National Council for the Arts. People live with visions of disaster too readily. Your healthy outlook would be a fine addition to the Council. I hereby request that you serve on it. Sincerely."

So she answered: "Dear Mr. President. I accept. It has taken me a long time to know what works in life and what does not. I will do my best to support what works. Sincerely." And she signed her name with a writer's hand.

Other Shoes

Who shall climb the mountain of the
Lord? Who shall stand in his holy
place? The man with clean hands and
pure heart, who desires not worth-
less things.

—Psalm 24:3-4

A man got off a subway train in New York downtown onto a platform crowded with comers and goers and he nearly stepped on a small boy who had the first looks of panic on his face. So the man stopped, forcing people to go around him as he looked down at the boy. He then looked up, over the heads of people, to see if someone was working back against the crowd with the same look of panic. No one. People were either aboard the train or flowing away from it. "I can't touch this kid," the man thought. "I'll scare him more." So he stood a few feet away hoping the boy's panic wouldn't ruin him for life and a man or woman would show. "But that has to happen in a minute or something's wrong." And something was. So the man sat down where the boy could see him at eye-level and gradually focus on someone he could move toward. Which he did even as his head kept swiveling and looking. His tears were very quiet, even his panic, as if he had been through it before. The boy came up to the man and put two small hands on the man's shoulders not thinking at all of what he was doing. "So the anchoring works," the man thought. There were people coming on the platform every minute and it was filling up. Another train came roaring in, emptied and filled, passing around the man and boy like water around a rock. By now the boy was glued to his shoulder, still not looking at him but around, around.

"She'll come," he said to the boy, just loud enough so he heard. "She'll come." He'd guessed by now that the boy had been swept out of one of the cars by a crowd and mother had been carried to the next station. She'd have to race up the stairs, over, catch a return train, race up more stairs, over, and would show any minute above the turnstiles like a steeplechaser. And there she was. She went over the turnstile dress and all, no shoes, didn't give a damn about concrete and broken arches. And the boy saw this fantastic leap and heard her flesh hit with a splat and her unbroken gallop as she spotted him at the shoulder of the man and came sliding into him on her knees. The man never saw panic disappear so fast from a human being as it did from that boy. There was a look of absolute belief that took its place. And the mother just held him. Another train came in, unloaded, loaded, looked at the three without a blink and left.

"Hey Lady, you left this stuff," said a voice. It was a man and a woman holding several shopping bags. They were older people. "We figured you lost the kid. So we brought this behind you."

"I had too much," the woman said. She could hardly talk yet, her chest was still heaving. She had the fierce look still of someone who would have gone through a wall to get to the boy. "You an athlete?" the man on the ground asked. "You came over that stile like a deer." The woman still couldn't talk. And she wasn't stifling the boy, just holding him, and he was back to himself and registering things around him including the man he had just anchored onto.

"You haven't got any shoes," the man continued. "I could go look for them." She shook her head no. The older couple had gone. Another train came, unloaded, washed around them, loaded, left.

"We look like a Christmas crib," the man said. "They'll be tossing us money soon. Come on athlete, I'll take you home. Look like a guy that beats his wife. Pregnant in summer. Barefoot in winter."

"I've some new shoes in the bag," she said.

"I have too," the boy said.

"Let me hold him," the man said. "Dig out the shoes." So she did, beautiful black pumps. She put them on and the three got up. She took the boy back.

"You going to leave the bags?" the man asked.

"Yes," she said. "They're a shame to me." There was some more panic on the boy's face as he started to bend toward the bags from his mother's arms.

"I'll take them behind you," the man said. "No one'll know."

"Okay," the woman said, "but I'm ashamed to look at you too."

"Ah," the man said, "it didn't take me a minute to figure out what happened. I really thought you'd come racing along that third rail, frig the current. You *are* an athlete, aren't you?"

"Yes," she said. "Marathon. I get into myself and forget some things don't take care of themselves. Men too. This one's father just walked out. Needed someone else. I was just buying stuff to distract us. It sure did. He was gone too before I knew it."

"Talk about being trapped," the man said. She just shuddered. So did the train coming into the station.

"Let's go one stop and find your shoes," the man said. "My bet is you kicked them and they're against the wall." So they got on, went a stop, got off, and there were the high heels, one under a bench, the other in a corner near the revolving grate. "Okay," said the man after he picked them up. "Everything back right."

"Just a man missing," the woman said.

"Won't be for long," the man said. "You have a magnificent form. Anybody'd love it. Though right now you look like you ran through a shredder." She looked at her legs and knees and so did the boy.

"You make me less cynical," she said. "I need to be less cynical. One man isn't everything." They got on the train, the woman with the boy, the man with the bags. It was crowded. They were pressed together.

"One man is everything," she said. "More when he's gone."

"You're sure?" the man asked."

"Yes," she said. "I'm not it for him. Never mind the magnificent form. Listen, thanks. We get off here and it's just up a block."

"Lead," the man said. She did, carrying the boy, up a block to a townhouse condominium, up the stairs to the second, and into two rooms with kitchen and bath. Her sweat stuff was hanging on a door and there were photos of her starting and finishing marathons. Not boasts but good runs.

"Really, great form," the man said. "You were full out even at the end here. How many miles?"

"That's twenty six," she said. "I was third. Best I've done." She was still holding the boy. As she had been since the station. He wanted down but she didn't.

"Please let him," the man said. "And get some antiseptic on those scrapes."

"You sound like a coach," she said. "Are you?"

"No, far from it," he said. "I'm a nurse. Work seven to three. Emergency room."

"You're like a priest," she said, "except you're free. Would you just wait a while until we're not shaking any more? I'll feed you unless you've got someone."

"No someone," he said. "But not frozen stuff. My stomach's my wife. Love her or leave her she says." Then he stopped. "Funny how words come out. I never say that."

"Well, you have to love a woman or you have to leave her," the woman said. "Man too now, I guess. How about a crockpot stew? It's been on."

"You got used to that man, didn't you?" he said. "And you nearly lost two today. And there's no substitute, is there?"

"No," she said. "And no make-believe. But I want to feed you before you go. It's so I can do something. You were just right."

"Okay, you clean up," he said, "I play with boy, you serve stew, I go, you win next marathon. World returns to normal."

"Damn, the stew is dried," she said.

"Okay," he said, "I go get pizza. Chef's caprice. Come back. World returns to normal."

"Let me do some eggs," she said. "Breaking them will be normal."

"You came over that stile like a deer," he said. "You have to know that."

Just a Touch

You shall no more be termed Forsaken,
and your land shall no more be termed
Desolate.
—Isaiah 62:4

A man was flying home from Europe the day before Christmas. Rome to Brussels to Boston. There was an elderly woman beside him. He had the window seat, on the left side of the aircraft, so he could see the south of Ireland, Dingle Peninsula, Ring of Kerry, a while after they had left the Continent and crossed England. He knew the old Irish from down below, in Boston, where they had come to visit up and down the street on Christmas Eve. They were long dead, they and their rote phrases about 'balls of whiskey,' and 'little sups,' and 'just a touch.' They had glows on by midnight Mass, though he as a kid was asleep by then. Mostly he caught their voices through the bedroom door, a life that was not his. What he saw later was the waste, the almost brute life they, many of them, let themselves lead. So their wakes were like old stock certificates from failed companies, beautiful engravings, sad stories. "Ah, I'm the sad one," he thought, "seasonal depression." His wife would meet him. She had one of those born smiles. It came with the face. Like the angels on the Rheims Cathedral. It was still hard for him to tell when she was angry.

The woman beside him had been taking metal shards out of a large cloth handbag. Looked like shrapnel. Twisted every which way. She would run her fingers over them slowly, hold them in one hand only, some were sharp still, but they were old and rust and earth had worked on them. Ireland was behind them, the sea was ahead, five hours of it. The woman laid each one on the food tray, there were seven, though she seemed to have more in the bag. She began to turn each as if to see what was their best face. She noticed him looking.

"These are from Bastogne in Belgium," she said, "the battle there forty years ago this Christmas."

"I'm hooked," he said, "even before you told me. Remarkable shapes!"

"Yes," she said, "took me months to choose these."

"For what?" he asked.

"For headstones," she said. He was looking at her now, not at the shrapnel. She had hard hands, the metal was at home in them. Her whole body seemed like something wrought, not something old and fragile.

"My tongue is hanging out," he said. It was his way of asking everything and nothing.

"I'm a sculptor," she said. "My young husband was killed at Bastogne. I was in England at the time, Women's Army Corps. After the war, I found where he was buried, and wanted to put something I made on his grave. But Graves Registration wouldn't let me. Just rows of crosses and stars. I finally bought the field next to the dead, there were only a hundred. I'm going to make another graveyard. I will use these shapes. I have been collecting them from the farmers in the area. Shrapnel turns up all the time, in the soil, in the wood of trees."

"You mean you'll sculpt the metal into larger sizes?" he asked.

"I'll do the design," she answered. "I can't do the metal work anymore."

"So just stand them on the ground in rows?" he continued.

"Oh, no," she said. "The design will be like a still explosion, an empty center, then these shapes flying outwards from the center, and they will be large so you cannot see over them, you have to move through them, and they will seem to be flying. I will foot them that way."

"What about names?" he asked.

"They will be welded on to each shape at a spot visible to someone standing. They will be welded on like scars, a different metal from the shape they're on."

"Just random?" he asked.

"No," she said, "like a shellburst. And I've researched all the lives that were lost, except for a few no one could trace. I've matched these shapes to those lives. These are the last few."

"It should be fierce, that graveyard, not peaceful," he said.

She put her head back against the seat rest. "I want no one to think that death is a repose," she said, "crosses and stars are a repose. Every death is different. I want their deaths happening right now."

"And the center," he asked, "bare?"

"Well," she said, "did you ever see, in the circus, those men who stand on aluminum poles? If you haven't, they sway in great arcs but always come upright, the swaying is random, like a stalk in the wind. I have a shape, aluminum, it's seventy feet tall, bends nearly to the ground. A very thin male form, but its head will be weighted to be like the man on top of the pole and that will bend the man in those slow and random arcs over the metal fragments. Like the slow motion trajectory of bombs or shells. It will move with the wind."

"I'm just stunned," the man said. He reached over and picked up one of the fragments.

"That went through someone," she said, "so the farmer tells me, imbedded itself in a post in a barn. He dug it out for me when he knew my purpose."

"I was looking down at Ireland back a bit," he said, "and thinking how many I knew from there finished their lives aimlessly."

"Better that than this," she said as she pointed to the fragment in his hand.

"Who was he?" the man asked.

She knew what he was asking. "I hardly know anymore," she said, "he's become all the men he's buried with." She paused. Then continued, "You see, I think men are nature's tragedy. Ever since then. He hid his bad eyes, memorized the chart, so he could be a rifleman, so he could taste war, and then write of it afterwards. I'm still sick to think of it. So I have never sculpted a woman shape." She was turning the fragments in front of her. Then she looked at him. "My life is unexpressed," she said, "his is not."

Ids and Egos

O sing a new song to the Lord,
sing to the lord all the earth,
O sing to the Lord, bless his name.
—Psalm 95:1-2

"Birth is not so important," a woman said to her husband. It was Christmas Eve and they were watching TV, a German choir group singing Bach's *Christmas Oratorio*.

"She's going on me again," the man thought.

"Rebirth's the thing," the woman continued. They watched more. "Look at our children," she said, "three heathens and parents of heathens."

"Have they phoned?" the man asked.

"Yes and I told them," she answered, "while you were in the shower."

"So you didn't call me?" he asked further.

"They hung up, one, two, three," she said.

"Ah, conference call, surprise. Global hookup," he said.

"Yes," she said.

"I'll phone them separately," he said.

"Don't you want to know what I told them?" she asked. He motioned gently with his hand, wait! There was a lovely section of the Oratorio being sung. When it was over and some coughs and page rattlings were going on in the Baroque church where the music was being presented, he said, "You told them to be reborn."

"Yes," she said like escaping steam.

"And they just hung up, one, two, three," he said.

"No," she said, again like steam.

"They said something," he continued.

"Yes," she said. There was an orchestral interlude going on, the camera was on the hands of the flautist.

"What?" he asked.

"Pretty much the same," she answered, "you should take me to a shrink." He could hear the three voices and he could hear her calling them to repentance and spirit baptism. "And that thing of a daughter, she's the worst!" the woman continued. The man watched as the camera moved on to the recorders.

"What did she say this time?" he asked.

"She said go screw the spirit," the woman answered. "The spirit is a woman," she went on, "you see how ignorant they are!" The camera was on the organist now, on the three banks of keys and his effortless fingers.

"You scare them," he said at the end of the organ interlude, "they'd prefer you depressed."

"They think I'm still not right," she said, "I tell them I love God and they hear ids and egos and superegos and I hate to think what else."

"That's what they know," he said.

"It's not what they were taught," she said. She was beginning to melt. He recognised the melt. It was dangerous. "Belief is something else," he said, "you know that. You have to leave them be." She was slumped now in her chair. A counter-tenor was singing. The man let the melody finish. She was watching her husband, not the TV.

"You believe?" she asked.

"Yes, but not as you do," he said. "I think you've brought yourself back, not the Spirit." He could see some fear on her face, a fear he knew so well. "I think that's what the spirit loves." Her head twitched as if she were brushing something away.

"Why don't you believe in the Spirit?" she asked softly. "I love the Spirit," she said further. Her eyes wandered back to the TV screen. The narrator was singing and the words were marching across below him.

"I do," he said, "but you're not a flute in someone's hands. Not in mine. Not in anyone else's."

"You're hard," she said.

"Oh," he said and said nothing more. The narrator had stopped and a bass was singing, the camera was focused on his face.

"You just resist me," she said.

"I do," he said. Then after some more music, "I'm jealous, I've told you."

"I never understand when you do," she said.

"I don't want you owned by anybody but yourself," he said. "I cannot survive by myself," she said, "I've told you." "Yes," he said, "you're right. I am hard. I resist that."

"I go back in," she said, now looking at him, her face open and flushed. He just nodded, now looking at her, the sound of the choir coming through softly like a lullaby.

"I believe in that Spirit," he said, "when you tell me, I believe in that Spirit."

"I am sorry I am this," she said.

"Oh," he said again, then nothing more.

"When she is here with me, everything is visible. When I feel her going, things start to disappear. When I talked to them tonight, the phone began to disappear." There was some pain on the woman's face. She continued, "Then they began to disappear. And that's when I told them." He was listening now the way a drum listens and responds to the slightest tap.

"Only the Spirit can keep what you love?" he asked.

"Yes," she said.

"Where?" he asked.

"Alright," she said. There was defeat in her voice. "In me."

"Dear," he said, "don't you see the way the Spirit holds you?" She straightened a bit.

"You mean crazy, holds me even if I'm crazy?"

"Yes," he said.

"Well, you're sweet," she said. She had half a smile on. "And you're clever." He was grinning too. As after a brilliant move. But there were tears in his eyes. And she saw the love. "So I have to learn," she said. He shrugged. "Now you're being cute," she said. "After being brave, now you're being cute." He shrugged again like an expert. "I don't want them shattered," she said, "not this way."

"It's not in the nature, love," he said, "it's not in the nurture, it's in time. We have to trust that."

"So they could be," she said softly, to him, to the screen, because the camera was focused now on the infant Jesus in the crib, plaster on real straw. Then the camera panned upward to the Virgin, then faded to the crucifix over the altar, then back to the conductor who was moving the orchestra through some hushed passages. "They never show Joseph," she said. Then, "Call them for me, they'll be worried."

"You want to talk to them too?" he asked. She thought, and they both watched the camera pan upwards again from the altar to the crucifix then to the baroque dove above everything, bedded in rays of gold light, then down to the boys' section of the choir. "No," she said when the music ceased. "Tell them my mouth is full. I'm eating squab."

The Body Click

It was for no reason except his own
compassion that he saved us.
—Titus 3:5

There was a kid about twelve who loved the hours before dawn. He milked the cows with his father then. Wintertime was most powerful for him. He could hear his father stir so he got up, always knowing he didn't have to. His father enjoyed his company more than his help. Because he wasn't much help, he loved school, loved books, but loved to talk most of all, about new things, supernovas, the gestation of volcanos, genetic engineering. And his father loved to listen, could do two things at once. His father was a very happy man. The kid would often find him just looking, at land, at animals, at machinery, with kind of a glow in him, not of power, but of someone who was getting a gift. This morning was cold, and double dark. The stars looked broken and the moon numb. Near Christmas. The kid felt a thrill at the way nature lived with the cold. His own blood flowed faster, his own heat shrank inside him during the short walk to the barn. He didn't look down, just up to see everything, so he slipped several times, did crazy dances on the ice, felt a hand in his back keep him from pitching. His father knew him. It was the looking up that made him spot an object falling out of the sky, a glinting thing, a tumbling thing, not a shooting star, it went straight into the pine copse at the edge of the great field half a mile away, and the snaps it made alerted his father too who stopped to figure out the sound.

"Geez, Dad," the kid said, "I saw something fall in the pines. Like a plane wing." So they both did a three sixty scan of the sky, saw nothing, but heard a high jet-roar echo drifting down around them.

"The truck," his Dad said. And they both headed back to the house, into the shed beside it, started, backed, then shot down their own road toward the pine copse. They slowed near it, both looking in to see what had landed, but couldn't. So his Dad stopped and said, "Let's do some circles, you left, I'll go right. Keep turning until I meet you, then we'll narrow it." "Okay," the kid said as they got out. It wasn't long before he heard his father shout, "Boy!" a word his father rarely used and only for deep occasions. He headed for the shout and came on his father standing in the debris of some snapped off pine branches. There was a funnel in the trees over him, and what looked like an airplane door at his feet, and a bundle, a human bundle, on the door like a body on a stretcher.

"She's living," his father said. "Give me your coat, run for the truck, and drive it right in here if you can, or as close, never mind what happens to it." So the kid ran like an Indian, spotting the best terrain for the truck as he went. He jumped in, backed it, aimed between trees and ran it in crazy jounces through the brush and saplings until he got to the plane door, the woman and his Dad.

"We've got to pick this door up, put it in the truck, then back out slow and hope we don't break anything more. She'll freeze if we don't." So the two of them picked the door up either end with the limp body covered by their jackets on it and moved it around toward the tail of the truck.

"We better carry her out to the road," the kid said. "I bounced too much on the way in."

"Right, boy," his Dad said, "can you walk backwards and not fall."

"Yes," the boy said.

"When you have to, put it down," the father said. So they got the door and woman onto the road. "Now out with the truck," said the father. The kid ran back, gunned the truck rearwards through the path he had made and swung it around facing up the road to the house. The two got the door onto the truckbed. "Now go easy but sure," the father said. "I'll hold her." The womenfolk were awake when they came up, the kid's mother and two older sisters who were in high school and had to be ready for the bus. They were stunned by the thumping on the porch, and the kitchen door kicked backward as their father and brother tilted a chunk of airplane into the kitchen and there was a woman's body on it, her shredded clothes underneath the jackets knotted around the door release.

"She's alive still," the father said. The mother just shoved the kitchen table out of the way, then grabbed the phone off the hook, dialed the police and said what she saw in front of her and said send a helicopter not an ambulance. She then went onto her knees beside the plane door, pulled the jackets away and looked at the woman. The wind had practically stripped her. She was a stewardess. It was her apron that had caught on the door handle and held her to it. She was blown out with the door.

"My God! Were there others too? Boy," she said, she never said that, "take your sisters and go look, use the car for the girls, you take the motorcycle. I'll phone along the line. We have to keep this one warm. Now go." So the three headed out the door. The girls followed the road. The kid went out into the fields. He had a Harley-Davidson, an old one his father treated like an heirloom. The fields were hard and ridged from the frozen rows, but he paid no mind. He did broad s-turns for a couple of miles beyond the copse. The sky was beginning to lighten and the thin snow cover reflected it so he could see if anyone else was there and there was no one. Along the road, one of his sisters had climbed up on the roof of the car to see better as the other drove. They saw some lights coming across the fields the other way. Their mother had gotten the word out quickly. But nothing when they met. So they started back. As they did, the helicopter came along overhead and set down so when they arrived the medics were already inside. They saw their parents and two medics lift the woman slowly off the plane door and onto a stretcher without changing her position. They had put an oxygen mask on her so her face was hidden. But the kid could see an ever so slight movement below her rib cage, the miracle of breath still going on. Then they had blankets around her and belts lightly tied to keep her from moving. The crew then took the stretcher out through the door, into the helicopter, and they were off in a hard roar and swung away toward the county hospital ten miles off. Cold air filled the house. There was a rising sound of the cows in the barn lowing to be milked. There was a red rim on the horizon. The kid's father closed the kitchen.

"If you hadn't seen her she'd be gone," he said to his son.

"You heard her," the son said.

"I've never seen anything so miraculous," the mother said. There was no more said between them. The father put his arms around his son, from behind him and stood there. They were both cold from not wearing their jackets. The school bus honked at the end of the lane. The two girls panicked and ran for their things.

"I'll run you down," the father said when they came in a jumble of books and clothes back to the kitchen. "And I'll run you in after the milking," he said to his son. "May God keep her," he said. When he came back, the two did the milking. Then the kid got his books, his breakfast, and they drove.

"Dad," the kid said, "do you know what the odds are for that happening even once? They say the body clicks off when close to death like that. She may remember nothing. And those trees really took up the shock. But for the door to turn at exactly the right split second. It acted like a nose cone for re-entry. I wonder what she broke. But it's fantastic the way bones come back if set right. Though they can turn into knives. That's why you all were so careful. If it hadn't been clear I wouldn't have seen a thing. Her skin was so smooth. There wasn't a mark. Skin is wonderful the way it heals. You can make it work its own healing. God, what did she go through!" And he stopped with his voice choked.

"If you hadn't seen her, she'd be gone," the father said. "It's wonderful the way you see."

Next to Nothing

Indeed from his fullness we have,
all of us received—yes, grace in
return for grace.
        —John 1:16

There was an old Buddhist gentleman riding a bus home on Christmas Eve. He was from South India. His daughters were both doctors. They lived in downtown New York with their young families, near the hospitals where they worked. They had married Christians, so they were celebrating and he had gone to join their festivities and wish them blessings. He loved the simple life, life with people, so he rode buses to and from where he lived uptown in a single room near the Institute where he taught. He taught Buddhism, mainly to people who wanted information, rarely to those who wanted to live it. But everything led to the truth for him. Sooner or later all the forms of life had to give themselves up and look into the nothingness, those exciting, fascinating depths of nothingness where anything new could happen if it ever wanted. At one of the stops Santa Claus got on. The stores had just closed so the help were going home. It was late enough. He was an angry Santa, fully done up right to the beard and he was hugging himself as if he were freezing. He sat right in front of the old Buddhist, in the sideways seat, so the old man could see his profile. And he was angry indeed, this Santa.

"What's up?" said the old man in his Indian accent.

Santa looked quickly and saw sympathy. He let out a breath and said, "Somebody stole my street clothes. Out of the locker. Stone-washed cotton jacket, a poet's sweater from Bananna Republic, and jeans this guy got me in Greece. Boots gone too. And the damn store wanted me to turn in

29

the uniform and go home in my shorts in a cab. So I told them what they could do."

"A Santa suit is next to nothing," the old man said, "you must freeze if you have far to go. I give you this scarf."

"No, no," said Santa, "I don't have far. I'll run it from the stop. Have to get the landlord to let me in. Hope he's home."

"You are young to run," said the old man. "And young to be Santa Claus. How do you fool the children?" There was a smile on his face.

"Best damn cotton jacket I ever had," said Santa. Then he adverted to the gentle question. "O, I talk in my belly and they fool themselves," he answered. "Like an Indian in the movies."

"Do I talk like that?" the old Buddhist asked.

"O, I mean red Indian," the young man said, "and I mean Hollywood. And I mean late night shows with all those dead actors and actresses. What a funny thing! They look younger than I and they are dead and gone."

"Then I must sound like Gunga Din to you," the old Buddhist said.

Santa laughed and said, "Geez, you're right. But more like Alec Guiness playing some guru with a big beard."

"It's you who look like the guru with that beard," the old man said. "I have only to shave very seldom. People say I must have stolen something from my women to have such hairless skin."

"The store wanted to take the beard too," said the young man. "I had this Irish scarf my girlfriend made for me. Mohair and too long. I used to wrap it around my head like a turban. Didn't need a hat. Gone! Boy! Merry Christmas somebody! She catches you with it and she'll ring your bell! Ho! Ho! Ho! Say, this beard is actually warm."

"It makes you look wise and good," the old man said. "And if as you say you speak from your belly, you must sound saintly to those who come.

My friends tell me if I had a beard I would be wealthy with people coming for advice."

"You really a guru?" Santa asked.

"I am not," the old man said, "but people want me to be. People want me to free them from this world."

"That ain't Christmas," said Santa.

"Oh, but it is," the old man said.

"No," said Santa. "It's really Mommy and Daddy that sit on my lap all day. Those little kids are like tape recorders. You know what they want now? They want dolls that can have organ transplants. They can put in Japanese eyes and English noses and Irish ears and African mouths and I'd hate to tell you what else!"

"Ah," said the old man, "you are right. That is a desire to be everyone else too. Is that not wonderful! But even that cannot last. And you must come back to the child who has only what its parents have. And that is nakedness. And it is wonderful too!"

"O no it isn't," said Santa. "I nearly had to walk home naked tonight. Honest to God, you don't take somebody's clothes!"

"Did not your Christian baby shiver in the cold?" asked the old man.

"Listen, I'm really not a Christian," said the young man. "And I don't know what that baby did. I know this baby got ripped off and nobody up there is singing."

"Yes, I had forgotten," the old man said. "Santa Claus is not from religion anymore. He is from commerce. You should have commerce pay for your stolen clothes."

"Fat chance!" said the young man. "They kept my paycheck until I bring this monkey suit back. I had to twist an arm just to get bus fare out of them."

"Please do not be unhappy," the old man said, "you will have a great story to tell your children. And it will be humorous to you as you run home and ring your landlord. He will think you are crazy. But maybe you should go to your girlfriend first. Perhaps she may sit on your lap and ask for some love for Christmas."

"You know, you are really funny," the young man said. "But come to think of it I am going to have trouble getting in the apartment. The landlord's gone away. Geez! And she's on the other side of town. I'll freeze walking."

"You will do this," said the old man, "my clothes are big enough for you. At least the outside ones. So we will exchange. The bus stops at my door far uptown. I will be warm. You can return these later. And repossess your Santa suit and go and get your paycheck."

"Well, we'll have to do it quick," said the young man, "next stop is the crosstown bus."

"It would be wise of us to do it," said the old man. "Here, take my overcoat. It is Donegal. My daughter's husband is Irish American and loves to give me old country things. And this beret is French. My other daughter's husband is French, but he will stay here to do brain surgery. And this scarf is from Bolivia, I don't know why. You will not mind wearing red trousers I am sure. We must not cause a scene. There, you look nice. Now show me how to put that beard on. Yes, under the hat. Now, are you ready to go? Here are the coins you will need. How do I look? Will someone sit on my lap and ask for gifts?"

"You look like a Santa from the South Seas," the young man said. "Where do I find your place?"

"There is my address sewn inside under the label," the old man said, "my daughters always do that for me. They do not think I am very responsible. But my things always come back. At least I think they do. Here is your stop. May you have peace."

"I feel funny in somebody else's clothes," the young man said, "maybe I shouldn't do this. I have you looking like a fool. I haven't got your key, have I?"

"O heavens, yes!" said the old man, "it is in the pocket also. And is my wallet there? It holds little, but in case they take me to the crazy house I will have an identification. Now you go and have peace."

"You do look funny," the young man said as he moved to the door of the bus.

"Then that is good," said the old man, "that is better than Gunga Din." The doors of the bus hissed open and the young man got down. He saw the crosstown bus over the intersection, so he made a dash on the yellow light, black boots and red pantaloons flying under the Donegal tweed coat and French beret. "You look funny too," the old man said looking through the window. Then he was startled to see himself in the window, long white curly beard, conical red hat, red coat with white collar. Then his dark skin and darker eyes. "And you are funny too," he said pointing his white gloves at himself reflected in the window. "You should go home and shave."

Balancing Things

" . . . you should be clothed in sincere compassion . . ."
—Colossians 3:12

A woman decided to smuggle a baby. Because she wanted life not to be wasted. She was in the Peace Corps, finishing her stint, and had seen too often what was left to die in the streets if the dogs didn't eat them first. And she had seen systems that did not work, orphanages that were like dog kennels. Back home there were unqualified people. But they were better than anything she saw in Cuzco in the public sector. So she married a gravestone name, bribed the certificate into the records, had a fictitious baby, i.e. picked one off the streets, and flew home with it. A discreet ad in the papers got a flood of responses to a P.O. Box. She had to work by guess. So she drove her car to various neighborhoods, to addresses on the envelopes. But that told her nothing. And the boy baby got complicated, not ill, just active, very playful, very noisy, not crying, just boisterous. He loved trying to tumble off things, including her. She had checked him out medically before she came home, though she had balked at the whooping cough shot because that did some kids in, she had read. Better to take a chance.

He was a copper baby. Must be pure Indian, had spikey hair and almost black eyes. But his face was not impassive at all. There was a fire and a glee to it as each new thing happened. Airplane door, window, clouds, mountains, runway, airplane door. He was fifteen pounds of hungry delight. And he was desperate to speak. What he learned first would be it. She had been using English and Spanish. His real tongue was Aymara, no doubt. She saw she was stuck with him. She couldn't toss him to the unknown. Better to bring him back and slip him into one of those orphanages, get a fictitious divorce, then return home and maybe work later

34

for a legal agency. So she spent almost all she had left on a round trip ticket to Cuzco and flew back with her tumbler boy. She was it for him, no doubt also, he had fixed on her smell, her feel, her sound especially. But when she got to the orphanage in an old monastery and saw the howling need up and down the aisles, she was staggered even more than she was when she first saw an orphanage. And her tumbler was quiet in her arms and a little afraid.

It wasn't a minute before some of the mobile ones began to go for her legs and wrap around them. There were some nurses who took a look at her as they worked or went by. One finally stopped and said in American accented Spanish, "You didn't just find that?"

"No," the woman said, "I stole it to give away in the States. And I can't. Now I'm stuck."

"You stole it off the streets?" the nurse asked in English.

"Yes," the woman said.

"You went home and back?" the nurse asked.

"Yes," the woman said.

"Of course we'll take it," said the nurse. "But if we do, you beat it, and you beat it fast. Because we have to report things. And jail is not nice down here."

"I wanted to do something good," the woman said.

"It was something good, but you chickened out on it," said the nurse. "That's the kind of thing you can do once and not come back."

The boy began to tumble again. It was the nurse who had to grab him. He surfaced on her and tumbled again so the woman ended holding him upside down like a folded blanket.

"He's really yours," the nurse said. "But he belongs here. So I think you're stuck. So I'd say give him fifteen years then he'll be on his own. You can work here and live in the convent with us."

"You speak like a judge," the woman said.

"O, better than a judge," the nurse said.

"Can I leave him for an hour so I can go think?" the woman said. The nurse answered nothing. She just put out her hands. But the woman didn't hand her the baby. "I'm trapped," she said. "I trapped myself."

"You want your own life, don't you?" the nurse said.

"Yes," the woman answered.

"Then leave the baby and go. I'll cover you. There's really no law here." The boy was still again. And she could smell him, his fear. She reached him to the nurse. There was panic on his face. She backed toward the door, bumping a few of the unsteady orphans, reaching down to straighten them, then she turned and went down the stairs and out into the narrow streets. "He will learn Aymara," she said to herself. "And Spanish. He will marry copper not white. He will be missing teeth by twenty. Be wrinkled by forty."

She had forgotten her period. Her blood began to flow. So she looked quickly for an alleyway, went in one, inserted a tampon, then readjusted her skirts. As she did she heard a telltale cat-like cry from a pile of rubbish further up the alleyway under a bricked in window. Not a cat. The last sounds of a baby. Indian baby most likely. So she picked it up in its filthy rags and ran back to the orphanage, up the stairs, in the door to the nurses cubicle and put it down. There was no one in. So she ran out. When she came to another alleyway, she went up it and found another abandoned baby and ran back. The nurse she knew was in the cubicle. So with a fierce look on her face she put the baby down. Then ran out again, up and down several alleyways. She found several more babies and brought them back. Until she was exhausted with emotion. "I could do this for fifteen years," she said to the nurse. "And never come back empty handed. So why don't you?"

"I haven't enough room," the nurse said. "There's some blood on you. From what?"

"From me," the woman said.

"You go," the nurse said. "You'd be wasted here. One more waste."

"Won't you go crazy?" the woman asked.

"I already am," the nurse answered, "I know what's in those alleyways. It's why I never go out. I take what comes."

"I can't move," the woman said.

So the nurse said, "I'm going to walk you to the Plaza. I'm going to put you on a bus to the airport. And have you take the next plane home. And have you know I decided for you. Because I love you from just a short time. And I'm going to have you use your blood for some new life. And you will balance this for me. Because I never know the mother."

"You are," the woman said.

"No," the nurse said, "I'm the father, would you believe it? Come, I'll walk you."

The Solemnity of Mary

Slap Shots

. . . you are not a slave anymore . . .
—Galatians 4:7

"If you take that game, don't come back home," a woman had said to her husband. She meant a hockey game. On New Year's Day. He was a pro referee. The game was to be televised. For those who didn't like football.

"Okay, no game," he had said.

So here he was bored stiff, walking around a house full of women, wife and two daughters, two teen-agers who were out hitting their friends houses to see who was going with whom before coming back for dinner at four then a party somewhere at seven. So he and his wife were face to face, in the living room, in the kitchen, the den.

"You could try," she said.

She sat with coffee in front of her. He had just come in the kitchen for the banana half he hadn't finished at breakfast. He sat down and ate the banana half in three bites then looked to see if anything else interesting could happen.

"I should be a slap shot," she said.

"I can't talk," he said, "you know that. It's like chasing a puck across the whole pond."

"You can if you love someone," she said.

"I love someone," he said. "Not the way you do. I told you that."

"I can't be a hockey game," she said. "Kids are grown. I'm like the hampsters upstairs. Except . . ."

"You used to love the game," he said. "You keep looking. It's all I am."

"It's not all I am," she said.

"Like what?" he asked.

"The girls and their bodies, for one thing," she said, "me and my body, for another."

"You look okay," he said.

"I'm not," she said, "I'm starved to death. And I'm starting to look around. Except all we know are old jocks."

He felt a surge of rage. "That's a slap shot," he said.

"It went off the glass," she said.

"So why do you keep me home," he said. She looked straight at him.

"Okay," he said, "okay. Nothing comes into my head except I am what I am. I get there and I breathe that ice and I see all those guys flying, and I'm flying with them, I feel so real, so alive! And when I come home, I find I go dead. I want you and I want them, but it's like I've been tricked. Not by you three. By what people do. You just marry, you have family, it's like a hitch in the service. Then the service drops you. Or the team drops you. And your tongue's still hanging out from the last game. Or last battle. And you haven't got anything to handle what's left."

"Doesn't your body tell you anything else?" she asked him. "Don't your eyes?" He opened his hands empty on the table. "Because if you live backwards," she continued, "like on a train, things leave you, you think. But it's you leaving them."

"I can skate backwards better than I can skate forwards," he said. It was an aside and he knew it. "What do I see if I look ahead?" he asked. "I see my girls go. I see you get old. I see you get empty. I see I have nothing to fill you up. I see I'm forgotten. Except on a wall, National Champs, we look like kids. I have this hunger to stay alive. And this is all I know. This game is all I know."

"You went to college," she said.

"They just about admit it," he answered. "They put the diploma in Latin so no one would look close. Bachelor of Philosophy. That means we could read and write."

"So do I get cheated too?" she asked. "I mean I could look but who's going to look at me? There are no milkmen. And women read the gas. And I'm in one direction."

"You're good still," he said.

"But not for you," she said.

He could say nothing. Until he said, "I'm an empty man." Then nothing, until he said, "You want me to be that way?"

She didn't answer. He looked for the longest time.

"Yes," she said then, "I want you to be an empty man. I'm asking, not telling."

"I'm afraid," he said. He was looking right in her eyes. "I'm afraid I might run."

"From what?" she asked.

"An animal," he said. He still did not take his eyes away from hers. "Like an animal," he continued. "That African stuff we see, those kills. There's something in me. It's really me. Someone else is talking to you."

"So you'd be a kill?" she asked.

"Yes," he said, "I think so." He waited. "So you can go if you want. It'd be wrong to keep you. You are good. There are more than milkmen and jocks."

She put her hands on her forehead and looked in the cup, then said, "Can't you face that animal? I've never seen you afraid."

"Could you?" he asked. "You can see it now. It's eating at me already. I want to crash into some boards. I want to cut loose a shot. Not make love. We're alone and I just see someone with a cup of coffee and a warm voice. I want to taste sweat. Like someone hooked."

He was shaking. He went on, "Remember that lady? In the story. She points out a door to a guy in the arena. Woman behind one. Tiger behind the other. She doesn't want to lose him. I think she pointed to the tiger door."

"She's dead either way," the woman said.

"So's he," the man said.

"Haven't I got anything?" she asked, "haven't we, even if we're women?"

"You have to do something more than this," he said, "I don't know what. You have to bite something. The same with them, they'll be home and it'll be all clothes and boys and school. We should buy them horses. Or let them climb mountains."

"There's one thing I'd love to do," she said.

"What?" he asked.

"Learn to fly a plane," she said.

"I can make extra money," he said. He was happy to be on a new topic.

"Well, what if I talked airplanes all the time?" she asked.

"I'd love it," he said, "you could teach me."

"What about them if I crashed?" she asked.

"They'd buy black dresses," he said. Then, "Sorry." Then, "They'd marry someone different from me."

"It's a tie game," she said.

"No," he said, "you win. I'll face it. But it's gonna be funny after."

"What is?" she asked. "Buying dresses," he said. He grinned and threw the banana peel perfectly into the dispose-all.

Squirrels and Birds

May God . . . give you a spirit
of wisdom and perception . . .
—Ephesians 1:17

There was a woman who was her family's historian. And that got her into a clash with the FBI. And into a crisis in her life. They wanted to know what she knew about a first cousin who was up for a Federal judgeship on the West Coast. She didn't know him personally. But as the agents sat in front of her and asked about him, a vivid picture of his lineage came to her, though she said not a word of it to the men seated in her living room. What right they had to this kind of knowlege she didn't know, nor did she know what use they would make of it. But they wanted to know about the past. It was certainly colorful. She knew her grandparents, all four, before they died, and got from them a history going well back into the last century. Even to the details of birth and death. Which helped her present family when they wanted to know the answers to medical questions—were heart attacks frequent in the past? or cancers? or consumptions? What about alcoholism? It was a knowlege that gradually became a burden on her. She saw a lot of depression back there. Easy to understand it. She had visited the several locales in the old country where all her people came from, beautiful but poverty-stricken places where the only entertainment was watching who conformed and who didn't, who stayed sober and who got drunk. There was no question of sex behind the bushes in the damp grass. A heavy cold would result more often than a pregnancy, as telltale a sign as a swollen belly. The non-conformists ran away. To another continent. To another family. And not a trace until a son or daughter came back looking for roots, stayed a few days, filled in some huge blanks with sketchy details, then went off to yet another continent looking for a home. The woman herself felt homeless because of her knowlege. Though she had a husband, a house, and four grown children. She floated with the family history.

"Give me a minute more," she said to the agents. Something about the Federal Judgeship didn't ring true. Her cousin was from the second family of his father who had been an immigrant and had left a first family undivorced in the old country. Back at the time of the quarrel among the rebels. The father had run with a price on his head and no future since the other side won the quarrel. But there were half-brothers and sisters left. And they spat fire when their father's name came up. To them he had a yellow streak down his back. The woman had met them only once and that was enough. Her cousin's mother, the second wife, came from eccentrics born in this country all the way back to the mid-sixteen hundreds. Religious dissenters, abolitionists, pacifists, prohibitionists. So her cousin, she knew from reports, was a volatile character with a brain like a steel trap for issues and the language of a drunken gypsy to describe them. She could not remember him ever becoming a lawyer.

She looked at the agents and said, "You're lying to me. What has he done?" They didn't twitch a muscle.

"If you'll just tell us about his background, please, we're simply going on what the Justice Department tells us and asks us to do." And they waited.

"His father was a saint and his mother more than a saint to have to live with the father," the woman said, "and if you believe me on that one I'll believe you." They said nothing. "This is criminal," she said to them, "isn't it? You suspect something. And don't quite know who to suspect. So if you dig the ground up you might find some worms. Find the worm you want." They said nothing. "I think you are looking for a spy type," she said. "Someone who's capable of working two sides of a street." They said nothing. "My family can produce anything," she said. "And so can yours, the two of you. Now go."

"We have the right to ask you," they said. "And we have the right to an answer."

"You'll be a long time getting it," she said, and she walked to the door to let them out. They left saying it only made their work more difficult.

She closed the door and knew she was right, they suspected criminal activity on her cousin's part. They used a lie to go after the suspect. The weight of the future was now added to the weight of the past. The woman walked to the window. Her whole being seemed to want amnesia. There was a hummingbird at the feeder outside. There was a squirrel on the wire above trying to get around the old phonograph record she had placed just above to protect the feeder. The hummingbird zipped off. The squirrel overreached and fell splat on the spring mud below. The feeder hung swaying on its chain below the wire, still half full of syrup above the sponge.

"My family can produce anything," she thought. "Easily produce a traitor. And just as easily not." The hummingbird zipped back again. The squirrel was starting out along the wire for another try.

"I hope he's not," she thought. Then thought, "I hope I'm not either, keeping my mouth shut." The squirrel was hanging by one foot now trying with the other three to keep the record out of the way so he could bite the feeder and let the syrup out. She hit the window a rap, scared the squirrel who let go and went plop again in the spring mud. Then she knew what the agents had really done. They expected her to call her cousin and tell him. And that would scare him into something if he were guilty. "And your family can produce anything as well," she thought.

So she picked up the phone and without dialing said into it, "You chose to be this way. That should tell you all you want to know." She put the phone down and the weight of her family with it. She went back to watch her hummingbird and squirrel.

Lighters

. . . it means that pagans now share the
same inheritance, that they are parts of
the same body, and that the same promise
has been made to them . . .
—Ephesians 3:6

A man saw a Buddhist monk commit suicide. It was during the Vietnam War. The man was a reporter, a print journalist. He had seen a lot of things, but never anything like this. He was sitting on the steps of the main government building, waiting for some politicians to come out so he could get a few answers from them, when he saw a group of monks in their saffron robes and shaven heads form a circle on the concrete about thirty yards away. One of them walked to the center of the circle, then they all sat in a lotus position and seemed to drift deep inside themselves into a sort of trance. The reporter actually heard the click of the cigarette lighter when the monk in the middle shot into flames. The monk did not budge. Nor did the other monks. He was a flaming statue of Buddha sitting there totally unmoved until the flames had consumed so much of him that he toppled, still like a statue in the lotus position, dead on the ground. The reporter felt as if his own life had been sucked out of him by the torched monk. And the smell of burning flesh made him sick. Everyone in the government building was at the windows watching. They had apparently been tipped off. The monks in the circle rose from their lotus positions and simply left the charred body of their fellow where it had fallen. The reporter ran to the monk in the lead of the file and started to shout, "Why? Why?" like a drill sergeant shouting at raw recruits, but the lead monk took no notice, nor did any other down the line as he shouted "Why? Why?" He was out of breath and weeping as the last one passed. And he was sick, faint. So he sat on a bench and put his head between his legs to get some blood back into it. After a while he noticed sandaled feet and a saffron robe standing just in front of him, someone waiting for him to look up, someone very feminine from the look of the feet and hang of the robe. So he sat back slowly and saw it was a Buddhist nun.

"Do you want me to tell you?" she said in French, which he understood. He was unable to speak but she could see he was still shouting "Why? Why?" like some painting. He motioned with his left hand would she sit. She was shaven also like the young men.

"Our teacher will be back," she said. He shook his head in incomprehension. "You will write about this," she said. He shook his head again, this time in horror. "What he burned was nothing," she said. "To show that what they kill is nothing."

"Oh, oh," the reporter said in a long groan and he just opened his hands toward her.

"People kill to cling to life and cling to power," she said. "Our teacher has shown them life and power are nothing to cling to. Therefore nothing to kill for."

"That's too logical," the reporter said.

"You would not kill now, would you?" she said.

"I wouldn't kill before," he said.

"Then you would give up life rather than destroy it?" she said.

"I guess," he said, "but not by suicide."

"Our teacher would not have someone else kill him. Someone else would sin to do it," she said.

"That's also logic," the reporter said. "Don't you feel for him? Don't you love him? Doesn't it destroy you to see that black heap?"

"It does destroy me," she said, "it destroys everything, if everything could only see."

"Oh woman," he said, "everything about you says the opposite. You can create life. It's in your body right now."

"It will not be soon," she said, "I will protest the war tomorrow."

"I do not exist anymore," he said. "This whole world doesn't exist."

"Then I have set you free," she said. "It's what our teacher has done."

The reporter sat there looking at her for a long minute. "If you do this tomorrow, if you burn yourself alive, you will put me in hell. And you will never come back as someone able to do good. In fact, I'm in hell already. And you will push me deeper." The woman said nothing. She looked at him as one looks at an object of meditation.

"Are you lying to me?" she asked.

"No," he said. "I am where your teacher has put me." She was silent again, thinking, looking at him without a stare, but almost without a blink.

"How can I wake you up?" she said.

"It's being awake to all this that is the hell," he said, "don't you understand? What your teacher did is a sin."

"It is the one sin permitted," she said.

"No sin is permitted," he said, "that's your logic." She rose to leave. "If you do not do this," he said, "I will become a monk."

"Why?" she asked.

"To free you with life, not with death," he said.

"You need not," she said, "I can free myself."

He could say nothing more. He began to feel sick again. And faint. So he lowered his head between his knees. The sandaled feet and saffron robe stayed there in front of him. He heard the snap of a cigarette lighter and he jerked upright on the bench. She was standing there holding the lit lighter, watching the flames calmly, peacefully. She let it burn and burn until finally the flame began to weaken and go out. When it did she closed the lid. Then she reached the lighter toward him for him to take.

"Will this free you?" she asked.

"Yes," he said.

"Then take it," she said. She turned and left him. And he sat on that bench until the lighter cooled in his hand. Then he pressed it. Nothing.

Purple Darkness

The Lord's voice resounding on the
waters, the Lord on the immensity
of the waters . . .
> —Psalm 29:3

There was a man who loved to sail. He was an old bachelor. It had just happened that way. Service in the war, then career in foreign service. Then boats, a love of boats, a love of navigation, among islands, islands of the Carribean, every chance he could. So when he retired, he had bought a manageable sloop and lived out of the north coast of Jamaica, St. Ann's Bay. He favored going up through the Windward Passage to the Bahamas and touching all the little ports. Next, he favored going east by Haiti to the Leeward and Windward Islands. That was the route he was on when he spotted a tropical storm heading his way out of the southeast. There had been no weather warning issued so it was probably something mild. Better ride with it though to be safe. So he shortened sail to a jib, one he could let go if need be, and swung around to the northwest on a course that would take him back between Haiti and Jamaica. The rain arrived with larger swells of the sea and some wind, but steady wind, not gusty. It was just a big, sweet rainstorm and some curling to the sea as the swells got large, and a wonderful purple darkness from the clouds. The rain was warm and fat. The man had on his slicker and hat and had closed in the cockpit with a tarpaulin to save some of the water. He ran with the weather for some time, two hours maybe, then the tail end of the storm passed him so he could swing around and reset course southeast, plotting his position as just between Haiti and Jamaica. He had lost about forty nautical miles. He got clear of his rain equipment, hoisted the mainsail and began his run southeast.

In about an hour's time he spotted a body floating in the water off to port. The water was still up a bit. So the man switched to engine power and steered in the direction of what he saw, then saw another body heaved up by another swell, then a third, then a flock of them. And it was not the storm that had just passed that was the cause. These bodies were bloating, so the storm had just moved them around. There was no mystery to the scene, just tragedy, Haitians escaping to Jamaica on rickety craft a soft breeze would sink. And this was the direct line between the two islands.

There was a change in the weight of the air and the man felt the wind shifting. That will bring the storm back. Drive me right on shore. I'll have to face it and hope to stay in place. So he kept his engine on and kept way as the storm swung back over him, still not too violent, still a drenching rain and some breaking waves and the same dark purple for light. At one moment, though, he spotted another craft bearing down on him in the poor visibility so he eased up on the tiller and let the sea move him out of the way. It was a barely discernible craft swinging in a top heavy way and propelled by a wicked engine that coughed up most of its strokes. Just before it disappeared in the purple light, it took too deep a heave to port and just kept going over dumping people off its topside like apples out of a barrel. The man saw its bottom, then its other side, then its bottom, then its stern, and there were its apples all around it and then the barrel was gone and a sheet of rain came between the man and the scene.

"If I pull in there, they will drag me under," he thought. "If I don't, they will," he then thought. So he throttled up, jumped down in the cockpit, grabbed his inflatable dinghy, his extra life jackets, cushions that would float, and got ready to pitch them to anyone he could see on his first sail through. He had to see whom he could pick up without ending in another tragedy. He fixed the rudder and stood up on the stern behind it and when he saw a group struggling in the water who looked at him in absolute amazement, he snapped the release on the dinghy and heaved the suddenly swelling thing into the middle of the terrified group who began a desperate life and death struggle to get aboard it. Then, still under way, he threw life jackets and cushions into other groups still afloat. He was now through to the other side of the floating heads. He jumped down into the cabin, hit the radio switches and pumped out a mayday call, giving his last calculated position and his guess at drift. And he indicated there was a boat down and survivors. He did this several times until he caught a voice back asking how bad. He clicked off knowing someone had the info.

Then back in the cockpit, he reversed course and headed again into the pack hoping some people were still afloat. First thing he spotted were people clinging to wreckage. He swung his craft right up to them but they were afraid to let go. So he looked for individuals who had no choice—on a beam here, or a crate there, some just swimming. And he hauled them up on the small deck. Then the people with the cushions. Now he had enough to attract people on the wreckage to reach for hands aboard his own craft, which got lower and lower in the water as more and more people came aboard. The boat was now sluggish and rolling with the heavy motion of the sunken craft, and the survivors still with strength kept shouting to him here, there, here, there. Until the man knew he had to head out and away if any life at all was to be saved. But he knew he had to fake it. If his survivors thought he was leaving, they would not allow it. He spotted a veil of rain just closing in so he throttled up and headed right with it, in its direction. Soon he was blinded by the fat, sweet rain, as everyone else was, and he was running before the great swells in a northeasterly direction. It took some time for that squall to pass, and when he could swing his heavy craft around again there were only a few feet of sea visible and no bobbing heads. Then his fuel gave out and he had to swing heavily, heavily around and run before the storm toward the Haitian cape which was not that far away. He did all this amid the shouting French of the survivors, the pointings, the shrugs of impossibility, the indications of empty fuel tank. He had had to set people to bailing out the cabin and cockpit so his survivors knew they were in danger of death again. The survivors were mainly men and young women. The babies and the old folk were gone.

The storm was by them now. And there was a sound that turned them; a navy plane out of Guantanamo spotting the people-thick sloop hoisting one sail and waving desperately to be seen. Within a few hours, a cutter was alongside. US. There were ladders over the side, and the survivors were hauled on board. The man shouted up to the crew the approximate location of the sinking and told them to get up there quickly, some more might still be alive. "Just give me some water. I can sail this back home. And got a can of diesel? I'm out." The crew got the water and diesel down to him and some food in a bag in case, and moved out toward the wreckage spot, but the man knew there was little chance except for those on the dinghy and cushions. He hoisted sail, swung around on a west southwesterly course and then sat at the tiller and looked at his filthy boat. Because that was what it was. There was vomit on deck, excrement, ripped clothing, a sandal, some blood, kerchiefs. All the cushions were gone, the dinghy, he saw remnants of food on the cabin floor.

"I'll head for Port Antonio," he thought. His equipment was still intact, so he plotted a course and made for port a day and a half hence. He fixed the tiller and took a bucket left from bailing and began to scoop seawater onto the filthy deck to wash it down. He dropped the bits of clothing into the sea. Then he looked at his wake and what was floating in it. Then he looked at the storm now far to the east on the horizon and heading away. Then he looked at his decision to save some and not others and to fool the some into being saved. "It would have taken God," he thought. The sloop was light again, and made easy way. "Right over their graves."

Ash Wednesday

Nowhere To Be Seen

Do not make your heritage a thing
of shame, a byword for the nations.
—Joel 2:17

A man was on a hunger strike. He was in prison for being a terrorist. *They* said. He said he was a freedom fighter. He would bring the spotlight on them. They were the terrorists. He refused food and clothing and did the smear on the walls thing, making the prison a place of excrement. He was at the stage of fast where they were force-feeding him, orally, then intravenously. And was flat on his cot most of the time. Messages got through, Do it! Do it! Usually from outside the window, a shout from the prison yard, the shout becoming a chant until a prison bell rang signalling the abbreviation of recreation, all back to cells! Psychologists worked on him. Mainly by recounting what terrorism had already done in the country. They wanted to crassify the noble cause by showing its innocent victims.

One day they brought his mother in, "O Jesus! What they won't do!" They stood around his cot until she told them to go. She had given them her real reasons for wanting to see her son. So they withdrew, out of earshot but not eyeshot. She looked at him from where she stood and said, "I hate you for what you've become. You kill in order to cure. And I'm going out of here to starve myself against you. The day you take food, I do. And the day you die, I go off something. And I'll be screaming peace against your war. Do you hear me?"

"You're a traitor," he said.

"I am," she said, "I am. And you have ways of killing me. A word from you. But I want this on your hands. You are going out guilty. Or you're coming back in with another mind."

"I'll send the word," he said, "now get out!"

"I will, and gladly," she said. She began her fast from that minute. She stood at a crossing of the Cromwell Road during the day. She had braided flags of several countries and several churches into a noose and rope and hung the noose from her neck and tied the end to the foot of Oliver's statue. Police moved her on. She found store entrances, church entrances, where she could stand. Until the police moved her on. But now two news stories were hitting the papers—two ferocious beings starving at each other, the one for war, the one for peace, the same flesh and blood. Family was no go in this, no pleading worked. And clergy were useless. And the son was weak to the point of blindness and under the camera's scrutiny every minute and in all the papers. The command was still on, Do it! Do it! And the mother had several close calls, trucks, taxis, but she stayed to crowded places, though she slowed with weakness after a few weeks and knew she had to find some exposed place that would get her equal publicity for his last days and hours. And she found it.

The season was Lent, the last week, and all statues and crucifixes in the Cathedral as elsewhere were masked with purple drapes. Including the great crucifix over the main altar, the one that would be used for the unveiling because it was such a beautiful carving and visible throughout the church. The priest would stand below it Good Friday and expose the right arm of the crucifix first, the left arm second, then the head and torso, letting the drapery fall so the whole crucified body showed and people saw the suffering Jesus. There was a space in the niche behind it where she could hide, if she could stay in the Church the night before and climb up there unnoticed.

"I will have to be dead," she thought. "It will take me weeks more to starve." So she dropped her exhibitionism for a few days and spent time praying in the Cathedral. Priest after priest came to her to beg her to stop this madness, until finally she said she would leave and not trouble them. She went out through the vestibule, took holy water, went out the center door, went left to the side door and back in, through the choir entry and up the spiral staircase to the loft. She saw the door into the organ casing, it was open, so she stooped and went in, pulling the door quietly shut behind her. Her exhaustion was now nearly extreme. So she slept a numb sleep and when she woke many hours had passed. It was nearly morning, and the first of the Spy Wednesday masses were beginning. Later the choir came in for practice and she was deafened by the organ sounds. The repeats of difficult passages. So she slept again after. Meantime she was missed because the son had died of starvation in prison, and the rebels were exultant about this defiance of foreign rule. And she was nowhere to be seen or quoted or interviewed.

There was a great Mass that Holy Thursday evening. And there were prayers for her son, and for the country. Then there was a procession to a side chapel where the communion for the next day would be placed and an all night vigil be held until the Good Friday service the following afternoon. Toward two in the morning when there were few people holding vigil and she looked like one of them, she came down from the organ loft and worked her way unobserved up behind the main altar through one of the side aisles and doors that led behind it. She climbed the scaffolding stairs, the ones used by the candle lighter. There were several hatches on the back of the altar where extra vessels were usually stored. The vessels were in use in the side chapel so the hatches were open and empty. She removed her clothing and hid them in a hatch which she closed. Then with what strength she had left, she eased up on the back ridge of the altar that held the candles and formed a walkway to the niche where the main crucifix stood. She carried a rope with her, a noose on one end, a short rope she had prepared. No one saw her in the dark church. She stepped into the niche and got behind the shrouded sculpture. There was a footstool there, one used by the sacristan to tie up the shroud. The shroud would be untied from below by ribbons run down to the altar table where they could be pulled by the celebrant. They were crimson and looked like streams of blood. She stood on the footstool and managed to reach the loose end of the rope around the upright of the cross behind Jesus' bent neck without disturbing the shroud. Then she tied it in a firm knot so there was very little rope between the knot and the noose. She put the noose over her head and tightened it around her neck then kicked the footstool away, a small noise in a large church, and strangled herself to death. The upright held. Her feet did not reach the floor.

The next day at three in the afternoon the Mass of Good Friday began, the long readings, the long chant, then the adoration of the cross. At the phrase, "Behold the wood of the cross," sung first from under the choir loft, next from mid-church, two of the ribbons were pulled revealing the left arm, then the right arm of the Crucified. At the third singing of the phrase, the third ribbon was pulled and the whole shroud descended softly onto the tabernacle top revealing the Crucified completely, and another pair of arms hanging down naked, and the naked curving hips of a woman. People with side angles saw more, they saw the rope and the hung body. There was a roar went up, partly from fury, partly from nausea. One quick minded photographer who was there to photograph the Cardinal, leaped the communion rail, ran up through the clergy, did a jump up on the altar table, took some rapid fire shots with his camera, then jumped further over the candle platforms and down onto the scaffolding behind the altar, then down the steps and out through the door behind, then through the sacristy not knowing what he had on his film. He had the woman on it, hanging dead from the the cross of Jesus.

It hit the world press before many hours were up. As did other photos of the melee in the Church, long lens shots of the priest untying the noose and the woman slumping down into another priest's hands, then the fire brigade people up on the altar table lowering the purpling body onto a stretcher and covering it with a tarp then running it out the side door. Everyone knew who she was in no time.

There were counter hunger strikes from then on until the hunger strikes stopped. Just the terrorism remained. And the need to reconsecrate the Church. Services were shifted elsewhere for the remaining days. Some people never came back to it when it was. They were as sick to death as she.

Grade Change

Then the eyes of both of them were
opened and they realized that they
were naked.
—Genesis 3:7

A woman was correcting exams. She taught Economics. More the history of it than the theory. The paper in front of her was very poor. A straight F. But the last line said, "If you do not pass me, I will kill myself." She looked quickly back to the first page and saw the student had forgotten to sign a name. Hers was there and the name of the course she taught and the hours and day. But the student's was not. So she wrote an F just below the last sentence, then wrote the following remark: "Please see me before you do. You haven't understood Adam Smith's theory of the invisible hand." At the end of the next class, instead of handing out the papers by name, she simply spread them across the classroom bench in front of her and asked the students please to claim their own. She had an appointment with the Dean and would be in her office within an hour in case anyone couldn't read her handwriting or had any questions on the exam material.

A little over an hour later a young woman came to the door of the office. It was open as usual, so the teacher beckoned her to come in and sit and close the door. There was not a word, just a heaviness, and a strange calmness.

"I really meant it," said the student.

"So did I," said the teacher.

"Tell me about the invisible hand," said the student, "then I will tell you about the suicide."

"The invisible hand," the teacher said, "is something that adjusts our lives so we can take whatever we have to take."

The student knew that was not the invisible hand of Adam Smith's. "And what if it fails to adjust our lives?" the student asked, "and we cannot take whatever we have to take?"

"We adjust things for ourselves," the teacher said.

"That is what I am about to do," the student said.

"You have a weapon?" the teacher asked.

"No, I have a capsule," the student said.

"I don't understand," the teacher said.

"I have a cyanide capsule. It's in my cheek," the student said.

"Where did you get such a thing?" the teacher asked.

"From an invisible hand," the student said, "my Daddy. He's CIA and when he travels, he takes one with him. So no one will find out what he knows."

"Ah," the teacher said, "you will take one on me and I will not find out what you know."

"You do not want to know what I know," the student said. "You want to know what you know, like every teacher."

"A teacher is a very small thing," the woman said, "she is not an invisible hand however she might want to be."

"You could have passed me and kept me alive. No one would have known," the student said.

"I have kept you alive," the woman said. The student said nothing. She moved her jaws slightly and the woman knew she had set the capsule between her teeth.

"Give me half of it," the woman said.

"Why?" the student mumbled through her fixed mouth.

"You have to know you never just kill yourself," the woman answered.

"You're trying to trick me," said the student.

"I put an F on your paper," the woman said, "you didn't have to come here. Now I want you to know what you will do to me as well."

"Okay," said the student, "but if you move, a bit of this is enough." So she took the capsule slowly from her mouth. And with half an eye on the teacher she separated one part of the capsule from the other so the powder escaped but a little. Then she turned both halves upwards to save the remaining grains. Then a curious puzzlement came over her face. She raised one of the halves to her nostrils and moved it slightly back and forth. Then she touched the capsule-half lightly to the tip of her tongue while staring almost wildly at the teacher. "It's sugar," she said. "They mean Daddy to talk if he's caught. He's away. He thinks . . ." She tasted the capsule again, then threw her head back and dumped the rest of the grains into her mouth. "Sugar! Sugar!" she said. Then she sat there as if reels of film were playing right before her eyes. The film then seemed to fade out and her eyes gradually focused on the teacher who sat there with tears coming down her face.

"You have done to me what he has done to you," she said to the student. "How much alike you must be."

"I have to tell him," the student said, "I have to tell him quick. But I don't know where he is." She was agitated and starting for the door.

"You tell him and he'll break before he gets caught," the woman said. That stopped the student. "Now sit," said the woman. "What you do is look for the truth in everything. You have to hope he comes home before you say a word. Then you sit him down and you tell him what happened here. But don't you presume that all those capsules are sugar. Do not use your tongue on them again. But there is something a lot more lethal than cyanide. You. You can kill someone and not know it until after. And that's what he's nearly done to you. Do you want now to understand the invisible hand?" The woman was flushed as she spoke. It was not anger. It was not relief. It was more like the flush of love. And her voice was shaking.

"Well?" she said. "Do you want to? I'm asking."

The student sat there. She looked almost the opposite of the teacher. She was empty. She was pale. But she was attentive. And nothing was spoken for the longest time. The flush subsided in the teacher and rose in the student.

"The invisible hand is . . . " she paused in her speech, "is a market force . . . that controls prices . . . in terms of supply and demand. If you have many gloves, you have a low price. If you have few gloves, you have a high price. Unless government intervenes."

"Very good," the teacher said. "For that I will give you a C."

"The invisible hand is . . ." the student paused again in her speech, ". . . is the power to use things for their own good."

"That's a little better," said the teacher.

"The invisible hand is. . . is . . . is the power to hold anything that happens," the student said.

"And?" asked the teacher.

"And," said the student, "and let things float again."

"Alright now," said the teacher, "I'd ask you to sign that paper with your name. And I will understand it contains what you just said. I will give you a B. Your answers were good, but you did leave something out. The invisible hand does not have to do what it does."

The student said nothing. She reached in her bag for a pen. She signed her name above the course and teacher and handed it to the woman who put a grade above that and handed it back.

"Maybe I haven't earned this," the student said.

"Tell me later if you think you haven't," the teacher said. "And I will change the grade."

"Yes," the student said. "I will tell you."

2nd Sunday, Lent

New Coat

I will bless those who bless you,
I will curse those who curse you.
> —Genesis 12:3

A young man was working at New Hope Inn, a hostel for down and outers. It was weekend work, part of his internship in social studies for a college degree. This was a cold weekend. It drove even the toughest off the streets. They had to shower, which they hated, they had to shift to clean clothes, which they hated, and eat a balanced meal, then sleep in a clean cot. Only the bitter cold would make them do it. The young man recognized one of the derelicts after he had been cleaned up. An ex-POW, sure, the one who had been tried for treason but acquitted, though the word was he really did rat on his fellows. His photo had been in the papers for weeks, and on TV. His defense had been he had saved people greater harm by telling lesser things about them. He himself had been severely tortured so the Courts Martial saw they couldn't inflict more.

The ex-POW saw the young man looking at him. He was sitting to his meal after the shower and change of clothes. He got up slowly like someone injured and walked to the young man and grabbed him by the shirt front and spat in his face. The young man who was very strong and well trained picked him up bodily by his own clothes and carried him back to his meal. The POW still burned with rage.

"No violence," said the young man, "it's against the rules. You'd freeze outdoors."

"Where are my clothes?" the POW hissed.

"You got 'em on," said the young man.

The POW tried to pull free. "Where? Where?" he said, "you give 'em back!"

"They're in the wash, most of them," said the young man. "If they're any good, I'll get 'em for you."

The ex-POW was now looking at him with fear suffusing his face. "Now," he said, "now!"

"They're wet," the young man said.

"Now, now, now!" the other said and there were tears running, tears like self pity.

"Just eat," said the young man. "No trouble, later we'll look, and then we'll sleep, and you'll go out set in the morning."

The other lurched again as if looking for the laundry room. "I'm dead, I'm dead," he muttered, "I'm dead again." And he struggled.

"Okay," the young man said, "you eat, I'll look. Your stuff wasn't much, they'll probably throw it out, not wash it."

"Please, please," said the other making to follow.

"We'll locate your stuff. We'll put it in a bag for you. You can take it in the morning. Now sit."

The other did but with a fixed stare at the young man. Who backed away and left the dining room and went into the locker space where there was a pile of discarded clothes waiting for cleaning or the rubbish. He remembered the wool coat the man had had on, the remnants of a suit coat underneath it. He saw the collar of the coat so he pulled to get it free, heard a few rips from the ancient cloth, then had it out. There was a grab from behind him as the ex-POW went for the coat.

"I'll just take it. I'll go back and eat. I'll just put it under my cot. It's okay."

It was a heavy okay, and bulging okay, as if it were stuffed with extra padding. Some drifters put scarves inside the lining, down through the holes in the pockets. This man had put some plastic shopping bags, it seemed.

"What you got in here?" the young man asked. He wasn't dumb. "This coat weighs a ton."

The ex-POW was near frenzy. "Just give it," he said.

"You're not running stuff, are you?" the young man said, and he jerked at a side pocket. Out came a plastic shopping bag inside which were some sausage rolls.

"It's not mine," the other said, as he backed away. "It's not mine. I have to finish. Need some food." And he went out through the door. The young man unloaded the coat and laid out from the stuffing seven sausage rolls of coke worth millions on the street.

"He wants revenge," he thought. "He lives like an animal. Someone knows him. And gives him a chance. He nearly froze. He doesn't want to die. He wants revenge." The room was empty. Everyone was eating or serving or fixing the dormitory or cleaning the showers.

"Well, he's dead now," the young man thought. "But not before he tries to tell them what happened. Then I'm dead." So he put the sausage rolls back in their plastic sacks. And he went to the next room and found a refurbished overcoat, pulled out the pockets and ripped open their bottoms, then distributed the sausage rolls wrapped in plastic and scarves inside the breast and down the length of the coat. He carried the coat back into the dining room and walked toward the man sitting in front of his untouched tray. The man was back to a state of rage. As if he were planning some further revenge.

"It's all in here," said the young man as he dropped the coat in a careful pile beside the other's chair. The other looked up with absolute puzzlement. "Sleep with that under your bed, and leave with it in the morning. It's the real stuff, not soap, and nobody'll kill you. Though you're going to kill somebody else. So I'm going to go phone the police. And they are going to follow you. And they're going to follow the ones you give the stuff to. And you're going to do people a lesser harm this way." A bitter look of hatred came over the ex-POW's face. "Your food is cold," the young man continued, "let me get you a hot tray."

"You're scum too," the other said.

"Right," the young man said. "So you just tell them who spotted you. They put a contract out on me. And you can laugh behind bars. But it's nice there. Place is heated in the winter."

The ex-POW was now staring at him with an empty look. "I could make a suggestion," the young man continued. The other's silence said make it. "*You* could call the police. Say you came in here clean already and were able to keep your clothes and your sausage rolls. Say you were trapped by your need for revenge. And you want to lead them no matter what happens to you. The dope people will get you one way or another. You just have to choose how you're going out and who you're taking with you." For the young man, it was like watching an earthquake in slow motion, the workings of the man's face.

"You're just trying to save your young ass," the other said.

"I could have called ten minutes ago," the young man said. "It would have made sense to everybody. Your pals included. I still can."

"You want me to lead 'em?" said the other.

"In both directions," said the young man.

"Okay, phone, but you're my killer," said the other. "And you'll look clean. Like everybody else."

So the young man went to the office nearby the dining area. He could see the ex-POW. He got on to the police and explained what he had done if they wanted to take advantage of it. Or they could come right by. The plan was good, they said. Let it carry. Tell the guy he'd be shadowed. And if he didn't get picked up at the contact point, to keep living as a runner, they would photograph all contacts and follow the sausage rolls wherever they lead. So the young man went back to the table and told the ex-POW.

"So now I'm double scum," he said. "To you. To them."

"It's the only way left," the young man said. "You can't join a choir."

"What do you know?" the other said.

"This," said the young man, "I know this."

"So you don't shit on my grave," the other said.

"So I don't," the young man said.

Hammer Thrower

'Is the Lord with us or not?'
—Exodus 17:7

She did fountains. For shopping malls. Soulless things, she knew, business people wanted no distractions from business. The one she was looking at came down a flat, simulated stone wall. It was like a curtain ruffled by a slight breeze, the wall canted outward from top to bottom ever so slightly to keep the water from splashing. "No splashing," they had said, "we want people to be loosened in their pockets, not lazy in their behinds." The water looked very busy going somewhere down a slot in the floor. A sheet thirty yards wide, thirty yards high, coming out of a ceiling, going into a floor, almost soundlessly. There was a reverse curve below the floor leading to the holding tank. They had had troubles, people throwing soap in so suds came out the top, but a few arrests and fines had stopped that. And they had had to put restrooms nearby. Men thought it looked too much like the old time urinals with their slate slabs and constant flush, but her backing was blond so the water had silver play in it from specially set lights. Women liked it, they would often put their hands through the sheet to the stone and have the water run up their arms. But there was enough water to scare off most.

"So, okay," the woman said to herself, "that's the hole in peoples' pockets." She turned to leave and bumped into a man who had stopped to look.

"It's a pisser," he said. He had this big grin on and didn't notice she had bumped him, or hardly noticed.

"Sorry," she said.

"For this?" he said pointing to the fountain.

"No, for this," she said and she shoved him back out of her way. He was a big man, football big. He reached out an arm so it was over her shoulder and across her chest and she came to a halt then backed under the pressure until she was in front of him. "Pisser meant great when we were kids," he said, "and you didn't shove anybody bigger than you."

"Well people have told me it looks like a urinal, men people," she said.

"Why should you care?" he asked. She was glaring at him. "Ah!" he said, "it's yours. I forgive you."

"For goddam what?" she said.

"Shoving me around," he said, "what else?" It wasn't rage now on her face, it was hurt.

"You can take it," she said.

"Ah!" he said, "I'm a gorilla." She saw her prejudice. He put a big hand on her shoulder. "This yours?" he asked nodding toward the fountain.

"Take your hand off me," she said.

"It's not a hand," he said, "it's a question, but it's gone, see!" And he removed it. "But you hit me first."

"What question?" she asked.

"Why are you so touchy about this wall of water? And how come you didn't put one on the other side so it would be like Exodus to walk between?"

"I wanted to," she said. She was flushed with feeling now. Detained by a gorilla with a brain.

"I guess you can tell," he said, turning his head but not his body. His neck was like a hawser rope. "This is the way underground rivers come out of the sides of cliffs," he said further. "And it's Moses and the rock, isn't it?"

"Maybe," she said.

"You Jewish?" he asked.

"Yes," she said, "can I go now?"

"Not until you say something," he said.

"Like what?" she said.

"You did hit me. I'm not a gorilla. I never played football. This is all hammer throw and shotput and javelin. I'm a mythical warrior. A .22 bullet would stop me. So would a woman who gives me a shove for nothing." She was speechless. Because she was really confused. He had a red carnation in the buttonhole of his suit. He took it in his huge hand and said, "Look!" and he ate it.

She started to laugh against her will. Then she said, "I'm sorry I shoved you. It was righteous anger. Good thing for you I wasn't really mad."

"I want to put my question back on your shoulder," he said. She turned to look at the wall of water. There was actually a vague reflection of the two of them in the fall. "Like evolution," he chuckled, "beauty and beast."

"You are scary looking," she said, "even in a suit and tie."

"The truth," he said.

"I deal," she said, "with these guys who are scared if anything has any feeling at all. I wanted to put some knobs in that marble, at certain places, and there'd be a barely discernible face sculpted in the water, tears in fact, but tears of joy, I know I can make them look like tears of joy. And the knobs would shift from man's to woman's face by a slight change in the flow of the water. And the disruption of the flow would make it look as if water were springing up out of water, so men and women are the same effect of life, the same cause of life. They nixed that the way they nix taxes."

"So Moses to Miriam," he said.

"Right," she said.

"And Jesus to Mary," he said.

"Right," she said, "both Jews."

"Eloise and Abelard?" he asked.

"Okay, not Jews," she said, "you can have your choice."

"I'll take 'em," he said.

"So," she said, "I have it tamed down to pocket books and bladders. You have to empty both before you leave." And she stopped speaking.

"I feel something else," he said. "There's a kind of desperation in that water. It's running from nothing, running towards nothing. But begging for a cradle and a grave. Something to stop it being infinite. This is God without Moses and Miriam."

"It's not God, it's me," she said. "As soon as I stop being smooth they don't want me."

"You'll go crazy like this," he said.

"No," she said, "there's a tank underneath and a pump you can turn off and on."

"So, this is a lie," he said, "and I am a gorilla."

She bent her head into her hand. "You do hit hard," she said.

"Not harder than you," he answered.

"We can't be what we make," she said turning towards him.

"We can mean it," he said.

"They don't let you mean it," she said.

"But this is you," he said, "they have the button, but once they flip it on, this is you." He waited, then said, "Flip it off and it's me."

"Who are you?" she asked.

"I told you," he answered, "a hammer thrower."

The Best Place

The things which are done in secret are
things that people are ashamed even to speak of;
but anything exposed by the light will be illuminated
and anything illuminated turns into light.
—Ephesians 5:12-13

A woman sensed her husband loved someone else. The knowledge came suddenly. And hurt as if adhesive tape were ripped off her whole body. They had a son who was a newsman in Europe and a son who flew for an airline after a stint in the Service. She was an editor of children's books. He ran a teaching hospital as its Dean of Studies. There was a glow to her husband that did not come from the job. Nor from her.

"Do I want to know who she is?" the woman asked herself. "Must be young. And fertile as the Velveteen Rabbit." So she went to the hospital one evening, just before five, went right to the cafeteria, got in a line at the food counter, a tray, some silverware, coffee and a roll. From just before the cashier she looked and she saw him with her over near a window that gave out on a wall but let in some light.

"Neat place," she thought, "would illustrate a book." She walked across the busy room and placed her tray on the end of the table as she hooked a chair with one foot and brought it across so she could sit as if between them making the triangle complete. "I came to see who you were," she said to the woman. "And came in peace. Some things one just knows. Like this." There was not a word more. The other woman was exactly her age. Much handsomer than she. When she spoke she had a mellow voice.

"I spent a long time in religious life. I was not prepared to love someone."

"You love him?" the wife asked.

"Yes," the woman said. "I don't have a measure for it." She was looking at the woman's husband as she said this.

"Please look at me," the wife said. The woman did. "I give him to you right here," she said, "but your love is not stronger than mine. It's newer."

"This is not a property deal," the husband said. He was flushed with rage. "I'm not goods."

"We're the goods," the wife said, "you're the catbird."

"So it is anger," he said, "you're here to do a little damage."

"No," the wife said, "I want you to choose me again. Or I want you to go from me. And I won't sulk if you do. I said I loved you and I meant it."

"This is no place," the husband said.

"It's the best," the wife said. "I didn't follow you. I just knew you'd be here."

"I am not wrong to love him," the other woman said. It was a soft, defiant statement.

"I never said you were," the wife said. "I am not wrong to love him either."

"I'm a ping pong ball," the man said, "I'm something impersonal between you!"

"Then tell me what I am!" said the wife. He said nothing but she saw his love for the other woman fill him with color. The other woman sensed it. Her strength seemed to increase.

"I see this only in the young," the wife said. And she felt the adhesive being torn off her body again. "Tell me who you are a little more before I go," the wife said to the woman. The woman didn't answer. "Then do you want to know something about me before I go?" the wife said. The woman didn't answer. So the wife looked at her husband and said, "If you return this evening, you return to me. If not, then to her."

"You have no understanding," he said.

"I find her attractive myself," the wife said still looking at him. "I'm glad I'm not you."

"I've been dying with you," he said, "you seem to live off yourself. Suddenly someone seems to want to live off me."

The other woman was losing her courage a bit. "Are we the same woman?" she said to him. "I mean am I warming up something? I've never loved anyone until you. I can live my life. But this is different."

He was caught. He put his hand up a bit as if asking for a time out. It was a long time out, a turbulent one. Then he said, "Yes, I guess you are."

"Are what?" the other woman said.

"The same woman," he said. "It's like the waxworks. Unveiling a statue. Perfect." He looked away from the two of them, out the window toward the blank·wall. It was clear who was which to him.

"So the one who moves is the real one?" the wife asked. "Well, I'm going to move too," she added. She put her hands on the tray before her and started her chair back away from the table.

"Wait, please," said the other woman. "I tried to tell you I haven't known this before. He said you didn't understand and I don't think you do. But I'm not going to be a surrogate for you. So *I'm* going to move. And try to be me with someone. Not you." Then she looked at the man and said, "I'm different." She rose and left the table to them.

"She is," said the wife, "and so am I. It's you who are the same."

"With you I am," he said. "With her I'm different."

"Then we are both facing that blank wall," she said.

"Not you," he said, "just me."

"I was ready to let you go," the wife said, "and I still am. As she said, so I say, I can lead my life."

"I'm the only one who can't," he said. "I'm dying on myself."

"Come," she said. She put a hand on his arm. "I'm really not blank and really not a wall."

"Then what is it?" he said. Now it was she who thought a long time, she who went through a turbulence, then a calming down.

"I was too satisfied with you."

"What does that mean?" he said.

"It means I have demands to make on you. Or *my* life is over."

A Life for a Life

I am now going to open your graves;
I mean to raise you from your graves . .
and lead you back . . .
—Ezekiel 37:12

A man saw a woman beaten to death by a mob. The mob thought she was an informer. He was the informer. He had made love to this woman to get names. But she had many lovers so the mob thought the reverse, *she* did it to get names herself. They kept killing her after she was dead. And lucky it was nearly dark or they might have spotted him plus some of the others and have done them some damage also. She was left lying in the open field where they had hauled her, outside the village. He knew he had one chance to keep suspicion off him. So when the kicking was done and the passions cooled, he walked with his hands open toward the body lying in its own space. He looked like love itself. And people took him as a lover. Crazy. They hesitated whether to kill him too, there was shouting, some attempts to rouse more passion, some of the crowd threw a few things, but passion had been satisfied and the ruse began to work.

He moved her corpse over on its back. She was beaten beyond recognition. But she was still limp. So he hoisted her up on his shoulders, her head and arms down his back, her legs down his chest, and he walked out of that field, not back toward the village but toward the burial ground away from it. He walked slowly. A scattered procession of jeerers formed for a short distance, then gave out with the light to go home and feed. A few stayed, children in fact, two children, girls of eight and ten, hers. They were the living picture of fear even in the dark. Whatever life they had he was carrying it. And he was stained with it.

He went into the cemetary area. It was Christian. There was a hut with tools. He opened the door with his foot, and with a free hand took a spade.

72

The girls were just beyond reach. "I have to do this right," he thought. He carried her body to an open space in a row, then put it carefully on the ground. He began to dig with the spade. It was a hard, clay-like soil but it gave as he dug it out almost in slabs. He felt the girls flutter by him and land on her body. They were choking with grief. When he had the hole dug, he took his shirt which he had removed for the digging and put it on the woman, it was long for a man, short for her, but covered her nearly naked frame. Then he took his handkerchief and tried to smooth away some of the damage from her face.

"Now lift her by the legs," he said to the two girls. "Move her to the edge." They did together. The man got down in the hole, about four feet. "Now let her legs down in," he said to them. He held her under the arms as they did. Then he lowered the rest of her onto the bottom, an awkward movement, but very gentle. Then he rolled up on the side of the grave, and, still lying on his side, he arranged her body so it was neat and asleep.

Then he began to sing a slow chant for the dead. The two girls crept close to him. And he noticed what he expected to notice. He was being watched and watched carefully. He could see quick movements in the dark thirty, forty yards away. People trying not to be seen. Then carefully, with his hands not the spade, he began to roll the clods into the grave as if he were reluctant to bury her. He kept singing chants for the dead. And he motioned for the girls to help him. Which they did, though they were still numb, they did imitating his gentle way. Until she was covered. Then he finished the rest with the spade. Now he knew he would have to go back with the girls to the village. He had to stay with them. If he made any move to leave, suspicion would be on him. And he had to treat them right. Or people would spot the ruse. And he had to fear that those who wanted his information would be angry at not getting it and might reveal him for revenge reasons and the scene of mob murder would be repeated only he'd be the victim. And who would bury him? Two girls? Who waited on his life for theirs right now?

"I"ll sit here until they come," he thought. "They'll come for the girls first." He sat with them on the grave the rest of the night. And true enough, some women came in the morning. And they beckoned to the girls. But the girls were afraid. Until he gave them a firm command to go. That he would stay with their mother. So they left him. And the man sat the whole day mourning. But watching those who watched him. It was well into the second day before someone approached with water and some food. He took the water but not the food. On the third day the girls came to him. They had some food and he ate it. Now it was clear what he would do. He would go into the village. Get his belongings, lay them out on the street for anyone who wanted to take them, everything, though the bundle of money would have to be abandoned in the wall of his house. Then leave as though to say he could live there no more. His movements would have to be slow, but there must not be a wasted one in case those he told names to got wise to him and got angry. And this is what he did.

But the girls wanted to go with him. No one wanted them around, even family, they were reminders. "I will have to abandon them," he thought, "but far enough away." So he motioned to them to walk ahead. They didn't know which way. So he took them lighly by the heads and began. Their heads were warm, their hair soft, they seemed not afraid anymore. "I could grow them and sell them as wives," he thought. And he sensed under his hands what they could be. "Maybe keep one of them for myself." The ten year old would be tall the way her mother was. "I'll have to do some begging," he thought more. "No one to inform on." They were at the edge of the village and his hands were on their shoulders. "I'll get over to the bus road," he thought. "Bum a ride into the city." He stopped. And they did with him.

Then he saw himself shatter as window glass would under a rock. He saw a mob come through the window, someone grab an arm and pull it from its socket and run, someone grab the other and run off with it, someone pick his genitals off his body like fruit off a tree and run, then someone take his head, someone his torso, and leave only one thing, his heart suspended in the air and sucking for life the way lungs do. And the heart started to fall toward the dust but he had no hands to catch it with. And he snapped back to himself on his knees with his two hands out in front of him. The girls were drawn even closer to him by all this. And women ran over to him with food. But food for the road. "My life has been taken from me," he thought. "I will be killed if I take it back. Someone will know every minute if I do." The someone was out there ahead of him. He could feel the pull. It was a life he did not want. But it was a life.

Extra Things

. . . one of you is about to betray me . . .
    —Mark 14:18

A woman was in a country illegally. She spoke the language but had no card. Back home she had been on the dole. An educated, young, strong woman, with one problem, no future worth anything. In the new country, the one job she could work she invented herself, selling flowers, at the edge of a college campus, under a live oak, where there was also a crossing and a bus stop, fumes and noise, but she handled beauty all day and loved it. She took the earliest Metro to the flower market across the Bay in the City, then came back in time for the early traffic at her spot. She would sell until dark. All cash transactions. Someone soon noticed what an excellent place she had. And someone soon found out she was illegal. So he came up to her and said he'd have a share of the profits or he was turning her in.

"Fine," she said, "but you have to see Big Joey about that. He's the one who put me here. I do a few extra things with the flowers for him."

The blackmailer turned a little pale. "Never heard of Big Joey," he said. "Then just stay here with me for a while. He'll roll by," she said, "to get his goods."

"Listen, I made a mistake, okay?" the blackmailer said. "I was just looking for a little. I don't have a job. So just forget it, okay?"

The woman said nothing. She looked hard at him as he backed away and went off. But off to watch. She could see him back under the copse of trees near the Engineering Building. He was a bum for sure, but a shrewd one. He'd see if there was a Big Joey and run if there was. Big Joey's didn't kill little bums. Hurt 'em maybe.

She was wrapping a spring bouquet for a man when he said. "You have a nice spot here. How would you like to keep it?"

"I have it," she said as she held the flowers up between them. He didn't take them.

"While I was looking," he said, "I saw some nice ways to pass things on to people. A rose here. A daffodil there. That's a nice pot of begonias."

"That's silly," she said, "you wouldn't make enough to live on. If you want to hurt me, hurt me. But get lost right now."

She put the bouquet down on her small table. The man left saying, "Go home early."

"There ain't no Big Joey," said the blackmailer who had come up behind her and overheard some.

"No, there ain't," she said, "there's just me, and this stick, and broad daylight. And you can tell whoever you damn please. Now get out of here."

"I just need something to live on," he said.

"Then get a job," she said.

"Can't," he said, "can't concentrate."

"Why not?" she said.

"You know," he said. And started to shuffle with both feet a bit. And she did know. He took some heavy stuff once, and the whole edge off himself.

"Well, work for me," she said. "Take this pot of flowers and get out in the middle of the road and do your dance there. Balance it on your head and never mind the traffic. And I'll think of something else."

So he got out in the pedestrian crossing halfway, put the pot on his head and did his shuffle. Someone in a ragtop bought the pot. There was a shouting of prices back and forth from the woman. And the man was reluctant to bring the money back. "No money, no pot," she shouted. He went the other way with the money, up the hill toward a market and a jug.

And the other man was back. "Okay, it's small but it pays. There's a whole school here."

"Go," she said, "Go!"

"Maybe I won't," he said. And he began to circle through her flowers, touching some lightly with his toe, knocking them over, but also scaring people away from buying. He had a mean look about him. The woman was helpless. She wanted notice from the Police. She saw the blackmailer come down the hill to the lights across from her so she said, "Look!" to the man walking through her flowers and she pointed across the street. And he did look. And the blackmailer saw what he now thought was Big Joey. He dropped the jug smash on the sidewalk and turned and ran.

The man walking through the flowers didn't understand. "Okay," she said to the man, "what do I do?"

"I just have some small packages. You put 'em in bouquets. People just pay you for the flowers. I'm around someplace. I tell 'em which flowers. And they tell you and you wrap the stuff in."

"Okay," she said, "but you don't give me the stuff here."

"Where?" he said.

"Down there," she said pointing to the hedges that boxed in a small botanical garden.

"I can play," he said. So they walked down toward the break in the hedges and when they got there she ripped her blouse then grabbed his shirt and pulled it free of its buttons then ran back toward her flower stand screaming and pointing back toward the astonished man.

"He tried . . . He tried . . ." she gasped, and people saw him standing there immobilized. Then he turned and ran, through the gap in the hedges, and once out of sight ditched the stuff he had in his pockets and disappeared out the back of the garden and onto the walkway down toward the Life Sciences building in which he then hid. She knew there'd be Police. So her flower days were over. But there'd be a report and a description, of the two of them. Her friend had better disappear, just as she had better. So she too went into a building, still almost running as she did. Engineering. Not too many Ladies Rooms in the old thing but she found one with a window that overlooked her flower stand. She saw the Police, both Campus and town. And people pointing in various directions. Then the Police began to load the flowers into their car trunks. But they sniffed them all, and prodded and poked. She sat in a booth for a long time. Later she left. It was rush hour traffic and the University emptying, great time for sales. As she came out the door, there was her blackmailer hitting people up for small change. He didn't see her. Then he did and froze. She was like a bomb to him. One that would go off.

"This is worth nothing," she thought as she turned away from him. She walked across campus to the Police Station. She walked in, up to the desk, and said, "You took my flowers."

The man at the desk said simply, "Then you got problems."

"No," she said. "You have."

Playing with Fire

. . . let us celebrate the feast by
getting rid of all the old yeast of
evil and wickedness . . .
—1 Corinthians 5:8

A man was in Jerusalem for Easter. A clergyman who taught Scripture at a Bible School in the States. A bachelor by accident, but young enough not to need to be. His studies had absorbed him. He was crowded into the Sepulcher itself, bent under the low, stone roof, leaning over the pink slab that was studded with small candles which ate all the oxygen the pack of pilgrims didn't. He had squeezed in with some from the Islands who had come with their priests.

He felt a hand working his wallet loose from his back pocket, someone lifting his jacket to get at it. He couldn't turn, couldn't straighten up. So he reached back in a flash of anger, just about able to, and grabbed a wrist and held it. The wrist pulled, pulled toward the hole out of the Sepulcher through which new pilgrims where shoving in, displacing the old. He stepped on his own wallet. He could tell, not see. It had little in it, the man was a shrewd traveler, his important stuff was zippered in coat pockets inside his suit. He held the wrist as he would hold a mountain rope. He was around a person in front of him, old woman already bent, and as he tumbled out into the crowd pressing the Sepulcher rock the wrist jerked free but he caught a glimpse of a priest in robe and headdress and panic stricken face. Who then raised his head in dignity now that there was no evidence. The look he gave the man was one of untouchable arrogance and that angered the Bible scholar more than anything ever had in his life.

So he moved through the crowd behind the priest not knowing what to do with his anger. There was a group marching in procession around the

Sepulcher, led by Turkish guards in old, brilliant uniforms, they smashed their pikes down on the stones in front of them and every foot got out of the way. Then priests and people followed with bells, books, and candles. The priest slipped into the procession. "Priest, my foot!" thought the Bible scholar, his fury mounting even more. He saw someone with a fistful of candles, someone who tended the procession to make sure all had them, so the man put a request look on his face, the din made speech deaf, received a candle, lit it, and began to work forward in the procession toward the bogus priest who kept checking around his veil over his shoulder.

"I'll light him," the man thought, "run a little fire up that veil. It won't get far. But I'll loosen his bowels a bit." The man's anger was hotter than his candle flame. He was almost possessed, "Theft! In this sacred place! By a bogus priest! Of a useless wallet! How could the thief know?" He started to reach with his candle over the shoulders of shorter people, toward the veil. The thief saw him and jerked away, furious himself at the victim for not being a lamb. The man reached again, singing now, singing the Alleluja he had picked up in the procession, singing it like an ecstatic who needed room for his arms and his soul. A big man next to him put a hand on his, smiled an intelligent smile, and brought both candle and hand back into a safe position, then patted the man on the shoulder. That way they all processed three times around the Sepulcher.

At the end of the third, the bogus priest cut out of the procession and headed through the crowd toward the door. Simply lost himself in the multitude. But the Bible scholar tried to catch him anyway, shouldering his way also to the door, out into the small square and the choice of going left or right through narrow, teeming streets. There was wax all over his hand from the candle, his skin was somewhat burned. And his anger began to cool. He blew the candle out the way he would blow out that thief if he caught him. Return to his normal self was very slow. And the shame that rose in his face rose very slowly. Until he felt that he was burning.

"What sweet revenge on me!" he thought. "This place could turn you into a wretch." He was now facing the entrance to the Church, being moved gently left and right by the flow of people. A group of whom stopped around him. And there was the voice of the guide shouting some information, in English. "Before you go in," she said, "I'd better tell you a few things. You wouldn't hear a word inside. Just remember nothing is exact in there. The hole where the Cross was put is a guess, the cave where the cross was found is a legend. And the Holy Sepulcher is not the real one. It's at the bottom of the Mediterranean Sea. During the Byzantine Empire, the real tomb was cut out from here, the way you would take a loaf of bread from an oven. It was loaded aboard ship down at the coast and sank with the ship in a storm. And remember the guards are here at the request of the various religions, they are not the State intruding. So be back in 45 minutes, there is no way we can group inside."

The shame in the man began to burn even more. "I lost a worthless wallet to a worthless priest in a worthless shrine, then I tried to singe his skull!" He wanted to laugh but tears came instead. The woman guide was still near him, holding her small flag so the group could know her.

"You sure about the Sepulcher?" he said to her.

"I'm sorry," she said, "I didn't mean to harm your faith. My group are not pilgrims." She was looking at his wet face.

"Oh, this is something else," he said. "A priest tried to pick my pocket inside and I tried to light him on fire for it."

"A thief is safe here," she said, "you should carry nothing."

"It was next to nothing," he said. "But are you sure about that Sepulcher, it's at the bottom of the sea?"

"It's a judgment on evidence," she said, "but it doesn't really matter, this one works."

"Oh, does it!" he said. "Turned *me* into one."

"You sound hard," she said, "but hard like that candle maybe. Most of us are." She put her flag under her arm and took out a box of matches. Wooden ones. Thin little things. She struck one and held it. He reached the candle to it, the wax still around his knuckles and thumb. She lit it. "Be careful you don't burn the innocent with the guilty," she said and smiled. The shame lit up in him again and tears came.

"I meant to be humorous," she said.

"You were," he said, "that was genius. I wish I had you in my hand."

"Oh, I go out too," she said.

"Goodbye. Thanks," he said. He went back inside the church and stood in the din and the shoving. He held the candle until it burned down and went out. Then he worked the wax free of his hand and dropped it in a candle tray. It was the mould of his fist he left.

Behind the Flags

. . . your faith will have been tested and
proved like gold--only it is more precious
than gold which is corruptible even though it
bears testing by fire . . .
        —1 Peter 1:7

A woman ran a day care center during the week. Weekends and some nights she was an urban guerrilla. Her group had taken out two soldiers in an ambush one Saturday evening, and had blown a pub full of enemies into the street on another. She hated the injustice of centuries. And she hated the compromises that had gained some freedom, not total liberty. There were no Peter Rabbit stories told in her center. More like *The Rising Of The Moon* and rebels gathering with their pikes. Which had stirring music to it. She was pregnant, she had recognised, though she had checked with no one, didn't have to, she was three months without a period. The weekends were spent in some cold lofts. And he, the father, was so wanted that he had to skip overseas.

There was another attack planned. It meant crossing the border on foot Friday night, walking until dawn, hiding Saturday, then on Sunday, during a parade, penetrating an army barracks by stealth and setting bombs in the living quarters, to go off in the evening when the soldiers returned. She was desperate to go on this one, and could conceal her rounding belly in baggy clothes. So she made the list. During the week she was law and order itself, and the nursery a smoothly run chaos. The fact is she handled parents' problems as well as childrens'. She's a modern nun, people thought, all care and no belief.

She met the other three that Friday in the back of a garage. They got inside the tank of a milk truck, down through the hatches as into a submarine and onto some ladders that had been run the length of the tank and hung from ropes. The tanker was half filled with milk to weight down the tires and shoot milk out a spigot if anyone turned it to see. A hatch was left slightly open to leave in air. Near the border the driver rapped on the steel and they came out into the dark and the open fields, which they then crossed after the truck had left. Her body was in excellent shape. The explosives were not too heavy on her back. Each device was self-containing, had to be, in case they were spotted, if they got away from pursuit there were alternate targets. All she had to do was turn a dial, as on a washing machine. In fact, they had agreed to blow themselves up as they surrendered if they were caught, lure their captors close, who cares how few, better be dead and a symbol than alive in a prison grave.

Well, they were spotted, and had to split, a patrol with dogs just across their path, uncanny, as if tipped off, moving right toward them. She was to wait in place as the other three split and drew the patrol away, hoping to escape them, but if not, taking a few out as planned. And she, in her extra backpack, had some women's street clothes, maternity clothes in fact, and she was to hide her explosive in a cotton bag that had laces she could tie around her back. The bag would give her the right look if she made it through the patrol and into town at daylight to her secondary target. It was to be the basement of a church where the drums and flags for the parade were stored, and just before, the place would be packed with marchers.

The other three did manage to draw off the patrol from her. But she heard shooting at a distance, then silence, then an explosion. There was a lot of vehicular activity on the roads thereafter. So her way across them was more difficult. She had to wait behind the walls and hedgerows. But she made it to the abandoned cottage they had planned on, made it just at dawn. She thought she heard one more explosion a good distance off but she was not sure. The plan was she would rest only a while then put on the maternity clothes and lay the bomb if she could on Saturday in the church then begin her escape a day early.

As she rested she began to feel some cramps, twinges more like it, in her womb. She might be in trouble from a miscarriage. That infuriated her. So she dropped the idea of rest. Best to move now, risk getting caught in her night outfit and blackened face. She could trigger her captors with herself. So she moved along the inside of the walls and hedgerows until she couldn't move anymore. Then behind some bushes she changed into the maternity clothes, cleaned her face, combed her hair, set the bomb well over her belly, put on a kerchief, then came out on the shoulder of the road and walked as she knew pregnant women walked. The place was abuzz with the news of what went on the night before and she feared capture, but somehow among the more frequent cottages and thin rows of houses she escaped halt and search. In the town itself she moved with greater ease right to the church. But for the last mile, the cramps had been increasing and she knew she was in real trouble from within. But she had to plant the bomb.

She walked by the church and saw it was busy with people who knew one another. They were preparing for the next day, and mostly men. They'd have to be distracted. She'd have to light a car up, around the corner, how do you do that in broad daylight, and as a pregnant woman? The cigarette trick they had been taught. Cigarettes she had. Take one and put it crossways in the book of matches after lighting it, close the book, and leave it in the neck of an opened fuel pipe. When the matches flared she would be gone and the fumes would ignite the tank. So she rounded the corner and found a car and leaned against it as a pregnant woman would, took the gas cap off as she leaned against the boot, slipped it in her pocket for later disposal, took out her book of matches and her cigarettes and did as she was shown how. She laid them carefully in the neck of the pipe, then moved as quickly as she could away. When she was fifteen yards off, the matches flared and fell down the pipe and there was an explosion enough to wake the dead. The blast shoved her to the ground and brought exactly the pandemonium she wanted and gave her the chance to look frightened as she ran in fear from the scene, disposing of the gas cap as she went.

The church emptied of its people, enough to let her slip inside and look for a place to put the bomb and set it, then slip out as an ordinary looking person. She went in behind a row of flags, saw some boxes of old hymnals, emptied one quickly, put the bomb in the bottom of the box, re-heaped hymnals back on top, put the extras on the other boxes, then started out from behind the flags. A severe cramp hit her. She had to get out before she was crippled by it or she had to hide and try to weather it. She got just outside the door when she had to fall with the pain. She had to avoid detection. So she crawled back inside the church basement and looked for somewhere to hide. There were some old flags near where she had hid the bomb and timer, they were off their poles and piled. She could get under them, there were enough. People came back soon after she hid, but the use of the place was over for the day because of the torched vehicle around the corner. So after an hour the place was locked.

She couldn't breathe well under the flags. The cramps were nearly continuous. She made it to the middle of the floor where she fainted with the pain. She lay there in and out of consciousness and cramps until the miscarriage occurred and then she was simply too sick to move. She bled so much she became delirious. She spent the whole night that way. The first people who arrived in the morning found her in her own blood in the middle of the floor. An emergency unit was called for, whatever the suspicious nature of her being there was. She had no identification. She seemed barely conscious and couldn't respond to questioning. She was young enough to be unmarried and to have tried to abort herself to avoid shame. They had to work on her right there before they could move her, so the scene became like a battlefield medic station.

She felt herself coming back to consciousness. She felt the effects of their swift medical care. She felt she could speak but she did not want to, she might discover herself to them. Their solicitude for her was remarkable. The way they lifted her onto the stretcher. The gentle pressure of the straps around her. Her baby was lost. The ones who discovered her would be lost too, in an hour or so. The stretchermen started to lift her. From somewhere nearby there was an explosion. The bearers put her down and everyone tensed as if for another one. Then people ran to the door and out. She knew on the floor the third of her men had escaped the patrol and hit the police barracks nearby, their original target. The confusion was great, the ambulance and crew needed. They thought she would maintain until the emergency was over, so they sent and got some women to come in and sit with her. And men came in who were going to do that parade never mind death. The women held her and stroked her as she kept the lid on her consciousness. And the men were quieter with the drums and flags. It was near time for that bomb.

Then something burst out of the woman on the stretcher. "I put a bomb in here. I put a bomb in here." It sounded like deranged talk at first. "It's in here. It's in here," she said louder. "It's nearly time. It's nearly time." The women caught on quickly that this stranger with her different accent was not delirious. They rose and screamed out of the place, screaming the men out with them. The woman on the stretcher could hear the new panic outside the door distancing itself from the place. She tried to get free of the straps of the stretcher but could not. She wanted to defuse that bomb. It was what she had really given birth to, not the poor flesh left in a plastic bag in towels there on the floor.

The explosion collapsed the ceiling and started a fire which brought the whole church down on her and everything was burned beyond recognition. And there was a strange, contradictory rumor among the crowd as they watched. "She warned us," it went. "She warned us." "The beast."

3rd Sunday, Easter

Objects of Piety

Remember, the ransom that was paid to free
you from the useless way of life your ancestors
handed down was not paid in anything corruptible.
—1 Peter 1:18

A woman was at a funeral mass. The dead man was a guerrilla genius. Killed in exile by a runaway truck on a mountain road, the news said. Knocked him and his small car over a precipice. She had made love to him, but so had others, during the terror days they had inflicted on government to gain independence for their region. Her pregnancy had put her out of action during that last daring burst so she was not caught when someone turned traitor and named names. The dead man had escaped the roundup, or series of shootouts that had destroyed their group of terrorists. But the man's tactics were ingenious and ready for anyone's hand.

She had the son, a two year old, with her. She was safe in this crowd, even the priest was preaching a eulogy about courage and integrity forced on people by tragic oppression. Outside, across the Plaza, there were bitter protests of the requiem going on, Catholics throwing their crucifixes, their objects of piety, rosaries, small statues, up against the steps of the church as a protest and statement that they were pitching their belief to the devil for what was going on inside. Her parents were out there she knew. They had taken her in for the sake of the new life, though they didn't know whose. They did now they saw her grief, when they saw her go where she never went, to Mass, and with the baby, who didn't belong in the crunch of people, but did, they saw, when she forced the matter, so they told her to stay with her murderer into the grave, and his son with her. His son was frightened by the anger. And frightened by the pack in the church. He was crying almost without sound. He was wet and dirty and he smelled but she had no change.

"Sacristy," she thought. So she worked to a side aisle and up, went into the sacristy. It too was packed with people but they were looking out the door at the preacher who showed above their heads in the pulpit like some crusader monk impassioning volunteers. She put the baby on the vesting case. It dawned on her she could leave him. No sense in him if the father were dead and the cause stifled. Or she could teach him the genius of his father. Here was a bomb with its clock set for twenty years. She saw a drawer half open and altar linens inside, squares priests wore under vestments. Perfect! She took a fistful, worked her way to the sink, and there removed the soiled things from the boy, washed him and put a half dozen sacred linens on using their strings to make a good diaper, then disposed of the other diaper in the basket for altar laundry.

The sermon was over. The congregation was singing a patriotic hymn. It filled the sacristy also with its passion. Then it blended into a roar of no, no, no, and she looked over heads to see another priest up in the pulpit. He had apparently grabbed the regional flag off the coffin, had run up in the pulpit and, knowing he couldn't speak over the din, had started to rip it to shreds in protest. People had leaped after and were trying to pull him out of the pulpit, but he had wedged himself in as he tried to rip more. The rage seemed to increase as something else was happening, she didn't know what, down by the coffin in the center aisle. She forced herself out the sacristy door with her frightened baby now stunned into silence. There was a fight going on around the coffin, some men were actually trying to overturn it, to demean it, they had it on its side and were kicking the carriage out from underneath it. And they succeeded before they were ridden off by those who could get their hands on them. Chairs and people and coffin, there was chaos and everyone looking alike, it made for terrifying confusion.

In the grappling, the coffin broke open, the supposedly sealed coffin, and a stench rose quickly, but it wasn't the stench of a human being, it was the stench of animal flesh, a chunk of bull 200 pounds in weight. The shouting got fiercer as the partisans saw what was in the coffin. And the word spread and the grief turned to a kind of exultation. They knew! Even though they had been tricked. Their chief was alive. The death was a hoax. The fight would go on though he would need a new strategy. Or what was it? They had seen photos of him dead. Someone grabbed the rotting beef and raised it overhead and mounted the altar steps and shouted, "Here is your chief!" People started to throw chairs at him so he dropped the carcass and hit into the crowd like a bull himself trying to make for the door. The woman was shoved around now. The anger in the crowd was at frenzy level. She could scarcely keep hold of the child. In fact she felt him slipping, almost being pulled out of her arms. So she began to struggle against the pressure of bodies, looking desperately to get against a pillar or into some niche where she could protect him and herself. She actually had to reach him up over her head, flooding with bitterness as she did at the parallel with the rotten meat. Somehow people then saw the baby and in irritation shoved her over against a pillar where she could flatten and bring the baby down against her chest and keep him from getting ripped away from her and trampled. He was almost choking in his tears and frightened out of the wits he had. People began to pour out of the church despite the shouts of a man in the pulpit for control, for no panic. And the people who poured out began to pick up broken crucifixes and objects of piety and hurl them at the protesters behind the police lines across the Plaza. The police had to move in. Jeeps and trucks came out of a side street to set up a wall between the two factions.

Inside, the woman had some space now, still with her back to a pillar, still nearly deafened by the shouts of rage. And the baby was soiled again and the altar lines were poor diapers so she was wet from him right through her jacket. She sank down along the pillar until she was seated against it and holding him as in a basket of herself. He had his two hands gripping her hair and his face against her. She had reduced him to this. Had reduced herself. There were raging figures still looming over the two of them. "You will not turn into rotting meat," she began to mutter to herself. "Nor shitty meat." Then, "If he did this as a trick to stay alive. . ." Then, "To disappear and live easy. . .If he set it up with the government. . . I saw him dead!" Then, "I saw him dead. . . He's dead and its their trick. . . It's everybody's!"

She got up and was able to push through the remaining raging partisans back into the sacristy. There were priests there but they were arguing. So she got some more linens, went to the sink and changed the boy again. He was in a pitiful state, even looking at her as if he had lost her. So she bent over him as he lay on that sink table and she began to kiss him very gently on the forehead, then on the nose, then on the cheek either side. And she started to tickle him with her tongue, quick darts to his eyes so he had to blink, and she started to make sounds in her throat like pleasure sounds. But in doing this it was as if she had taken an ax to herself and split herself open like a melon. It's what the guerrilla genius had done to her. The boy was calmer. He had someone. She picked him up and went home.

She stood outside without knocking or ringing. It was her father who came out. "If I leave him with you and go . . .?" she said.

"Go kill?" he said.

"No," she said. She reached the child toward him saying, "Please. I don't know how."

He held up his hands. "How is it I know if I brought you up?" he said. Then he took the child, who was happy with the difference. "You go in first," he said. "Or I have nothing."

Something for Nothing

You had gone astray like sheep but now
have come back to the shepherd and
guardian of your souls.
—1 Peter 2:25

A man had to go for food stamps. The first time in his life. The packing plant was closed. For good. He knew it. And the land outside of town was still in winter so no jobs on a farm, if the farms were still working. He looked around and saw mainly women and children in the several lines to the several desks. There was a young woman at his desk. She asked him to sit when he reached her. He could barely give his name. He was a big man. He could carry a frozen carcass as if it were made of styrofoam. Though lately he twinged where he had been injured in football. State champs, his high school. He didn't want college, books were not for him, even the simplest. There had been Korea. He had married a cousin after, big woman, lovely woman, she died hard, but with tremendous faith. The two sons were service people with their families and overseas. Most of his savings went to her death. Now there was a dead plant and maybe a dead future. He said this all to the woman behind the desk. Between pauses as he tried for composure. Unemployment had run out. She was okaying the food stamps, but she kept testing to see what kind of job hunt he had tried. Food stamps run out too.

"You'll have to move someplace," she said. "We know there's nothing here."

"It's funny," he said quietly, "when I have nothing, you have something." She saw what he meant. "Don't get me wrong," he said. "You work. It ain't easy."

"So all your money went on her illness?" the woman asked.

The man nodded. "I'd have given more. I've got so much." And he waved his hand up and down his body. "I could carry her like a broom. And she used to be like a tree." He turned his head a second. "I should pay you for this," he said.

"I have to hear," she said.

"I'm shamed," he said, "I'm asking a woman." He said that to tell her something about himself, not her, and she knew it.

"She would have carried you like a broom too," the woman said. He looked up and at her. "So I'm in her place," the woman continued.

"You're like a girl," he said.

"It isn't the size," she said and he nodded.

"I mean you should be carrying someone else maybe," he said.

"I will," she said and he nodded.

"It's that I won't," he said. She saw he meant her young life and how she could create with it as she wanted. It was not envy. It was exclusion. The life was taken. The love was left with nothing.

"You can't just hang out," she said.

"No," he said. Then he sensed her looking at him with a funny look.

"I have no gun," he said. "I could never kill. Except in the war. But we didn't see. Just numbers the guys called in."

She untensed and said, "You know you can walk around dead."

"Yeah, I know it," he said. "And walk in here dead too."

"There's a line," she said and he knew she didn't know any more. She handed him the envelope with the stamps. "They're not mine," she said.

He heaved himself up and saw she wanted him not to say thanks but something else, goodbye. He thought to say "See you," but that was off. So he saluted her with his huge arm up quietly to his forehead, not military, family. And he started out along the line of women and children and the few old folks. Halfway down he opened the envelope, took out the stamps and handed a block of them to each woman and child he saw, then the last one to an old guy who couldn't figure it out for a minute. Then he left the office and turned along the row of stores toward where he left his pickup.

She ran up behind him with the books in her hand, pulled him by the arm and said, "They'll get their stamps." She was shivering.

"I have to do something," he said. "I can't eat off other people. I should just drive out and stop."

"No," she said, "believe me, no!"

He held his big hands out to either side of him, the blocks of stamps looked small.

"What happens to me if you do?" she said. "I just make believe you never were?" She was really shivering now.

And he said, "Go. You'll catch your death."

"Not until you say something," she said.

"I will use these," he said. That didn't seem enough. "I will use them on myself," he said further. And that didn't seem enough either. She stood there, arms wrapped tight against the chill. "So I can carry . . ." and he didn't finish because he didn't know what.

"Me?" she said. He nodded and she turned and walked quickly toward the office. Even the doorway was crowded. "She's a girl," he said as he walked to his truck. "I carried her in a race once. Had my face right between her breasts and couldn't breathe and didn't care. And we won a sack of corn that weighed what she did. It was so big. I had it on my head like an Indian when we went home. And we ate corn forever. There's gotta be a woman who lost too. Just gotta be. We can swap stamps. I look like a dog. Just wash these things and they're ok. Maybe fix a smile on my face. Get this ring off. Jesus!"

The Scheme of Things

Do not let your hearts be troubled.
—John 14:1

A man discovered one day that his marriage was a lie. She had been given a new identity and background before she met him. That's what it said in the letter on his desk. Along with a foreign ID photoed by a polaroid which gave her real name. No doubt it was she, name or not. The letter had come inter-office, not postal delivery. The bank did as much correspondence with itself as it did with the market. She was out shopping this morning. The two children in day care for a few hours.

"Criminal?" he thought. "Witness? Relative? Why tell me? Someone wants me to do something. Or I'm about to be nailed. Or she is. Pure revenge? I'm supposed to tell somebody about this. I'm sitting on too many portfolios. Once I tell someone, I'm out of this position. Someone else is put in. Who? There are only three who can do it without risking a loss of accounts. Someone wants concealment. Who could possibly know she had been given a new identity? Had to be the government. If her enemies knew, she'd be dead. For whatever reason."

So this letter in front of him came from a government source. Had to be from a covert branch. Intelligence. Law enforcement wouldn't dare anything but a scam. This letter asked for nothing. He had Spain, Italy, and Greece. Investments in energy production. The purchase of nuclear fuel. Not for Greece or Spain. Too impoverished. So Italy. He always thought she was Italian. She had gestures that were perfect. And her English was flawless now that he thought of it, the product of superb schooling even to the carelessness with which she used it. So a covert operation with the Italians. To slip someone bomb material.

"I have to force some moves," he thought. He turned to his computer but saw a hand laid on top of the screen and his immediate superior who held a copy of the letter in his other hand.

"Just leave things," he said. Security was standing right behind him. Then his superior said, "We'll have to run a check on your material. I have to suspend you until it's over. Then we'll see about this."

"Makes perfect sense," the man responded. "You'll find everything in right order. All whoever sent that letter needs is a few days."

"Who sent the letter?" his superior asked.

"Our government," the man answered. Then continued, "Who are you going to put in to do the check?"

"Has to be government, you know that," the superior said.

"I didn't know that," the man said.

"So it wouldn't be wise if you left town," the superior said. Then, "Sorry, but I have to play this straight."

"I'll go," the man said, and he got his jacket and left the cubicle. "It's not supposed to happen this way," he thought. "I should have gone to him and suspended myself. They must have a backup plan too. Such as I don't get out of this building alive if I show suspicion. Or they have her somewhere. No, she's right here. They have the kids."

His wife was standing in the corridor near the elevators watching the entry to his office area. She stood but she was ready to fall, just about. He walked over and put his arms around her, speaking to her softly, "Tell me, tell me quick and straight. We have to decide in minutes."

"I was mistress of a banker in Italy," she said. "I saw who came for a secret meeting just before a bank fraud was uncovered. There were Americans too. I was asked to give names in return for a new life, or I would be left to be killed. I am to wait here for a signal. To stay if you did not act rightly. And tell you it's your children and me for your silence. I am to go if you behave and not tell you more than I have to. If we move out of the normal pattern . . ." She stopped.

"We will not," he said. "But I have to know, am I just cover still for you."

"No," she said, "I don't want life anymore."

"Then I can't leave this building," he said, "not until I fix it so no one dares move. We get in the elevator. I get off at the next floor. You go to the lobby and stay until the crowd comes. I'll pull a fire alarm and get back upstairs. To a machine. And start a run on Italian energy stocks. So everyone will be watching them. Then we'll worry about staying alive." They did what he planned. The alarm brought the elevators to a halt and people down the stairs. He managed to climb against the stream and slip into the office in the confusion, reach a terminal that was behind a partition. In several swift moves he triggered the automatic sell for certain energy stocks, large blocks of them. That would signal something to the market. It would be sleepless concerning these stocks for months to come. No fuel sold or bought except under a microscope. He got down the stairs then into the crowded lobby. She spotted him coming out the exit door.

"I'm a criminal now," he said. "Those investors will be after my scalp. So we just have to stay alive for a few hours."

"You will go to jail," she said.

"Maybe," he said. "But I'm going to say I was being blackmailed to cover the sale of nuclear materials to an unknown customer. And that someone suspected. And I tried to cover my tracks by causing a wave of selling."

"What will become of us?" she asked, and she meant him and her children and her life.

"The FBI will come in and they will smell the rat in their own back yard. There won't be a peep out of anybody. And I'll be back at work in no time. And the nuclear stuff will stay put."

"The people are going back in," she said.

"Then it's time for me to phone," he said. "And you have to stand at the booth. You have to get hit first if there's any hitting. No good for them now to kill the children. They know the stock news and that I did it. If I get that phone call in we are safe."

They crossed the lobby to a phone rack. She stood blocking as much of him as she could. The phone rang on the other end. Secretary answered and he asked for his superior who was on to the phone in a second. The man said to him, "Call off your guns. And I'll take the rap for this. It's sitting in your lap right now. Security knows you took over from me. And the rap won't go any further than a secret session. That CIA crowd will cover the losses to our accounts."

"Okay," the superior said in a voice without emotion. "Where are you?"

"It's not where I am, it's where I'm going," the man said, "and going dead or alive."

"Okay," the superior said, "but don't talk to anybody."

"Everybody knows," the man said, "they just don't know who. So call off the guns or you're it." And he hung up. "Now I go back upstairs. And you go get the children. As if nothing happened."

"Yes," she said and backed away from him as if she didn't want to. He took the elevator to his floor. Walked into the office, to his cubicle. It was empty. He sat and brought the energy stocks up on his screen. They had taken a great loss. He sensed the presence of his superior behind him. So he typed in a buy command. The bank would be the buyer. It would admit computer fault and pay the penalties. And no one would look further.

Little Flowers

And if it is the will of God that you
should suffer, it is better to suffer
for doing right than for doing wrong.
—1 Peter 3:17

A man loved Mexican tapestries, or rather the woven blankets that had ancient designs worked into them, some could be quite powerful and look like tapestry. He had one on the wall behind his bed, depiction of an eagle with a snake in its beak and one of its claws, the other claw gripping the lobe of a cactus. This was the prophecy about where Mexico was to be founded. His love had turned into a good business. He would get a solid school bus, the short type, beat it up a bit so it looked ready to die, then drive across the border and head south, changing to Mexican plates when it was convenient. He would hit the markets in the various cities and towns, argue mightily for a blanket that caught his attention, then stash it in the bus under the seats.

To conceal what he had, he would buy religious art of all kinds. There were rosaries hung on the windows, pictures of the Sacred Heart whose eyes followed you wherever you went. There were many sizes of Virgins of Guadalupe and Theresas of the Little Flower. By the time he got down to Oaxaca his bus looked like a sanctuary. And he threw in other stuff as a concealment, ropes of garlic, coca cola cartons. But under the seats was kept free for his tapestries. He would have twenty or more by the time he got back to the border. He would then unload the religious junk on the side of the road, get rid of the other stuff, though this trip he stayed on an extra day for a flea market. Then he would drive up to Customs with a list of his tapestries, their cost. He would show his import license, pay the duties, then head for home and his attached studio, ready to sell what he had bought for a huge markup. He just had to advertise in the paper. People knew how good he was.

Naturally, Customs went over his bus with a fine tooth comb. So no one ever hid in or under his bus. He always slept on board, had a gun to defend himself and never parked in an out of the way place where he was not known. So it was a stunner to him, after he had left Customs and was heading north, to find someone had gotten aboard and wrapped inside one of the tapestry blankets. He noticed in the rear view mirror a line of water running across the aisle. "What the hell!" he thought and pulled to the gravel alongside the road. He went back and smelled the urine, then reached under a seat and began to drag on a resistant roll, stuck his hand inside it and hit the warm flesh of a foot. "Good God!" he said knowing someone might be stifled to death. He pulled the blanket out from the others, then simply stood up and unrolled it, tumbling whoever it was inside of it out on the aisle floor, a girl of about ten, and she was nearly asphyxiated and had been incontinent.

"She can't be alone!" The thought shot through his head. He went down on his knees again like a squirrel digging in each of the rolled blankets and hit the soft hair of a head this time. "Jesus, I remember! Two days ago. The guy that threw in the extras for the Aztec Eagle. He and his son, they loaded these kids on. Is this a kid?" He wrestled the roll free and did the same, pulled it up and tumbled someone out of it. "A mother, for Christ's sake, and she's gotta be dead." There were some bottles of water with straws in them that tumbled out too.

The women weren't dead but close to it. So he got down and did mouth to mouth on both of them until some breathing was established, then leaped to the front and brought his canteen back and put some water in them in a way so they wouldn't choke. "They look like sisters," he said out loud. "Who missed them at Customs? God dammit! Murder to put them in those rolls. That sonofabitch took money!"

He jumped into the driver's seat and wrenched his bus out onto the road. Then just as suddenly ran it back onto the shoulder again. The two were breathing, just about. He ran his hands down their bodies and came to the packets of cocaine strapped between their legs, one packet well soaked in urine. "Ah," he said, "someone on the other end. Two nice females. Two nice kilos. Money makers both. One is a kid! I just drive until dark and I lay them down in some field. Then I go home and get my head blown off by the guys who want to know what I did with them. Or I can explain to the Police who will sure as hell believe me." The mother was coming around, trying to sit up and say something to her girl. She saw her skirt up and the package strapped to her thigh showing, then she saw her daughter a bit further up the aisle still out but breathing, and she reached through the squatting man's legs to touch the girl, do something. He simply pushed her back down and said, "Save what you have. I'll get the two of you to help soon as I can." He stepped beyond the girl and into the seat and started the bus out again. He wasted no time.

Someone else wasted no time either. He was just underway when a pickup truck moved past him, then slowed down in front of him. Two men in the back with some hay bales, and between the hay bales he could see rifles the size of cannons. One of the rifles waved him toward the side of the road. He caught it. You can do this dead or alive, they were saying. What he did was slam on the brakes while still on the road, then at the last second he pulled onto the gravel, grabbed his gun out of the holster under the dashboard, flung open the door and leaped out and ran down alongside the bus, jumped the drainage ditch, and headed out into the scrub where they'd have to catch him to kill him. And he ran with his gun visible. They were smart. He watched them go aboard the bus. They came out lugging the women and the kilos, threw them up on the back of the truck, shot out both front tires of his bus, but with a pistol, more discreet, then sped off.

"They'll get me, but later," he thought. It took him hours to jack up the bus, reduce the back tires from doubles to singles, put those on the front, awkward looking beasts, store the shot tires in the aisle, then start again for home, going easy so as not to strain what he had. It was after dark and still on this long, lonely stretch of road that he saw the young girl again, ahead, in the lights of his bus, standing like a drunk someone had just propped and stepped back from. He knew immediately the cannons were off to the side of the road. So he hit the accelerator and drove blindly to his right into whatever was off there. She fell to the left of him. He heard some thumps then his bus bucked and reared like a horse and a blast took out a rear window. He wrenched the bus back up on the gravel shoulder, again it almost tipped over, and how his wheels held he didn't know. He sped some hundred yards down the road, stopped hard again, doused his lights and leaped out holding his gun into the safety of the dark. They couldn't go back the other way. They couldn't wait until dawn. They had to go by him. After a long while he saw the lights of the pickup truck flick on. He saw the two women hung out the side window like rags. He saw a gun over their backs, but it looked propped not held. Some of the men had been hit by his bus. When they shot his tires out again he'd know. They didn't shoot his tires. "There's one left," he thought, "and he's not steady. I'll find him." So he got back in his bus and drove without hurry for a long time, until three in the morning. That's when he saw the reflectors. He drove up slowly behind the truck, with his high beams on. He could see the two women still hanging out the side window. And a man slumped forward on the wheel.

The man in the bus took his gun, went out the door and approached the driver side an inch at a time. Something in the man was smashed, ribs, something, he had lost consciousness. The man with the gun edged back around the bed of the truck and went forward to the women. They had no pulses left. They were dead. He looked over them into the cab. The kilos of cocaine were on the seat beside the driver. "I'll just leave this," the man thought. "I didn't see a thing. This guy is not going to make it. Even if they find him."

He went back to his bus and drove off. "I'll have to wash that blanket," he thought. "I killed three guys tonight. And they killed two women. And who knows we did." He reached for his windshield wipers before he knew it wasn't raining.

Someone Please Explain

If you can have some share in the sufferings of Christ, be glad, because you will enjoy a much greater gladness when his glory is revealed.
—1 Peter 4:13

There was a woman priest whose son was up on a rape charge. She had talked to him just after the arrest and knew he had done it. He had evaded her question. Her husband was an MIA, he was a few bones left somewhere in Vietnam and she'd never know. She had been a pacifist and entered theology school when she was fairly sure he was gone. She had been a priest a few years, campus minister. Her son was in this school. It was a night of drinking, then a night of violence, then a nightmare. Father a warrior, mother a priest. And yet a woman was a woman whoever she symbolized. That thought was no comfort as she prepared to say Mass.

The chapel was small and people were in close on three sides of the altar and they knew. They may have thought she wouldn't come out, but there was no one else. So she walked to the altar, intoned a hymn because she was without an organist that day, and when the singing was over began the introductory rite which was deeply penitential. The ceremony carried itself until after the Gospel reading when it was time for her to preach. She took the text, "If you can have some share in the sufferings of Christ, be glad, because you will enjoy a much greater gladness when his glory is revealed." She waited a minute for people to think about the text. Then she began, "I am not glad. I don't know how to be. Will someone please explain rape?" They knew it was not a rhetorical question because she came out from behind the lectern and stood with her back to the altar leaning against it and looking at the people in front of her.

No one spoke. It took time to think. They knew she wanted a spiritual answer, that she knew the psychological ones. A man stood up in the back and said, "It was my daughter. I came to hear you. To see what you were like." He would have continued but a voice broke in quietly, "She didn't do it." It was a deep voice from a heavy man.

"But he did," the man down back said, "and he is hers. And this thing is senseless to me too."

"She still didn't do it," said the man with the deep voice. And he stood up. "So speak to us about God, the two of you, or we are trapped oursel- ves." He was looking at the man as he spoke.

"God has abandoned me," the man said. "And abandoned my daughter. To something awful. She's scarcely able to speak." He waited then a minute. "But I can help. She seems to turn to me. Not like a girl. Like an old friend. It was never this way. So I can do what God didn't. Maybe."

"My son has not turned to me," the priest said. "Some days I think he intended your daughter to be me."

"I wish it had been instead of her," the man said. Then said, "No, no," before the rest of the congregation could murmur it. Which they did.

"It's come close to me in other ways," the priest said to him. "I can sense it, even smell it, and this collar is no protection. It's also why I said to you I am not glad."

The man with the deep voice was still standing. He said, "So God has abandoned you also." It was a question but came out as a gentle statement. The woman at the altar did not answer right away.

"I don't know," she said finally. "What I do know is that my love is still alive. For everything. It just has no way. Or it has no power. The things of life go on without it no matter how much I wish . . . I wished his father not to go to that war. And I wished God to stop the killing there. And I wished that my son would be peaceful. And my priesthood would be a grace. And here it has become suspect and sterile."

"I don't sense that," said the man with the deep voice. And he sat down. Then the man in the back sat down also. They sat as if to listen.

"It may be," the woman said, "that I now know what St. Theresa meant when she said that all sins are committed in God, and that God is forced to be an accomplice. And it may be," she continued, "that God is reduced to doing only what we can do. I wish I could tell my son what it meant to be loved by a man. And not violated. And what the child of one's own body means. What I will be glad of, sir, is if you can restore your daughter to a trust in a man's love. I do not know if I can teach my son ever again. But if I could, it would be to trust a woman's love."

She stopped, but they knew she was not finished. "I am resting on someone now," she said. "The way something smashed rests on a floor. Like a pot of flowers. You can smell the earth and see the veins. I will not pick myself up, nor put myself together. Someone says it will be done. I am frightened by this someone. Who leaves me here before you. To pray for you. When I am . . ." She paused.

The man down back rose and said, "You didn't do it. And I am grateful you are where you are. It may be that I can trust something will put her together." He sat again.

"When I am not glad you suffer either," the woman concluded. "So I can only say this scripture belongs to another world than mine or yours. But I will wait for this scripture to come true. I will be glad if it does. And if it does not, I will have no one."

"The way your son has no one?" the man with the deep voice asked.

"No," she said, "love with no one is different." They agreed. And asked her to continue the Mass.

Duplicitousness

You take back your spirit, they die.
—Psalm 104:29

A man was an art restorer. Anything to do with paint. Canvases, wood, plaster, even the black paint used on stained glass. He had reached his maturity working in Florence after the Arno flood, even though he was a foreigner. He was that good. He had another gift, he could spot the authentic among the fake, more among the ancient artists than the modern. The modern expressed itself with less technique so there was less to go on. Finally, he could himself create fakes that were nearly undetectable. He knew he could because he had been asked to copy Rembrandt's portrait of his son Titus for the Dutch Embassy in Washington. They wanted it in the foyer to create a mood for business people who came, give them the impression of Holland as an old art as well as an old bank. His copy was perfect. And he did it for the challenge, not for the small stipend.

The US government approached him one day. It wanted him to copy the Rembrandt Lucrece in the National Gallery. But not copy it in the gallery. It would be removed on the pretext of it being restored. It would be brought to CIA headquarters and put in a special room. And he would be asked to work there but tell no one, and this under oath. He told them they would have to make more sense than that. They said they could get some important information from a foreign source if they pretended to give the original to that source and hang an undetectable fake in its place. So he had to make the copy perfect. That would go to the source. The original would remain.

"You really ask for blind faith," the man said.

"No," they said, "you have eyes no one else has. You can walk up to the original any day and know it is right there in the Gallery. And we will have the info."

"Who gets the copy?" the man asked.

"We do," they said.

"And what info?" he asked.

"Whether someone has the bomb or not," they answered, "so you have to be better than Rembrandt."

"Someone who knows about a bomb loves Rembrandt's Lucrece?" he asked. "An Israeli? A Pakistani? An Indian?"

"We can say no more," they answered. "We've told the source the switch we intend to pull."

"Okay, I will make a copy," he said. "When I am done, I will hand it to you and stay with this one until your delivery is made. Then I will accompany this one back to the Gallery and see it safely hung."

"Agreed," they said.

He worked a year, the greatest year in his life, the feelings, the moods of that tragic woman became his soul and so entered his technique that the match between copy and original was perfect, though like the difference between new and old skin. So he got permission to clean the original even as he darkened the copy. And on that last day he stood and knew that he himself could scarcely tell. He also knew he was being observed. Those people watched themselves sleep. "A few days drying and they can have the copy," he thought. But after the few days both paintings were gone when he returned.

"We simply went ahead," they told him, "and the information we want will be in soon."

"You've rehung the original?" he asked.

"Well, no, we have to keep it out of circulation for a while more," they told him.

"You're giving your source the original, are you not?" he said flat out. "And your source can tell. And even if I prove the one in the Gallery is a fake, it will be an argument, no one will believe it, right? Or people will think the forgery is ancient, not modern, right?"

"There was no other way we could get you to do this," they said, "and the information we will get is priceless, where the bombs are, what they are like, and where they can be reached."

"So no one will be the wiser as they view the fake," he added.

"Maybe some experts, but we will get to them too," they said.

"And you're watching me," he said, "to see how angry I get, to see if you have to lock me away somewhere."

"We are ready to blame a lot of things on you. There are many forgeries looking for an author."

"Lucrece," he said, "that's what you make of me." They were a little puzzled.

"I mean I'm silenced," he said. So they let him go. He went to the Gallery every day until the painting was rehung. It was his copy. Viewers were delighted again. Rembrandt was back. So he got permission from the Gallery to copy the copy. And again he did an astonishing replica, one that unfolded day after day to the amazement of people who walked by. There began to be a crowd every day. Soon someone wanted to buy it when he finished. Named a very high price. It took him only six months. The fake of the fake was perfect. And he sold it for the high price. Then asked if he could make another copy and was told to wait a while. But he insisted he was breaking no rules so the Gallery allowed him after a few weeks.

When he began again he noticed he was copying the copy of the fake. Someone had pulled a switch, a robbery, right in the National Gallery. So he began again his exquisitely detailed work and drew more admirers. He even started to talk to the crowds about the story of the woman and the colors that interpreted her. He explained to the Museum that the Vatican had asked for this copy, not for its Museum, but for the Papal Apartments, a room for visitors to be graced with pagan themes. For pagan visitors probably. He sold it when finished. Then filled with anticipation, he waited a few weeks, then returned to renew his request. This time saying it was the Swiss Embassy that had asked for a copy.

When he came to the painting, it was exactly as he suspected. The original was there. So he watched the newspapers for what had happened. And saw. Terrorists had killed an extremely wealthy businessman in Paris. His nationality was uncertain, though he was carrying a Lebanese passport, the dime-a-dozen kind. And the terrorists were more like Secret Police in the way they had managed the assassination. He had been killed in his home and it had been ransacked for something, though his works of art were not stolen. Paris Police suspected politics not hooliganism. It was discovered most of his works of art were rare and authentic, but a few were elegant copies, a Rembrandt among them. The French Government confiscated all the art until ownership could be or would be claimed by next of kin.

So the artist, the copier, went to the press and simply said to them that the Paris Lucrece might be the original because the one in the National Gallery was probably a fake, and he pointed to the story in their yesterday's edition. There was a storm after the allegation was published. The CIA could say nothing. No foreign government could claim the man or his artistic holdings. They ended up in French hands.

In the next day's paper there was a claim from three different sources that they were holding the original and that the others were fakes, fakes made by, and they named the man. "You just have to look," he said, "line them up against a wall and look, and you will be able to tell the real one from those that are not." But no one was willing to. They kept asking the man to tell which. But he kept saying, "You just have to look."

Trinity Sunday

Shaker Craft

True, they are a headstrong people, but
forgive us our faults and our sins, and
adopt us as your heritage.
—Exodus 34:9

A woman had learned to hate men. Not for their centuries of oppression. That was really abstract and she was very concrete. Two men in succession had married and divorced her, and for the same reason, she was no comfort, she read and talked and took up issues of environment and diet. She was not a campaigner. She chose exquisite plants for the house, marvelous bulbs for the garden, cooked tofu to perfection, sprinkled oat bran on strawberries, and drank only bottled water. And linens and cottons, she loved them. The bed sheets were linen. But she used these things, used them with delight, it was the thrill of living that led her to fresh and exuberant choices. Her men had seemed that way. But the flush of health in one of them turned out to be the flush of alcohol. And the other turned out to be the flight of a bumble bee, he pollinated everything with a petal. She was a home decorator with a flourishing business and had picked up traces of his house visits. He was a bond salesman who should have been downtown looking at a screen. Soon she began to hate the women who picked up with her two exes. They were bumble bees of their own kind. "I hate men and women and love everything else," she thought, "what stupidity!"

She was in the house of a retired Admiral one day, at his request, to look the place over and redesign it. His wife had just died. His son had died too, from Agent Orange in Vietnam. Son had been on patrol boats. "I've decided to give my things away," he said, "to the Armed Forces Museum. I won't have you look at any of it. Because I want you to design

110

a house of peace for me. Nothing soft. I'm not that. And I'm not a jock athlete either. You're good at design, so I'm told."

"I can't build you my house," she said to him. "Men seem to hate what I build for myself."

"Well, okay," he said, "I love the sea. I love wings. On anything. Gulls even. Great flyers. And I love craft. Right down to the pirogues I used in the bayous when I was a kid. So it's shape against nature, or with nature. Did you ever ride a giant turtle on land? Then hold on to its tail underwater? And I love rhythm. Not machine rhythm so much, though that's comfortable, but wave rhythm, or the rhythm of hills from 20,000 feet. And I love stars. To navigate by. To tell stories by. All that stuff is flooding in on me now. She liked her own things, and sat me in the middle of them, medals, life jackets, propellers, photos, in the middle of navy wife stuff. How she kept herself from going crazy I don't know, but she sure kept me from the madhouse. I'm near the madhouse now without her, and my son is gone. Left no kids. He wouldn't have any when he knew he was tainted. So I want something to live in for what's left."

"You want a design that's very masculine, but not warlike?" she asked.

"No," he said, "I want something very feminine. But for me."

"Like some bowsprits from the old whalers," she said and laughed.

"The old gang'd love it," he said. "They'd put liquor spouts in the tits and hang the gal right over their heads."

"What about a woman," she asked, "the real thing?"

"Ah," he said, "she's here. Can't you tell?"

"No, I can't," she said. "The only thing I can think of right now is Shaker furniture. It's neither man nor woman really. No sex to it and these days I think that's better. You can put only simple flowers around, simple cloth. You have to wear baggy clothes, funny enough. And you have to dance without touching anything. But shells go great, and preserves in the cupboard, and old bean crocks serve a lot of purposes. Andirons and a rack for logs. And brass candlesticks. Maybe a cast iron stove fitted with gas. And bread boards. Very lived in stuff."

"That'd cry for a woman," he said.

"That's what you want, isn't it?" she asked.

"I want to be one," he said. "And have no one know but you and me."

"The Shaker furniture will do it," she said. "You'll have to use it and use it for people. It has a way of dancing you too."

"Is that what you've got?" the Admiral asked.

"No," she said, "my materials are more raw. I'm committed to the natural but not to any specific form. I go for a while then change."

"How about rocks and things, in here?" he asked.

"They'd fit," she said.

"And what about slabs of wood?" he went on.

"Yes, if they are left unlacquered," she answered.

"What about flowers? I used to love the Ikebana in Japan," he said.

"Yes, but you'd have to learn," she answered, "I don't know of any artists around."

"That'd take time," he said.

"You have time," she said.

"I don't," he said. "I have a year at most. How quickly can you do this? Whole house?"

"What is it?" she asked.

"Lou Gehrig's," he said. Then he waited for her next question but she couldn't ask.

"There's a moment when things start to go," he said. "It's not yet. But when it starts, I go. Meantime I want to live another life. As though I can give it. All my life I took it."

"I can't design a suicide place," she said, almost unable to say it.

"Well, Shaker is a kind of suicide, isn't it? Or haven't I heard right. It's a place to entertain guests at a wake." He said this without arguing, said it as a conclusion one draws from someone else's speech. "And it's a woman who cannot breed, but is a woman without you noticing, with some life on her hands. That's what I want. I don't know why except what I told you."

"I have nothing I can do for you," the designer said. "I'm afraid of you."

"She was not afraid," the Admiral said. "When she knew, she simply went. Nothing I could say. But she said to me try a woman's life and then I would understand."

"O God!" the designer said. "Why didn't you just go together?"

"She was not against life," the Admiral said. "And she asked me to see it from her side. Then this diagnosis came."

"Can I ask you please to die like an animal?" she blurted out. "The way things of nature die?"

"Why?" he asked. It was a calm why, as if over a map of the sea and orders to ships.

"What if I design the house that way, like lairs, or cradles, or boneyards, rib chairs, rib beds, spindles and white hopsack curtains? What if I put in a crucifix or a menorah or something sacrificial so you can have a friend? I just can't . . ." she stopped, very confused.

"Maybe you make sense," he said. "Why do you want life so much that you want me to die like an animal?"

"I don't know," she said, "I might not face it myself."

"You think I should be able to?" he asked.

"Yes," she said, "it's like childbirth in the old days."

"What's born of this?" he asked.

"I don't know," she said, "maybe somebody who's alive but forgot it."

"Then do the rib design for me," he said. "Make it look like a childbirth. But so you and I are the only ones who know."

"I will need some time," she said.

"Time for what?" he asked.

"To believe this," she said.

Brawn and Brains

It is not enough for you to be my
servant . . . I will make you the
light of the nations. . .
                    —Isaiah 49:6

There was a woman who caught a child thrown out a window to save it from a fire. And someone caught her in a photo that won a Pulitzer Prize. Stopped the moment perfectly so her face and the face of the child were utterly clear. The child coming down in a dive with head thrown back. The woman bending underneath to catch the child with her chest as well as arms, her face tensed for the impact. The two faces, one terrified, the other focused and fierce as a hammer thrower's, the two became famous overnight. Because there were tears visible on the corners of the woman's eyes as if a mighty compassion was at work, not just an instinct. And the child's face showed he saw her and was trying to bend toward her. The impact broke both her arms but saved the boy. People died in the fire, a townhouse converted to condos on a street between two important shopping districts.

The impact also broke the woman's marriage, which had been fragile anyway. His wife's heroism was obvious to the man and too much for him to live with. He couldn't enter the hospital room without finding news people, interviewers, cameras. He had to care for her while she was in her casts. And when the prize was given for the photo and people picked her out when they were together, he said they now had different lives and had better go different ways.

She worked selling air time on a local TV station. And that job began to sour on her too. Customers couldn't talk down to her. Bosses couldn't. Personalities couldn't, especially the women. She was moved out of the job into something with higher pay and lower visibility. And no one from the boy's family came to thank her. Her personal life had been stripped from her like artichoke leaves.

She was in the gym one day, her old college gym, working out the injuries to her muscles on the nautilus machines, then around the eighth of a mile track. And she had started her jogging when she sensed a huge man come up beside her then stay at her elbow taking one stride for every two or three of hers. A huge man in marvelous shape but with knee braces laced on so she knew he must be a pro something who got ruined, pro football most likely.

"I see you here," he said. "I saw your photo. You have your courage." And he put out his hand to shake hers. She reached across and did.

"You're Atlas," she said looking at the size of him.

"From the knees up," he said with a grin. "Mickey Mouse from the knees down."

"Pro football?" she asked as they rounded one of the curves.

"No, Marines," he said. They went down the straight just breathing. "Beirut," he said at the curve.

"The explosion?" she asked.

"Yeah," he said. "Can't catch a whole building." They went down another straight. At the curve he asked, "You mind me?"

"Well, no," she said, "but I'm a little out of your class, you're just walking practically."

"You're a healer," he said.

"Tell me," she said ironically, "everyone else has beaten it."

"Well, I'm ashamed of myself," he said. "I was fast asleep and someone blew a roof in on me. A footlocker busted my knee. I was carried afterwards, like a baby, for 6 months. Now I run like I'm made of glass." They were actually running a slight bit faster, but free, with good breathing.

"I don't get it," she said.

"Well, you're weak and you did something strong," he said.

"I'm not so weak," she said, "here, feel my muscle." And she bent her arm and made a bicep. Which he wrapped his hand around easily. "Fierce," he said.

"I still don't get it," she said.

"Okay," he said, "I looked at that photo and said I want that woman."

"Why?" she said.

He started to laugh, at himself. "I was thinking my brawn and your brains, but what if your brawn and my brains. You remember that joke?"

"Yes," she said, "Bernard Shaw and the american beauty queen."

"I want to live with a different kind of bomb," he said, "a life bomb."

"So I'm a life bomb," she said, "that's better than Bernard Shaw. You're absolutely right."

"It's harder to catch hell than a kid, isn't it?" he said.

"Right," she said. "Look, I'm out of breath. I'm going to walk this lap then cool down."

"Me too," he said.

"How did they get you out?" she asked.

"They didn't," he said. She looked up at the big frame of a man. They stopped and he looked down at her face. "I was under too much rubble, they couldn't see me, they couldn't hear me."

"Your legs were pinned?" she said.

"One," he said.

She looked down again at the braces. Then saw there was an artificial limb under one of the high stockings. "Did you cut it off?" she said with no breath to say it.

"Not quite. The locker and concrete did most of it. There was a hole behind me if I could get free. They were moving stuff with a crane. And it was shifting." She saw the rest.

"I can't say a thing," she said. "I wouldn't have the courage. The animal that bites itself free of the trap."

"It's only one kind," he said, "I need another."

"You must have that too!" she said.

"I can't find it in myself," he said. "I did when I saw your photo. And when I saw you running."

"I'm afraid of you," she said, "you were right to cut yourself free, but I'm afraid."

"I am too," he said.

"So that's why me?" she asked. "You're falling."

"Right," he said.

Like a Scuttlefish

The people that walked in darkness
has seen a great light;
on those who live in a land of deep shadow
a light has shone.
—Isaiah 9:2

A man was assigned the task of making sure the wounded were photographed. The news media were forbidden the zone. Anyone seen with a camera disappeared. Maybe in a grave. So concealment was the trick. A woman's clothes were essential, a loose bosom dress, shaven legs, and some padding on the hips, a kerchief of some kind. Part of the game was to run up to someone shot and pretend to help while taking close-ups of face or wounds or both. Just open the blouse and bite on the trigger, a plastic cord to the camera hung around the neck, then the fake grief, the hands thrown back, quick snaps of the oncoming soldiery, then flight in fear, awkward flight like a running crane. So not really a target. Though the man got hit by both sides, rocks from the one, tear gas, even a bullet nick from the other. The photos were quickly developed and sneaked out, how, the man didn't know, but they showed up in the international press within a few days time and they infuriated the government.

It found out through an informer who the man was. But a counter informer tipped him off so he would have a chance to escape. Then he knew his own side had to kill him to keep him from naming names under torture. He would have to get away in a riot, dress like a woman again, but wear a soldier's clothes underneath, or what would pass for some. So he asked his leaders for the clothes. To be brought to his cellar darkroom and left. He knew some hit men would come, kill him, toss his body into the next riot as a casualty, a well photographed one. So he rigged an explosive device to the door handle, to go off when it was turned. They came and knocked.

He shouted "Come in!" from behind a heavy table he had turned on its side. He covered his ears, they turned the knob, bam! The three of them were flattened against the stairs badly wounded. The man jumped his table, went through the door, saw the packet of clothes blown up to the top of the stairs, leaped and got them and went out the door, ran down the narrow street toward the valley road and escape south. But at the cemetary wall he got over and in behind it where he changed into soldier's clothes.

The explosion brought several trucks of troops down from the neighboring hill camp. Maybe someone making munitions in the town had messed up. When the trucks went by, the man went up the road behind them and began to mingle with the troops. He saw some young men throwing stones and he led off after them throwing stones back and a squad of angry soldiers followed suit. He ducked down an alleyway, up some stairs, into a home where a woman was huddled with some children. So with a stick he menaced her into taking off her clothes which he bundled under his arm and left, running upstairs further, then along ladder like roofs until he could drop down into another alleyway.

Just before, he got rid of his soldier's garb, changed into the woman's and walked back toward the riot. He picked up a jug to put on his head and sidled toward the action. When it swept past him, the rock throwers that is, he seemed to be caught in the middle and ran a little back and forth until the soldiers came even with him and gave him a shove out of the way behind them so he was actually free and had shaken anyone off his trail. He went back down toward the valley road with his veil up and his eyes wet from tear gas. He got back over the cemetary wall at a higher spot and looked carefully down toward the place where he had left his clothes. He noticed someone hiding behind a mound and headstone. An extra killer, who had lost him, but knew he had to come back, or gambled he would. Kill with what, a gun? No one had a gun. A knife? Or a wire? I could just brain him with a rock, the man thought. I need those clothes and I need to be undetected. Then he thought, "Whose side am I on? My own. No one else's. I'm killing both sides. Both want to kill me. They won't."

So he slipped back over the wall, got his jug, raised his veil, and went down across the road over another wall and hunched behind some stones until nightfall. Then he moved toward the river. He knew where it was from the downslope. He would have to make ten miles in a night. Then go a day hiding and without water, slip between patrols the following night, then swim the river, make up a story and get asylum. He did this. It was a brutal test of strength and luck. He was at the edge of the river when darkness came and across it before the moon rose. He was barefoot and nearly naked. The air was cooling quickly and he knew no place he could go. The word would be out with his name on it.

A flare caught him in the open, from the other side of the river. There was a burst of fire from a machine gun jeep, a bullet hit him in the thigh and brought him flat on the gravel of the bank. A burst of fire came from his side of the river back across it. Another flare froze the scene, from which side he didn't know. He had to get back in that water and drift with it south and hope he didn't bleed to death before he could come ashore. So he slid on his belly through the shallows to the deeper current, ducking under water as often as he could and pulling himself along the bottom. "Like a scuttlefish," he thought, "and worth about as much." He put his head up for air in the blinding light of more flares, drew a rain of fire, ducked under again and began to swim, trailing his useless leg, downstream, down toward the Dead Sea.

There were small sand bars that protected him. But flare after flare overhead as the jeeps, more and more of them, began to build up on either side of the river. And whenever the fire of his homeland's jeeps got too close to the other shore, there was return fire, return flares, until it looked as if a kettle of light, a kettle of hawks, was moving down river. The man knew he was finished. He was losing blood and feeling shock. And swallowing too much water. "Enough to make me a Christian," he thought. "They'd kill me too." He was holding to a sand bar and its shallows. The river was open below him in the terrible darkness. "I'll light it all the way," he thought, "Dead or alive. Give them something to live for."

He let go the bank, slid back into the deeper channel and began to swim again. They fired on him and this time they hit and killed him. But they didn't know it. His body kept drifting, bobbing up and down. The flare light was so intense no one could see the spread of blood in the water. It moved faster than the body, ahead of it like torn shreds of a flag. Finally at daylight it was clear the man was dead. But the jeeps had to follow the floating body until it came up on either shore. Which it didn't do. It seemed more like cloth, catching, uncatching, moving like a dancer, still bleeding, still sending out shreds in front of it.

Finally it caught on a gravel rise in the river, in the middle. Where it stayed. There were vultures on it soon. And jeeps watching the whole day. And every fifteen minutes at night a flare. Which revealed jackals from both sides of the river at work on what was left. Which was very little by morning. Some of the bones even had been carted off. The blood reached the Dead Sea by noon. It showed up on a beach by about four. Some animal, the people guessed, rubbing it off their feet on the sand.

4th Sunday, Ordinary Time

The Mistral

... at the time when you were called,
how many of you were wise
in the ordinary sense of the word ...
—1 Corinthians 1:26   .

A woman was laughing to herself one day. She was at a small desk and looking through French doors at a lighthouse just across the narrow entry to a fishing port in the south of France. She was a writer there on a grant, and her laughter was at the ridiculous, not at the funny. Her sister's letter had just arrived, younger sister by eight years. In it she said she could finally tell that their father had abused her when she was young. The woman who was laughing thought this capped everything and made writing fiction seem insipid. She herself had lost her lover during the past year, a woman quite unlike herself, and had lost her to a man who loved to sail and was sailing around the world on the Guess Who with guess who? Now a scene from the past at home made sense, an explosive quarrel between her father and mother just after she had graduated and was working as an editor but still living at home. In fact her mother was waving a gun. Everyone knew it wasn't loaded but her meaning was clear. "Go, or I'll kill you somehow."

The woman writer thought it was the demon of alcohol her mother was driving out. And it was bad. However the war and getting shot several times would excuse it. Her father had made men very unattractive to her. Women were easier to love but not easier to hold. This was the second she had lost. And it had been a wild argument too, but her lover had started it, calling her ice cold Katie and fugicle and other frost bitten names along with crudities she only saw in print, never heard spoken. Crudities. Here in France they were wonderful, shredded carrots, hearts of palm, of artichoke, beet slices. They had agreed she should go seduce some good guy,

122

get pregnant and not tell him, have the baby, keep it if it was a girl, adopt it out if a boy, then try again, her lover this time.

So here she was pregnant in the south of France. The father was a priest. She started to laugh and cry as she looked out that window toward the lighthouse. "I've got to be making this up," she thought. "Like Voltaire with Candide." And amniocentesis said she was carrying a boy. She still had time to get rid of it but she waved the thought away as not hers, as something she saw on TV between two women cops, the discussion of it anyway. "So, dear sister," she thought, "what do I say to you. You're floating a flower on what you think is water. It's a sheet of glass. That wretched man! What do I know of him? What do I have to know?!"

She remembered the priest and his scared ecstasy. She had plotted it beautifully, summer cottage, long lazy day, long lush night, then goodbye. Then the silence when she didn't call, when he didn't call. Then the call and the coldness and his obvious relief. Then her pregnancy and split up with her lover. Then this grant for the south of France with a boy baby riding free along. She stood up and went out on the small balcony. Twenty feet below were the chunk rocks on which the house was built, then the water across to the seawall and the lighthouse in its fist. It was like a muscular arm with a candle. She was in the other arm. A what? For whom?

"I have to be something for her," she thought. "I have to pretend it happened to me too but I never told anyone. And it's my fault it happened to her. But it's a lie on him. And mother will load the gun and go look for him again. Though she won't have to look far. He's at Crusher Cronin's every third month. So I can't pretend. God! She needs some innocence. Her own. But who can tell her she is?"

The woman looked beyond the lighthouse to the blackened face of a long cliff topped by a plateau. A few nights before, the cliff had burned the whole night. Fire equipment had driven out on top and poured some water down the sheer sides, but there was little water. The next day, Canadair seaplanes had bombed the fire to death, landing on the water to fill their tanks, then taking off to hit the fire again and again until it was out. Which made fascinating watching.

"How will she stop the harm?" the woman thought. "Maybe if I tell her what a mess I made. I ran to anything but a man from him. But they were loveable! Everything seems loveable. That goddam fire that nearly burned us out!" She leaned on the balcony railing. There was a sloop under power entering the neck between her and the lighthouse, a woman at the tiller and she was topless, but with one hand she was trying to get into a sweater. And a man was lying on the cabin top looking aft at her, as nonchalantly as a king lion. He was finishing a croissant and talking with his mouth full and she was grinning. She let the tiller go a second, yawed a little, but pulled the sweater down over her head and torso. He rolled on his back and looked up at the sky, spread out like a crucifix. She reached down and took another croissant out of a canvas bag and pitched it so it landed right on his chest. And he went into an animal writhing, chewing on it like a kill.

"I can't play with her on this," the woman thought. "I can't anything. It's got to be somebody innocent. Not somebody who understands. And I'm carrying the only innocent thing I know. I have to pretend I didn't get the letter. I have to write and tell her I'm in a tough spot. The whole story. I have to ask her to come and live this time through with me, and help me with the adoption. She is going to want the baby. She'll want to shape it her own way. Then what'll I be?"

She began to notice light fan patterns on the water and a slight chill in the air. "Mistral," she thought. "I'll see a show now, goosebumps." She reached for her own sweater. "If I could straighten that bastard out maybe an apology would do it. That poor bastard! He's got two tongues and they're both thirsty." She watched the fan shapes grow larger on the intense blue water. "I can't hold my life and do it good," she thought. "I'll apologize to her," she thought further, "for everything that's ever harmed her. I'll say I'm the everything." The light was beginning to change to rose, and the fans were rose on blue. "I'm not the everything. I'll say let me love you. I know how. I really know how. Come over here and let me love you. I've got all kinds of unused love. I'll tell her she does too. Just tell her I'm a mess with loving."

The lighthouse was on, two shorts, a long, a break, then again. And there were people coming out the breakwater to sit in the rose light and mistral breeze and watch the whip-fans on the water. Like the shiver of a horse's flanks. "Well, at least it'll be no lie," the woman thought. "A little self-serving maybe, but no lie."

She turned back into the room, and sat at the desk, wrote the letter. The light was cobalt blue when she finished. The blond stone across from her was like a woman's skin. And the lighthouse? "I won't say," the woman thought. "I just won't say."

5th Sunday, Ordinary Time

The Right Blankness

If you do away with the yoke, the
clenched fist, the wicked word, if
you give your bread to the hungry,
and relief to the oppressed, your
light will rise in the darkness,
and your shadows become like noon.
—Isaiah 58:9-10

A man worked as a memory for the CIA. He was that much better than computers. He was creative. His assignment was to know the weaknesses of government personnel, the ones a foreign power could use perhaps to do some blackmailing. He got into the work through the service, an ROTC lieutenancy, work with Intelligence, then, tour of duty up, an offer from the CIA. He would be watched every minute, he was told, what he knew was that valuable. He would surely be approached to become a double, a triple agent. Or someone in government with a score to settle might commandeer his knowlege. So he was actually responsible to no one. He was to make all initiatives, if he spotted something, and he was to approach only a permanent special prosecutor who would then approach a grand jury. His job had been set up by a CIA director at the instruction of a congressional committee in the aftermath of some bad use of intimate knowlege by the intelligence community.

The man knew every possible weakness or vice that could be part of human nature. And he knew virtues that could be tricked as well. He had to let them all be until he saw them being played on by someone to the potential damage of the nation. He had banks of computers, banks of TV screens, banks of tape recorders, he could do an instant biography on generals, congress-people, judges, the men and women who ran things. Someone approached him one day, in the boldest of all possible moves. It

126

was a woman, an older woman, a philosopher type maybe. She was central European, linguistically superb, and she knew what his job was. He was at lunch in an outdoor cafe in Georgetown, had a table for two to himself. She sat down almost unnoticed in the second chair and said, "May I?"

"Yes," he said. He was reading an entry in the Congressional Record, a tribute to someone who had died, a case closed on an alcoholic, really, who had done well by accident, but almost ruined a lot of people in the process.

"I need to know something," she said looking at him. Wonderful lined face, lots of crags and sensitivity, gray hair, but mop-like, wavy, a bit tangled. He said nothing, looked at her with the right blankness. "I need to know if your State Secretary has AIDS."

He still said nothing.

"The man we gave him went home to several of our Secretaries. He was very good."

The man put down his Congressional Record, took his sandwich and ate some, then drank a sip of his cooling tea.

"Some odd judgments are being made at home, by several of our Secretaries." The waiter came and handed her a menu. "I know." she said. "I will have a salade julienne and white wine." Then she spoke again to the man. "We will tell you what your Secretary told our young man, give you the tapes. You will know they are not edited."

He took another bite of his sandwich, then of his pickle, and sat looking at her while he chewed, then sipped some tea.

"The judgments being made at home are warlike. Personalities seem to be changing." She sat there as if she would keep saying things until she got an answer. How she knew who he was made little difference, to him, or to her. His face betrayed nothing. "You have tested," she said. "We cannot."

He took the last bite of his sandwich. Her food arrived, and she set to eating it as if she knew what she was eating. He was looking at his counterpart from the other side. Maybe a psychologist. A faint smile showed on his face.

"The young man has disappeared. You must know that." She drank some wine, brushed her hair back a little from her forehead and let the light fall on her more fully. "We have to know before the symptoms develop," she continued, "or we will be embarrassed before the world." She took a leaf of lettuce in her hand and began to eat it elegantly. "And our shame will ruin you."

He had signaled to the waiter for the check and was reaching for his back pocket and credit card.

"If not kill you," she continued. "And kill us as well when you shoot back."

There was a light smile on his face as he examined the figures on the credit card, then added the tip and signed it. But looked at it again as if puzzled, called the waiter and had him go check the prices. The waiter left and in a few minutes brought back the adjusted bill, which the man then initialed where the changes had been made. He redid the tip.

"We are both now compromised," she said, and took the last of her wine. "You will live and I will not."

He looked at her now, the jewelry on her lapel, her wedding band earrings, simple, necessary stuff.

"It's in my hair," she said, as she lifted the mop of it again just above her brow, and he could see the thin head of a mini-mike. "And the video is on the second floor across the street facing you. Someone will wave if you look."

The man ripped the customer copy free of the bill, ripped the carbon, put it in the ashtray, then looked back at her again, but as someone who saw her as part of the scenery, two people sharing the same table who do not know each other.

She signaled to the waiter. The man delayed a minute to see what for, and he tilted his own face to the sun for more.

"I will have some chocolate mousse," she said, "then some espresso." Her life was over. She had revealed everything and gotten nothing. His Secretary could be removed in a day. Hers not. At least not in recent years. The man rose and left her at the table. She finished the mousse.

Then sipped her expresso. The carbon of his bill in the ashtray fluttered but did not blow away. A Susan B. Anthony silver dollar was holding it down. She took the two halves of the bill and matched them, saw the etching of his name, the changes, then the etching of okay, plus his initials, on the corner next to the new tally. Which was identical with the old. The peacefulness of death left her face. Her people were not sick. They were crazy.

Triage

. . . before us lie life and death,
and whichever we prefer is ours.
—Ecclesiasticus 15:17

There was a woman who had a life and death choice. Over her husband. He was a painter. But it was not painting that kept him alive. She did, her sensuality, she had to fill him before he could fill a canvas. During her two pregnancies she noticed him slacken, he needed total possession of her though he was not conscious of it. The two girls were nine and seven and he related to them better as they grew.

But as she grew, her other powers became visible to her, not just the one of being his source of painting. She found she was very good with disturbed children, she had ways of inventing language for them so they could grasp situations, be more independent. She could invent stories they understood. Then she began to do that for her own children, began to write the stories down, began to publish them and get surprisingly large royalties. He, in turn, began to recognise his dependence on her, and recognise he was losing total control over her.

One day she sensed her girls were disturbed, but she could not get them to speak. Then she knew he had shifted his sensuality to them and they were locked in fear and had no voice to tell her with. When she told him that all three were leaving him, he nearly went mad with rage, it was only a kitchen knife that kept him off during the turmoil. But after it, he told her as she stood near the front door with the girls behind her that if she left he would kill himself. She thought he meant it. But three lives were more important than one. She opened the door behind her and pushed the frightened creatures out.

"Go downstairs and wait!" she said. She did not take her eyes off him. He jumped into the small room where he did his sketching, yanked open a drawer, then jumped back out into the hallway with a gun in his hand.

"I just shoot you and I have them all to myself. Shoot a crazy woman with a knife. Crazy, jealous woman."

"They won't do it for you," she said, "they're still empty."

"I'll make you empty," he said.

"Like you?" she said.

"You stay," he said. "I won't touch them."

"I can't trust that!" she said.

"You can, you can!" he said.

"You will find someone," she said. She reached behind her and opened the door again. He was frozen. She backed out, then pulled the door shut. The shot and the door seemed to slam together, but nothing went by her. She opened the door again and saw him lying face down on the floor, his head towards her. She was appalled. But then she sensed something not right. This was a fake, to tear into her with an image of what could be. So she stayed inside the door but closed it behind her with the bang of someone stomping out. He jumped up cursing sonofabitch! and saw her standing there, knife still in her hand.

"There will be someone else," she said, "someone younger, someone lusher, someone who knows no rules. You can live off what you've already painted. There are redheads and blondes, they have wet tongues and they are grown up." She spoke softly, not with any scorn. "They will see what they do for you and want to do it."

"No, you," he said, "you!" And he began to wave the gun under his nose like smelling salts.

"You," he said, "you!"

"Then shoot one of us," she said. "And I don't care which. Those children are out of your reach either way."

"I didn't do much," he said.

She started to move toward him with the knife.

"Much!" she said, "much!" He backed a bit.

"You took me on," he screamed, it was a scream. "Like a shirt," he said. "You throw me off! Like a shirt! Dirty! You know!"

She stopped at what he was saying. She held a shirt in her hands, by the collar, off the ground. "Yes. And someone else will do the same," she said, "but not at nine and seven."

"Send them away," he said. "Your sister."

"You will find someone," she said. "They are waiting downstairs. Maybe I can save them. Maybe I cannot."

"You're good at that!" Again he screamed. "You choose who it'll be! You save yourself!"

"You fool no one with that," she said. "Not even yourself. For the first time." She turned and walked to the door, opened it, and walked out, leaving it open this time. She heard a second shot. She was at the head of the wooden stairs down and she saw the faces of the two girls staring up. They looked like souls in damnation to her, there was no time, just torment they could not control. They had heard the second shot also. They saw the knife in her hand. She turned and threw the knife through the doorway. There was a third shot. She walked down the hollow sounding stairs slowly, deliberately. There was a shot at each hollow beat. Until a click. Then the sound of a weapon clunking off a wall and clattering along a floor. Then there was the sound of a door being slammed, just as she reached the foot and the two girls.

She sank slowly down on the last step and put her head on her knees. She heard the door being pulled open. He came to the top of the stairs and shouted, "Okay, I'll get someone. Better. Better. Take your goddam knife. Use it on someone else." He threw it down the stairs so she had to jump out of the way, but she saw fear in him until it missed her. Then the terror of loss suffused his face as he looked down at the three. "Damn you too!" he said. And he collapsed there on the step.

She moved the girls toward the front door of the building. There were some sirens coming down the street. All that gunfire. "I will explain to them," she said. "You even use blanks." Then she continued, "When I have them safe, I will find you someone. She will know."

"You!" he shouted, "you!"

The police came through the door, made a quick judgment that the situation was not lethal, then one sprang up the steps toward the man who stood there with his hands out empty. The other officer picked up the knife and looked up toward his buddy waiting for a signal. Then the doors up and down the corridors began to open and people come out shouting, "Throw those maniacs in jail! Get rid of that garbage! Take 'em away from here!"

The woman's husband was standing like a zombie, looking down as if into an empty well. An officer had the gun and saw it had blanks, saw it was a marriage dispute. So he got everyone back inside their doors. "I'll take you in overnight," he said. "Disturbing the peace. People will feel better. You have to stay with the kids, Lady, or I'd take you in too. So come on," he said to the man, "close your door and come on." They came down the stairs past the woman and her two girls. He was like a dead man. But only like.

Funny Switches

. . . if any one of you thinks of themselves as wise,
in the ordinary sense of the word,
then they must learn to be fools
before they can be wise.
—1 Corinthians 3:18

A man had a problem. His wife. She drank herself silly. Often. He loved her silly. And while they were childless it was okay, he could call her job and say she was sick, she was a magician with a computer when she was sober. But they had twins her first pregnancy and the twins would be drinking scotch and milk if she had kept it up. She stayed sober their first six months, but the thrill wore off of being the wolf nurse to Romulus and Remus. A couple of days he came home and they were fiercely hungry and she was lying on the rug with the bottle in her mouth sucking on scotch and going goo goo at him to get a laugh. He just didn't drink. He loved high spirits, they came naturally to him so he didn't like the fog that followed the booze.

He tried to lift her off the rug and she squirmed as if tickled, then began to pull at his clothes to get them off. Meantime the double howl for food played in the background. So he let her pull his shirt loose but he backed into the kitchen toward the bottles of milk stored in the fridge. He and she had to stay far ahead of those appetites. He got the plastic bottles into the microwave and hit a few seconds on the timer before she got his trousers loose and down around his knees. At the buzzer she had his shorts off. He stepped out of them and her grip, did a dance across the floor into the bedroom, closed the door, locked it, then put the babies' bottles in the right position so they could feed. They set up a noise like a suction.

There was no noise outside the door. He opened it a crack and there she was in his trousers and necktie swaying on the couch back. She'd break her skull. She had the real bottle in her hand, Cutty Sark, and she tilted it slowly skywards as she kept ogling him and drank and drank until he knew she wanted oblivion, and more, more if she drank that bottle whole. So he danced out toward her to keep her off guard, around behind the couch, then grabbed her down, pulled the bottle out of her hand, and hit her a light punch in the stomach which made her spit a lot up. Then held her while she kept vomiting all over him, unable to be enraged, just heaving. She sank then in his grasp. So he struggled her dead weight into the bathroom and washed her and himself under the shower, toweled her and put her to bed. The babies were back crying. So he went into the kitchen again, heated baby food, then spoon-fed them one, two, one, two. Changed them after washing them, and set them back in their cribs. "Three babies in one night," he thought, "too much for anybody!"

Something similar happened in succeeding weeks. She was drunk a different way each time. She wrapped scotch bottles in babies' diapers and put them in the cribs. The babies were on the shelves in the liquor cabinets with labels pasted to their bottoms. So he got a nurse to come in one night and he took his wife to a detox place. She wasn't silly that night, she was violent, and drink was nothing to the resentment he saw smouldering in her, that as much was being sucked from her as she sucked from her bottles of scotch. She wasn't coming back to those babies. Nor to him. Unless he wanted a different disaster every day. So he asked his brokerage firm if he could do night shift work, at home, with a phone hookup to international markets. He was also very good at his job. They said yes but he'd be on commission only. And that worked. Because she went from detox to a hospital for depression.

He actually loved the life of those babies. He typed them into the computer so it would keep him alert to things to do, order food, make changes, take temps. But the hands-on knowledge was best. And they slept. So he had long hours he put in on his work. The strain showed on him. He looked up a psychiatrist, one close by, so he would walk the twins, park them with a receptionist, see the psychiatrist, come out perky, and go back to being the total woman.

He thought he had an appointment with a male. The psychiatrist was female. Toby. She took his breath away. She was not young. She breathed maturity, physical, emotional. She breathed peace. "I can just sit here and look," he said. "I feel better already." But he didn't. He broke, like an orange between two thumbs. She had his story before she could say a word. The story of a woman who would never come back to herself, nor to him, and he couldn't fill the hole with two babies and fat commissions, and there she was, the psychiatrist, like some divine being that whetted every appetite and didn't know it, and here he was with a ton of love but loaded into an impotent mule for a laugh.

"You ever hear a mule laugh?" he asked her as he was sputtering out. "It's a donkey in hysterics." He caught some breath. "I thought you'd be a man," he said. "I could get some distance. No distance. I'm in it deeper. Jesus, what a soul transplant wouldn't do! I'm really not a pity-me type. I'm a pigeon coop again. I'm flapping at the wire. You're so close, older, but so close!"

"I'll bet I'm not," the psychiatrist said.

"How much?" he said.

"A million. Confederate." she answered.

"I used it to ransom Red Chief," he said. "You're right," he went on, "she's rounder than you are, and when she's sober, she's like light on rippled water. You're trim. You're the sloop, not the water. This is all TV stuff, I've never been on a boat."

"What is she like drunk?" the psychiatrist said.

"She's like some ecstasy that doesn't know . . . doesn't know it's a killer." He stopped at that. The way he had stopped once on the Cliffs of Moher, within a foot of the drop, near the warning sign about the wind and its push. He told the psychiatrist that. "She was beside me, and everytime the wind pushed her a little, she leaned as far as it pushed her and dared it to push her more."

"Is she Irish?" the psychiatrist asked.

"Yes," he said, "the kind they say walk the beach at sunset with the sun, and just as it goes below the edge of the world, the kind that leaps after it."

"Then we are alike," the psychiatrist said. "Not in body."

A look of fright came on the man's face. "So you leave me holding the baby too?" he said.

"Funny switch, isn't it!" she said.

"I like that part of it," he said, "holding the baby." Then he just looked at her. "What did you land on?" he asked.

"Nothing," she said. "It's a free fall or a free rise, whichever. But nothing."

"So she couldn't take that, the nothing," he said as a question.

"No," the psychiatrist said.

"I must be pretty shallow," the man said. "All I see is something. Every minute something. Lovely stuff."

"I envy you," the psychiatrist said.

The man looked at her. "So alive nothing is better than dead nothing?" he asked.

"Yes," she said, "and I should pay you for this."

"So I'm right, she's gone?" he asked.

"Think so," said the psychiatrist. "There's something to do, but . . ."

"I love her," the man said.

"That's clear," the psychiatrist said.

"It's a nothing love," he said.

"Yes," she said. "Unless someone is there. I have someone. If he goes . . ."

"You land someplace," he said, "you land someplace. I know that now." He had a huge grin on his face. "It tickles. I can feel it. It tickles."

She stood up to shake his hand because he made to go. "They'll think you're crazy," she said.

"They can go jump if they do," he said. But his grin faded. "I make them jump, don't I?" he said.

"No," she said, "but where you got it does."

"Got what?" he asked.

"The tickle," she said.

Old Age Croak

"Does a woman forget her baby at
her breast, or fail to cherish the
son of her womb? Yet even if these
forget, I will never forget you."
—Isaiah 49:1

"Let me tell you about blight," a woman said. "My daughter. She's a Carmelite nun just to spite me. She hates my writing. Too much sex. So she has no sex. She's in a cast like a broken leg." The woman was speaking to an interviewer, a younger woman from a supermarket magazine. The question had been about her blighted marriage, and maybe her romances had been a substitute. She was the queen of the romances, had been for years. She could do one in three months, sell half a million copies.

"In fact, she's in a body cast like some plane accident survivor, you kiss plaster, you hug a statue. She's been in there twenty years. Singing sweet and fluttering her hands over holy cards or convent jam. She runs these bazaars to keep the place going. She's the young one, and she's not, the rest are like me with their old age croaks. You know what she's really doing? She's making sure I have no more life. I'll never see a grandchild. Your books, she says, and that's twisting the knife. I kept her alive with those books. Jesus, she found this guide to sorcery when she was in eighth grade and I used to find pins stuck through the dust jackets or the covers depending. Always through the woman. Never through the heart. Always through an eye, left eye, right eye, and she'd put the book inside the letter drop on the floor on top of the day's mail.

So I got the nuns after her and one of them turned her into a simp, a pious simp. Then one day, senior year, she goes to the bazaar at the Carmelite Convent and she sees the holy cards and convent jelly and falls in

138

love with the place. I screamed at her all that summer right up to the door. Her father found out and doubled with laughter in his bank vault.

She's white pink all over, I can't describe it. She says I should love that for my nymphomaniacs. Nymphomaniacs are a soul, a damn bruised soul, I tell her, and she asks me to spell soul everytime, so I say its steam, steam off stupidity. Then she reads me St. Theresa about the poor butterfly looking for a flower to land on. That's what men are, I say, only they are not poor and they are bumble bees. So you should be happy, she says, no bumble bees in a cloister.

She's got these granny glasses she looks over, at me, lessoning me, knowing its like ripping rags. And she turns up the heat in her voice, it's like burning charcoal and sweet gum if you know what I mean. She turns into one of my books for a minute, then there's that pin again, right through an eye. I want to kiss her hands sometimes, they are like my mother's, the veins show beautifully, a purple you never saw, you can watch her pulse almost. Then she puts her hands inside her scapular. Yes, they are old time Carmelites, lucky I can even see her. Then she rides her hands up and down inside that scapular as if she is feeling up her own body. Like she's flinging chapter two at me. But she knows I love what she looks like. So she wraps it up from me then plays with it to mock me.

Blight! Like a soak in a dry season! How anyone can stick to that life for that motive I don't know! Maybe I should join. That'd do it! She'd leave and have a hundred kids by a hundred different men and abandon them on the convent doorstep with the milk bottles. That dates me, doesn't it! Wouldn't I be good as a nun! I could wear their ragbag outfit the way I wear my skin now. I tried the suicide thing. They said she came and watched the monitor screen until the blips were regular. Then she stuck a palm woven into a cross onto the top of the oxygen tank next to my bed. I nearly threw that thing! You know she can really think dirty things in a good cause.

So what's the difference between us I asked her after I was out and mobile. You know everything I know. And can you ever put a twist on it! You'd make a fortune in the sicko market. Well, she hit me for that one. I still feel it. But it was symbolic and she doesn't know it was like a love, she doesn't know she gave herself away, she doesn't know why it was not a smile of triumph on my face, that little bitch, what am I saying, big bitch, she loves me. That's the only thing that could fuel that crazy convent life of hers. She doesn't know her father just wanted mastery over me, she doesn't know he was a cold bull, if you can imagine it, impersonal anyway. She doesn't know I was afraid she'd be like him. She almost is. But the day she hit me, I knew. She wasn't. So I stopped going to see her.

Now she has to do that Carmelite stuff right or she's got to come out. It's not too late. But if she did, she'd be like pastry. And she'd have to be like a porcupine. What I know wouldn't do her any good. Doesn't do it for me. I still get taken by those old bulls, still think they have eyes and know what they're doing. But if she's in there for a sacrifice for me, then that's the last pin through the eye, it's the one that works. I don't want to be saved. Not by her unbloody sacrifice.

What's so wrong with me? The stuff I write is soft. And I squeeze happiness out of stones. Real life characters just fizzle. She zings with life, even with the lid on tight you can hear the hum of bees. So that's why I stopped this kind of writing. So she'd have nothing to sacrifice for. And I wrote the life of that Huron woman who became a saint in the middle of savages. It's a goddam message to her, but she won't read it, everybody else does, it's been on top ten weeks, and I've got three contract offers from movies. I know they want the gore, the tepees full of screwing savages while she says her beads out in the snow for God to help them. Well, she gets killed by her own people. The beads are bad magic, white man's.

So what do I do now? She's blighted and I'm the blight and nothing I do works. I can't fake a conversion, that'd be too cute. Maybe if I did one on women's bodies she'd understand. Slave market scene. Medieval saint. Superb auctioneer. Sultan looking for just the right one. She's it. Long description. Sold to Sultan for half a kingdom. Ship to Byzantium. Hung in cage so she won't leap. She dances naked to God, in all the lights of sun and moon. It's a canticle. He opens cage, subdued. She moves to prow, leaps, will never be sold again. Rainbow touches wake of vessel. There is peace. I won't have her climb the rainbow. She'd hit me again for blasphemy. But it'd be something. So, does that answer your question?

9th Sunday, Ordinary Time

Legend

*See, I set before you today a blessing
and a curse: a blessing if you obey . .
a curse if you disobey . . .*
        —Deuteronomy 11:26-28

There was a young monk of the desert a long time ago who was given the task of making rounds of the caves to check on the well being of the other monks. It was tough terrain out in the Wilderness. It didn't take much strength to live there, but it took a lot of strength to travel it constantly. He had the youngest legs, he needed the most schooling in the life of a monk, so he was chosen to be visitor and pupil to the four hundred or so who lived in caves over thirty or forty square miles. They were hardy souls, but what they did to their bodies often reduced them to physical or mental wrecks. He was not to be a guard but a guardian.

He loved the travel, the rocks, the stubble of grass in the wadis near the smallest water source, the butterflies there in season, he loved the feel of his own body as he climbed sheer faces to some cell and without a word gave the sign of peace to a Paphnutius or a Zeno who acknowleged him with a blessing then returned to contemplation. He would descend the cliff face imagining it was God's and wonder did it itch. But sometimes he had to carry a Paphnutius or a Zeno to a village for care. An unwise fasting or dehydration. A few times he found madmen who hurled rocks down on him as if he were a devil and a woman. He was light skinned and had little beard though it was good so at a distance he looked womanly. Then he had to speak and dodge rocks at the same time until the madmen were exhausted. Not so exhausted that they didn't grab at him and try to make love to him as to a woman. He did not bring those back to the village. He fed them instead on the special food he carried, honey in the comb, figs, dates, food reserved for the kingdom. And he sang to them, the joyful

141

season texts, blurring the words so they could be like love songs, not hard-line psalms. They would often end up masturbating and weeping, but over a period of several days they would learn a strange lesson from their sins, that it was the devil who hated the body, not God.

Most times the cure worked. The young monk had learned it from the one who had preceded him in the job. But he knew it from his own good spirits. He found it hard to hate even the devil, though he was wary. When he had to travel by moonlight he was respectful of chasms and loose rock and he kept an eye out for bats. They veered off at the wave of a cloth he held in his hand. Sometimes the cure did not work, it drove a few to suicide instead. It was pitiful to see someone in just bones and skin screaming for love race to the edge of a precipice and hurl themselves off. He had to go down for the body, then build a cairn of rocks as a tomb for it, mark it with some cross, then hope the jackals were not strong enough to remove the rubble and eat the monk. Jackals were possessed.

He knew there were some women disguised as men living as monks in some of the caves. His predecessor had finally trusted him enough to tell him, though not who or where. He had some fear of finding one starved or crazed because he would have to nurse her too or bury her out of the jackals' reach. His fear came true one day. He had taken a short cut over a waterless segment of ridges, on a moonlit night. He took an extra skin of water. At dawn he came to a wadi. The stream was flowing at the bottom, there must have been rain to the east. Easy enough to go down and get more water. Near the bottom he saw a figure lying face down in the small run. A monk, a dead monk. Whom he turned over to see and saw a starved woman. She was in a fierce hair shirt and wore chains he could feel as he moved her. She must have heard the water and just made it down, tried to drink, fell forward, and had no strength left even to roll over. He buried her there, under rocks.

Then went looking for her cave. He found it, went inside, found her few living things, and by a candle the skull of a small child. "Hers," he thought. "She did something. The skull is here to remind her." He went to the door of the cave and looked south along the wadi toward the Dead Sea. The beauty had gone from it. It was purple with rage now, it was gray with revenge, it was blue as the heartless sky. "She's tempting me even dead," he thought. He took the small skull down with him, opened the rock tomb and put it at her bosom which was slack from starvation. Then he closed the rocks in on them again. He filled his skins with water and prepared for a few more hours travel before the sun got too high.

But something held him. There had to be a man here. He climbed back up and went into the cave. Nothing. At the entrance again, he saw a small stone to the right, flat stone, set out over the drop down to the wadi floor. He tested it with his foot, it was firm, so he stood out on it, back to the cliff face, if the pedestal gave he was gone. He looked to his right, something, a niche in a wall of rock within arms reach, just, and in it a skeleton of a man in monk's robes. There was still a bowl in the man's lap. He had been cleaned by vultures, no doubt. She fed him from here until he died, there could be no more sin between them. She must have wanted to jump many times into that wadi. There was no jump back from the niche.

"Can I reach him?" the monk thought. "If I have a stick." There was one, a walking stick in the cave. It was thin enough. He lifted the skull off, then lifted the whole skeleton and its few rags and swung them gently in an arc and around to the mouth of the cave. He put the bones in his own cloak and went down the cliff face to the mound of the mother and child. He opened the rocks again. Then he set the skeleton beside her and closed the tomb for the third time. He added extra stones, then extra stones, until he realized he was acting compulsively.

"Am I killing them for their sin?" he asked himself. "Some avenger from the law?" He waited for his breath to come back and his soul to clear. "No," he thought, "no, I want to protect them. I want God not to know where they are." He took out his honey, his dates and figs, and he laid them on top of the tomb. He looked up toward the heavens and said, "They are for you." And he waited for the stroke of anger. None came.

Instead he saw bees, bees. They circled after eating and flew up the wadi. He followed them as if following a sign. They led to a small crack in the rock and a seepage of water. The crack was filled with honeycomb and there were small flowers growing, giving off a light smell of perfume. "These are for me," he said as he looked up the sheer face to what showed of the sky. "They are you." He took some flowers back to the tomb and laid them on top. "They never knew," he said. But then, "They must have. They must have."

He left that wadi. He called it *Not Knowing*. It is the name people use for it today. Few know why.

Fragile People

What am I to do with you, Ephraim?
What am I to do with you, Judah?
This love of yours is like a morning
cloud, like the dew that quickly disappears.
—Hosea 6:4

"The man we bury today lived a lie," the preacher said as he began the eulogy over the flag draped coffin. "He told me to tell you when I gave him the last rites." There was attention among the mourners. A new way to draw a spiritual lesson, a new way of burnishing an old hero. "But I was not to tell you unless I told you something else." There was almost no breathing now. "To tell you I live a lie as well." There was a slight movement of anger as people breathed again. "He was not a hero in the war and I knew it. And I said nothing when I came here ten years ago. Too much life would be ruined. I was a corpsman in Korea."

The preacher stopped. One of the sons had risen. "Just wait one more minute, please," the preacher said. The son waited. "I ran from an attack," the preacher continued. "I jumped into a bunker with all my first aid stuff. And I landed on someone who was hiding in that bunker before me. We hid there as the fight went past us in one direction, then by us in the other. Then we crawled out. We dirtied and bloodied ourselves on enemy equipment. There was so much confusion! Another counter attack and people spread all over. I finally helped someone because I had to, then a few more because I had to, and I lost my companion in cowardice until the day I came here. And for helping because I had to I received a medal. And he received a greater one. For being captured and tortured and keeping faith with his country. You know he could never inflict violence on anyone. There was tough talk. He was hawkish. It was all bravado. But he could sustain violence. As I could not. When I was captured, I broke. I mean I

145

babbled so they threw me away as useless and our government got me back as useless. But he had something he would not betray. That's why he told me to tell you this. But only if I told you about me." The son was still standing in the pew. Standing as if to bear the weight of all that was happening. "So he was a hero, but not the kind you think. And he was a coward, but not the kind you think."

"You make no sense," the son said. "There is no one to verify what you say. You can say anything you want. You cannot wipe out this man's record. And you are babbling again. Now leave this off. Let the sexton read some prayers and we will go!"

The mother stood and went to the head of the casket and looked up at the preacher. "What you say is true," she said. The breath went out of the congregation. "It is written down in his will, but only for his family. I did not know he told you. I do know he kept your secret. You know you are ruined along with him. Does that do us any good?"

The preacher said nothing. The son was immobilized. "It does if I can have my real self back," the preacher said, saying the words in a slow and halting way. "It's what he said to me he wanted. His real self back. But he would have to die without it. He said to me it's worse than death. He said to me get it before. He said shame was nothing to pay. He said he wrote the will so I should not worry. Worry? Did he know you can take someone out with you?" It was almost a soliloquy the preacher had fallen into. Almost like the babbling he had mentioned had happened to him as a prisoner of war.

"Let me tell you what all this means," the woman said. Then she realized she could not be heard by those behind her. So she moved to the foot of the flag draped coffin and she turned to the people in the church. "We have a man who is close to breaking again." And she pointed to the pulpit with the whole of her hand, like a dancer lifting something. "And we have a man who was close to breaking until the day he died." She began to draw the flag toward her from the coffin, began to fold it awkwardly upon itself. "Fragile people should not be sent to fight. And they should not run churches." Tears were showing on the woman's face. "That is why my husband could not shoot. It is also why he could never betray. It is also why he was caught between. Do you see? He has this man in that pulpit for this reason. It is a coward's courage! He loved the life of things. Even the false life of things. But at the last . . ." She stopped. Then she turned, holding the folded flag against her, and leaned against the foot of the coffin. "And you," she said up to the preacher in the pulpit, "is this your funeral too?"

The preacher had calmed a bit. The son still stood erect, not so rigid now, but still firm, and listening with every pore. "No, it is not," the preacher said. "I feel a life in me again. I don't know what it is. Some of us are just. . . just here, we are not killers . . . we are like stones for a wall if you stack us right . . . if you throw us we harm people . . . we watch the morning and the evening, we watch the night and the day and we love all the differences . . . I cannot say more, except we are like the zeros that make sense only if you add ones and twos." He stopped again, again near the babbling point. "He said to me," the preacher began again, "that I would see myself like a clear drop of water hanging from a copper wire and growing quietly larger, and that I had a chance to catch it on my finger, or a chance to let it drop and hit the ground. That was the something he thought he could catch if I would promise to tell you all the truth."

This was too much for the people in the pews, too personal, too remote from what was real and they began to stir and the stir meant stop this. And the preacher knew it, so he stood down from the pulpit and walked backwards, slowly, to the sacristy door behind him, then turned and went in out of sight.

"I want you all to go," the woman said in a loud, stern voice. "Wait outside if you wish. I will bury him. The real him." And she hit the coffin a knock.

But the people in the pews were beyond reach, were deeply embarrassed. They couldn't go, they couldn't stay, they needed some escape. The woman sensed it after some long minutes. So she put her hands on the coffin and began to push it down the aisle. Easily. The flag over her shoulder like a serape. The honor guard was left up front, the pall bearers along the side. At the end of the aisle, she turned and said, "If I have to do it myself."

11th Sunday, Ordinary Time

A Break in the Cold

*"The harvest is rich but the laborers
few, so ask the Lord of the harvest to
send laborers to his harvest."*
—Matthew 9:37-38

A priest was a prison chaplain, a downtown prison, with wings for men and women. A pretrial place as well as a death row on appeal. He had one fear, the cold criminal—cold killer, cold thief, cold rapist. There was a cold killer after him, he knew it.

He had broken up a prison escape. He was in the cell blocks on the way to the infirmary, the year before, when three men took him hostage and holed up in the dispensary just off the corridor between the blocks and the sick bay. It was in a low building connecting larger ones, accessible to ambulances, to police vans. It was a straight run to the front gate and an artery out of town. There were phones. And over those phones the prisoners said they wanted an armored truck, Brinks type, brought to the emergency door, left running and empty, or they would blow the priest's brains out and run a fire into the two buildings on either side. There was oxygen stored in the dispensary. One of the men explained how he could create a fireball with it. Through a ventilating system which the men had access to, which couldn't be blocked for a couple of hours. So armored truck or a lot of dead bodies. Move any men out and the fireball starts now.

The priest kept his composure. These were the cold men he feared. "I will be cold too," he thought. The armored truck was sent to the emergency door within a half hour. The men were surprised. There usually was an attempt to delay, to talk violence down enough to set up an unbeatable trap. But they knew their own record of killing would have succeeded and within the time they set. So they sent one man out. He scooted onto the van, checked gas, the box, looked for explosives and tear gas, took a mighty chance and actually checked beneath the hood while under a dozen sharpshooting rifles. He went back in. One by one they came out, the last with the priest and a gun to his head. As they emerged the priest screamed, "Shoot! Shoot!" and he sagged like a sack, and shoot they did, one shot went through his shoulder and killed the prisoner holding him who had fired at the same instant and taken the priest's eyebrow and the bone under it away. Another shot went through the flesh just above his hip and into the belly of his captor. Within a few seconds the tires in the truck were out and a backhoe with its bucket up to shield the driver had come around a corner and simply tipped the armored truck over on its side. The priest and his dead captor were scooped up by a team and hauled to safety. Both men inside the truck surrendered.

It took months for the priest to recover and go back to his job. He had never betrayed a confidence. Had never betrayed the law. But he had caused one of the prisoners to die. And had been willing to die. That put him in a special category. So now prisoners brought him real problems, not bragadoccio. They took him into killers' confidences. But one let him in on a secret.

"There's a contract out on you," he said, "a heavy one. You're gone. Enjoy your meal." The one who told him waited to see if the priest would inform. Then they would ask the prisoner some questions which would guarantee that he would be killed for tipping the priest off. But the edge of death was the only place to live for such a man.

"It will be cold and quick," the priest thought. "So I needn't worry about pain." The healing of his face, the orbital ridge, his side, had been very painful. Not as bad, though, as listening to killers brag. "My killer will not brag," he thought more. "But I would like to see who hits me."

After a few weeks the tipster came in knowing he was safe. So the priest said, "Man or woman?" The prisoner didn't know. But he would. When he did, he said, "Woman."

"Movies," said the priest. Then, "Well, it's their money."

The prisoner said nothing. Then, "You shouldn't have done it. You should have done nothing."

"When it's my life," the priest said, "I do nothing. Somebody else's and watch out for me."

"You can't watch out," the prisoner said. "She's a kid who needs drugs. Or she's a hooker who loves Daddy. Or she's a woman with a rep and a bad story in the closet." He was toying with the priest.

"So you go now and watch the papers," the priest said. "Read the comics first. Get yourself ready." But the toying worked. There wasn't a woman he passed who couldn't kill him. Until he remembered his own wisdom. Cold. Cold. How do you reach the cold? "There are people damned," he thought. "Maybe I'm one. I don't want hell for those people, I don't want heaven for them either."

He spotted her in the oddest way. He was in a pastry shop, one oozing with glorious stuff, on a crowded gourmet street. Coffee and a danish for late breakfast. She came in and ordered coffee. A person of remarkable stillness, a quiet voice. "Coffee, just coffee, no menu, thanks." The place had small tables. Hers was near the door. It had mirrors and brightness. And there was a free lane between them. Though people were passing. Her pocket book was on the table. The thinnest leather he ever saw. It had a throat and string so she could reach in and pull out a kleenex. It was stuffed with a lot else. The coffee sat in front of her. And sat.

He reached down to his briefcase everytime he thought there'd be no one passing. Or drop something and pick it up. He had her in the mirror behind the cashier's stand. He saw her hand go into the bag and stay there. He waited a split second then flipped his table, the bullet hit it, the silent bullet, and deflected past his cheek burning his ear. The second grazed his shoulder as he dropped toward the floor. She was accurate but he was moving and lucky. She didn't fire a third shot and no one knew really she had fired two. People saw a commotion, upset table, man on floor with some blood on his ear, strange hole in butcher block table.

The priest righted the table apologizing saying he had tripped trying to get up and took the table with him. "She's right outside that door," he thought. "She's window shopping. She's furious she missed. She won't miss again or her future is ruined." He saw her standing on the curbstone, half turned down the street. She had every option ready. If he went to the pay phone, she stepped in the doorway and shot. If he made a scene, then she'd take out whomever she needed. She had a crowd to disappear into, probably a wig to drop, a coat to reverse, a hospital to hide in for a while. She had an eye on him, a hand in her bag, the way a french horn player has a hand in the bell.

He had an eye on her. A scarred eye. He waited until the door was clear and his clothes straightened. Then he walked toward her. Whoever came between them, he didn't do it, passersby. If none, he was dead in that doorway, if some he had a chance. There were some. Entering. He knifed through them and deflected her silent shot so it cracked the plastic facing of the coffee shop. And he held the bag down. She could shoot the sidewalk if she wished. Or give him the bag. Which she did. People were looking around for the reason the plastic had spattered. Traffic was heavy on the street. The two were looking eye to eye. She was absolutely cold. She had done everything right and she knew it. She could knee him but she saw he was stationed protectively, his hand on her arm. There was the traffic and he could shove. But there was a look in him that he would not kill.

So she reached up and took his hand off her arm. Then she reached again and took her bag back with its three frayed holes. She tightened its throat and let the bag hang from her hand. He put his arm through hers and began to walk her toward the subway station. He could feel the cold break in her and a rage and hatred begin to well up. She could do something wild now, careless, murderous. There was a litter basket near the subway entrance. He raised her hand and bag over it. Her rage was now volcanic. She was looking at him with pure hatred. And she saw he wanted her that way. That it was a trick, a classical trick, he had played on her. Get her to feel something.

"Go," she said. It was a hiss. She had tasted hatred of herself. For not being cold. Uncontrollable hatred. "Go," she said again. She shot herself before he was ten feet away, his back to her. The unrecognisable sound he recognised. People thought she had a stroke and fell. Those who stopped to help. And those who didn't.

"You drop it in the trash!" he said in fury. "You drop it!"

Crudities

. . . everything that is now covered
will be uncovered, and everything now
hidden will be made clear. . .
—Matthew 10:26

A woman sensed she was becoming crude. She had a dog she had gotten from a previous owner. The dog was wonderful but hadn't learned you don't copulate with people's legs. She kept him away from outsiders as a result. But he became a metaphor for a lot that was happening in the inside world. She had other metaphors, and they began to get cruder too.

"You have to be gross or nothing makes sense," she thought. "My son is a goddam liar. And my husband is a friggin cheat. And my daughter-in-law is an asshole to marry that creep and go hot for money in the art world." She was actually looking at her language as she said it to herself out loud. "And I fit right in with this talk."

The dog was at her leg. He was a soft fornicator. It was the love he wanted back. The big brown eyes and spaniel ears. She grabbed him by the tail and held his hind legs off the floor so he was puzzled out of his jerking. You needed a good golf stand if you were a dog in rhythm. Then she lowered him and he sat down eyeing her with absolute devotion.

"You're not a fucking liar," she said to him. And he agreed with his ears. "My son is," she said to him. His nose tried to sniff what she meant. "I tried to tell her. But I said he sometimes fooled himself into feeling what he didn't feel. But she thought I wanted someone socially better. I should have been crude then. Not now. No, sit!" she continued. He was up on all fours and going for her leg again.

152

She was at her writing table in the parlor. She was quitting this whole thing. For a while anyway. "Big brave!" she thought. She was writing Mother Theresa's group in Haiti. "Let me work for you for a month."

"My motives stink," she thought. "I want to come back here smelling like crap. Proud as crap. Strip them a bit to their essentials. They'll run me through a carwash with the windows open."

The dog was on his belly and actually trying to nip the toe off her shoe. She played that toe up against his nose a while. He had a dog smile on as she rolled his nose around. Then he was back up ready to screw again when she had to reach down and hit him. He stopped and stood there waiting to be told. "Sit," she said, and he did.

"I trained as a nurse but am out of practice. Yet I think people's needs are simple. And I know you take volunteers for periods of time. I was a pediatric nurse."

The dog moaned a bit out of neglect. "Lie," she said. And he lowered his chin to the floor and raised his eyes to the ceiling. "You're a husband alright. It's the way he pretends he hasn't been in someone when he comes home. Internist is the right word." The dog sniffed to find out what that meant and his ears tried to row him across the floor and his pelvis began to love the rug. And she burst into laughter that had him up on his feet and ready to run and chase something. He was a spaniel after all.

"You're the only one that will play with me when I get back," she said, now leaning toward him from her chair, her elbows on her knees, her hands out together and cupped. Sure enough his muzzle went right into them and his tongue worked on the heel of her hands. She grabbed him over the ears, the curly haired ears, and moved him back and forth, his eyes going from one side of his head to the other to stay fixed on her. "That's devotion, you dear," she said. And she gave him a shove which rolled him over and had him up and panting back at her hands. "Sit! Lie!" she said. She repeated it sharply, so he did.

"My life right here," she said. "The lady and the dog. Every dirty joke. I'm the crap I'm going to clean up. Clean myself up first. How quick the woman goes out of the woman. And they see a funny looking Mom. Not quite. Enough to honor the past. And look for another future. You know why I keep you now?" she said to her spaniel. He got up and hung his tongue out to see what she meant. "They see you too. They don't enjoy it. You know why? So I put you on the veranda."

He sensed she was going to do it now so he started to back away and look for places underneath things, like the piano. "He was right when he called you a fucking dog. Your mother's got this fucking dog! My mother's got this, my mother-in-law's got this fucking dog!" There was anger in her voice, and the dog started to move in retreating circles, a dog's way of waving surrender. "You know what they think of me?" she said as she rose and followed the dog slowly. He just kept making S patterns in the room. "They think that's what I want from them. You little symbol you! I hope he never touches me again. And I hope that other one forgets where he came from. And that soft wench of his, I hope she can keep his eye!"

The dog was under the writing table now and sank slowly to the floor but kept his eyes up. "Yes," she said, "finish my letter." She sat and wrote, "I'm a stable person and can get references. And I am able to sustain a hard regime. If it works out, I can return on a periodic basis." The dog had placed his head over the top of one of her shoes. She could feel his warm throat right through to her bones. "You'll sleep now," she said through the lid of the desk. "And hold me here. We have to let sleeping dogs lie." "No we don't," she said further, "this one maybe, not the other three."

Then she stopped. "Who's the sleeping dog? And who's the lie? I run off to Mother Theresa. The three will love it. She's in some crazy fuckin' place! She's with this crazy fuckin' nun! Haiti, for chrissake, we'll all have AIDS, kiss her going but not coming. They'll love it, though. I'm like a mobster's wife. Keep a hole in the sky open. Listen to me! I have poetry in my head and love in my body. And I'm left talking crud to a dog!"

She sat back without moving her foot. "You're not asleep, are you," she said down to him. He didn't move. "This is possum, isn't it, calm me down time, so you don't have to walk around ahead of my anger." He still didn't move, but his breathing had slowed. Then an eye opened, big brown eye. One. To see if the possum had worked. It had. So he closed the big brown eye. "They'd kill you if I left you to them," she said to him softly. "Get someone to put you to sleep the right way. They'd say sleep too, not kill, and what they'd remember was Mother had a fuckin' dog before she went off to that fuckin' island. They don't know what love is, you poor little beast, but you do, and isn't it a pity." The one eye opened again. "So I will put you in a kennel, before I go. It will be a lonely month for you. Or I could shift you to someone old." She laughed. "They might like your leg work."

She concluded her letter: "So I will proceed on the presumption that I am qualified and get all the necessary shots. I am clear of responsibilities here, my family is independent. And I too want people who are to die to die knowing some love holds them." "There," she said, "I'm not a brute anymore. Whether they take me or not." The dog snorted a bit, a dream. "I have to move my foot, honey," she said, "have to go get stamps."

Sunburn

*"Anyone who finds his life will lose it:
anyone who loses his life for my sake
will find it."*
—Matthew 10:39

There was a young woman on winter break vacation in Florida from her northern college. After banks of snow, a hot beach was heaven, and a body nearly naked in the sun. She came back to her motel for lunch, near the end of her stay, and found that her father had phoned. She was to phone back. She knew his business was having difficulties and knew she might not get a vacation like this again, would have to stay up among the snow banks for her junior and senior years. But the call couldn't be about that. She hoped it wasn't someone sick. So she called and got him at his architectural firm. It was nothing serious, just would she do him a favor and change her flight plan home to go through Miami and pick up some architectural drawings someone would bring out to the airport and give her if she'd do it. Of course she would and she would phone back after she made the change of flight and knew the times and numbers.

So she hummed her way through the yellow pages, found the airline, made the changes, and would pick up the ticket at the counter. She spent her last day baking like clay, or running into the surf like a kid, or Indian-wrestling college football players, or eating junk food like a hunger victim. She had to get up early so she left the clambake at like two in the morning to get some shuteye and hope to pack before the limo came at six for the airport. It was a short flight up to Miami. She made it with her eyes still closed with sleep. And she was still digesting; she left her breakfast tray untouched.

At Miami, she went out onto the concourse where her father said to go when she had called him back. The duty free shop at the display where the watches were sold. There was a messenger there, from Expedita or some other service, and he had her sign for a long tube that had a strap attached. It looked like a bassoon case. She could carry it on her shoulder like a rifle, or in her hand like a ram that could hit people. So she carried it like a rifle back to her new gate, plunked it on the scanner with her beach bag, her purse, her couple of tennis rackets. She picked her stuff up on the other side. The guards were as sleepy as she and they kind of groaned at her in sympathy.

"You really burned, baby," one said.

"Even the word hurts," she said back. Then she went to a corner where she could lean her head against a wall. It was forty-five minutes to boarding time. As she tried to stand the tube it kept sliding toward her like a falling tree and thumping her sunburn hard. Which kind of woke her into thinking, "This tube is too heavy. Plans are just rolled paper. Should be light as a feather." So she lowered one end to find the opening, saw it was like a shampoo cap. She lifted the cap off and saw a styrofoam plug inside. She worked that free, but it was long, maybe six inches. Then she saw some white plastic packages.

It was a tube of cocaine she had! There were maybe three pounds. How had she gotten through than scanner? The packages were wrapped like thick scrolls, like that Danish she couldn't eat on the first plane. Maybe Security thought posters. Or maybe they didn't think. And no one would check her further. He had risked her whole life. He was risking his life. He was committing a crime and she was helping. She was now helping formally because she knew. The tube was addressed to him. He was in despair to do this. He was crazy or blackmailed. And her life was over. Or was it? No one would check her further. There were millions here. And if she didn't deliver this, he was dead, she was dead, they were dead.

Then she sensed she was dead either way. She could not live off this money. She could not bring this tube to her father. "I'll take it into the Ladies Room," she thought, "and pour the stuff down the toilet. No, no, there's that messenger, I know his face, he's changed uniforms, he's Security now. I'll do it on the plane. Unless there's someone to watch me there also. I'll have to tip somebody off to this. I'll have to have them all caught."

The tube was like an atom bomb to her. The announcement for the flight was made, inviting those who had small children or who needed assistance to board first. "Sunburn," she thought. So she rose as if in pain and went to the head of the passageway, looked at the attendant, looked down at her sunburned shoulder. The attendant was most solicitous. So she went achingly down the passageway and into the door of the plane. The cockpit was open, and the pilot was standing just inside with a cup of coffee. So she edged slightly into the doorway and said, "I've been tricked into carrying cocaine in this tube of architectural drawings. You have to tell the police from the air. I'm followed, and maybe on board. It's my father who tricked me." And she stopped speaking and seemed to turn to stone.

The pilot said, "Quick, give me your ID." He took the phone off the jack and said to the passageway attendant, "Hold boarding for a minute." Then said, "Now give me that tube." He took the top off as she had done, the styrofoam plug out, and saw the packages. "My hand's too thick," he said, "your's isn't. Put your hand in and break one of the packages and bring some powder out on your finger. I have to be sure its not explosives or sugar."

So she did. It was cocaine.

"Okay," he said, "take the tube back with you. I'll get Narcotics on the radio. We can make a repair stop in Washington, a few minutes to check something and get someone on board. You go back with the tube and sit tight." He took the phone again and said, "Start boarding."

So she went back and sat in her assigned seat. Her old life was gone. Overhead was the tube that destroyed it. Whatever scenario Narcotics worked out for her over the crackling radio between Miami and Washington, the truth meant death. Just as the tube meant death if it ever got to the people on drugs.

"Better mine than theirs," she said.

As the plane lifted off the ground, she said it again, "Better mine than theirs." And she fell asleep from grief.

14th Sunday, Ordinary Time

Pious Pilgrims

"... there is no necessity for us to obey our unspiritual selves or to live unspiritual lives."
—Romans 8:9

There was a woman touring by herself in Jerusalem. This day she was walking a crowded Suq near King David Street, shops to the right of her, shops to the left of her, people in motion every which way. Someone pinched her buttocks through her khaki wrap-around skirt. Instinctively she swung the purse she gripped in her hand, swung it without looking, to hit the pincher. Who was gone. She hit instead a thick rope of garlic and sent it scattering down on barrels of spices below and onto the stone pavement. A shopkeeper roared out angrily from behind the spices with his hands spread to grab her, so she kicked a barrel of spices over and tumbled him into the street, then turned fast and blended in with the crowd which scarcely noticed, though the shopkeeper did a lot of cursing in her direction.

"Good thing I don't understand," she thought. "I'd go back and hit him instead of his rope of garlic."

She felt a hand brush over her buttocks in the crowd, where she still smarted from the pinch, so she whirled again, this time to look before she swung and make sure she hit what should be hit. It was another woman tourist like herself with her hands up for self-protection and a huge grin on her face saying, "Okay, okay, I was just taking the wrinkle out of your skirt. Pinchers leave creases." So the first woman let her breath out and said, "I'm ready to bop the Dome of the Rock or Jesus in his grave. You know I haven't got a clear inch of behind left! They're uncanny, they

159

pinch only the unbruised parts. Their hands have a damn radar. Who are you?"

"I'm a pious pilgrim like yourself," the second woman said, "and I'm paying for my sins. What do you say we walk back to back?"

"Hate to think what they'd do to our fronts," the first woman said. "This is worse than Italy. How about some Arabic coffee. We'll be hard to get at if we sit."

"Good," said the second woman, "at the end of this street and to the right."

"Think we can make it?" said the first.

Just then a Greek Orthodox priest began to edge around them in the crowd. He had on the beautiful Orthodox headdress and long black veil, then the flowing gown with its flared sleeves, and black shoes just peeking out from under the full skirts. He had a wonderful cachet to him, as if he stored his clothing in sandalwood or some other aromatic chest. So the first woman reached out quickly and pinched him on the buttocks, then as quickly, turned her head to look up at some lace blouses hanging from the awning of the shop. The priest stopped. And turned slowly as if to survey the whole world. He saw the two women minding their own business looking up toward the blouses but nearly bursting with laughter. And the priest seemed to know the blouses weren't funny. The women could feel the cachet of him come closer. So they looked over either shoulder hoping a storm wasn't ready to clobber them. But the priest had a beatific smile on his face. It showed through his glorious soft black beard. His almost black eyes were luminous.

"So," he said to them in thick English, "it's a pinch for a pinch. That's a severe law. But better than a tooth for a tooth." And he put his hands on either of their arms. And his hands had the same black hair on the fingers and up to the wrists, but they were soft hands, and touched softly.

"You just got it once," the first woman said, "and I'm sorry. I'm black and blue. And my friend here is green and red."

"If my wife were here," the priest said, "I'd ask her to take you home and rub you with balm until you are pink again. She does this very well.

This is not the first pinch I've gotten either." And he began to laugh deep inside his beard and black eyes. "They treat me as a woman here. My wife is my only defense. She hits them with things because she walks behind me as is the custom and she can see who did it. She's away with her sister who is having a child."

"Don't they pinch her?" the second woman said.

"No," the priest said. "She is not pretty as you are and she wears many skirts. But she is pretty inside and has only one anger. It's for those who do this to me, what has been done to you." His hands were still resting softly on the women's arms. And people as they slid by were now staring at him for what he was doing. But he stood there calmly looking at them. "She is pretty inside because she loves me so much," he said. "And she loves me too much. I have to tell her I am no more than a wildflower that dries in the wind. She combs my beard for me before I can leave the house. You see today it is not combed well." He was almost talking to himself as if he were not there but off with his sister-in-law who was having the baby. "And she would rub you back to being pink if she were here," he said. "You do not pinch very hard. May God be thanked." And with very gentle motions he stroked the skin of their arms a few times then turned from them. But stopped and looked over his shoulder like a luxuriously bearded nun and said, "Am I safe to go?" And he laughed that deep, deep laugh. And the two women instinctively touched him on either shoulder to tell him go. And then they fell into each other with a kind of release and they laughed themselves back into good spirits.

"He could have taken me home and rubbed me pink himself," the first woman said.

"His wife would walk in and bop you," said the second.

"It'd be worth it," said the first. And they both started to laugh again leaning front to front against each other under the lace blouses. So they saw the shopkeeper reaching out to pinch one and a passerby reaching out to pinch the other, and said to each other, "Watch it!" They leaped apart and the two pinchers were pinching air.

15th Sunday, Ordinary Time

Control of the World

*It was not for any fault on the part of
creation that it was made unable to at-
tain its purpose, it was made so by God,
but creation still retains the hope of being freed . . .*
—Romans 8:19-21

"You know I am not a visionary," a man wrote to his wife. "But yesterday I had a vision of damnation. Food and water came in, the guerrillas let
the Red Cross through, though usually it's the government that doesn't
since we're in the disputed territory. So the people were eating, some of
the hunger sounds had diminished. If you could ever hear them . . . ! Just
after the sun went, I was standing outside our tent, at the edge of the area. I
turned and looked east, that's when figures seem to rise out of the desert
and come in. Refugees arrive by night. When the moon is up, the figures
seem to be like souls arriving after judgment. Well, a purple color seemed
to breathe out of the dirt. It was the earth's shadow, no doubt, but it was
the most beautiful purple I have ever seen, it was living color, immune to
death and drought, it moved me the way you do. I wanted it to make love
to me. A night wind came and it brought me the smell of death. We bury
only at night so we don't lose the diggers to sunstroke. And there was the
truck, I could see it moving through that lovely purple, to go out some distance before unloading. The color kept rising and it even reached the
moon low on the horizon and the moon was exquisite, like some of the
women's faces who have purple tints.

"This has to be hell, I thought. The loveliness is the torment. It tor-
mented me. I hope this isn't a bad sign for when I come home. You are
dark and beautiful. The sun of many summers has scorched your skin also.
I know what to recommend here. I know where every drop of water is. In
the cloudless sky or on the tips of beetles' tails in the early morning. So

162

the sky must yield it primarily. If it does, people must plant with their minds, not with their instincts, their instincts have created this beast of a drought. And they must reforest and not burn their stripling trees. Those instincts are part of the damnation.

"Yesterday I passed a tent. I help out the medical crews when I'm not flying or out in the Rover. I know the woman, we stabilized her baby in a few days with treated water, marvelous the way it works. She had some tea and with every grace in the world she made me come in and sit. She brewed the tea over what I don't know, ersatz fuel also brought in, and served me the tea as if somehow she had control of the world and was using it to thank me. I could not refuse. I did not, though I'm dark and beautiful too, the way the Project feeds me.

"Well, the whole night was purple. And I saw some figures going out into the desert by moonlight. They were men from the look of their dress. I know what they were doing. I got it from my pilot. There is a belief that if the male dies into the desert, there will be an odor that attracts the female sky. The female sky will become moist with desire and will lower itself down for love. And the earth will be wet for planting. So these men who have brought their families leave them, they, the men, are not going to survive much longer anyway, so they act on this belief. They enter nature as men, not as accidents. They even dig shallow troughs for their bodies, they retain their male power until their breath stops. The terrifying thing is, by removing themselves, they spare precious resources for those they leave. And they cut down on procreation. There are few men around. There is a scientific result from a strange belief. Again a beauty that masks a beastly reality. I don't talk this way at home, you know it.

"Why was that so beautiful last night? That woman's hands as she made the tea? Those silhouettes of the men walking away from the camps to turn the desert male so it could draw the female sky? The women think something else, my pilot tells me, so they can put up with living after the man goes. They think they are freeing a god with their suffering. The god is the very beauty I just told you about, the beauty I see as diabolical. The god entered a jealous woman at the creation of the world and she trapped him inside her sex. Only if other women suffer will he be free. They saw him freed last night in that color. He is freed in music. And that tea ceremony, it frees the god from the jealous woman. The women surely support pain. The way no science could. Do you see what I mean by something beautiful masking something beastly? Or do I understand anything more than water?

"Water is very beautiful. More when it is absent than when it is present. Some people when they come in are so parched they can't drink. They are looking at it and they can't swallow, it runs down their chins, and some try to rub it into their bodies with weak strokes. Then they look at their fingertips in disbelief. That's the god I find imprisoned in this earth. You get him out by digging deep holes in the right places. You get him out by catching him on tent flaps in the early morning. You get him out by running pipes from the salt sea and evaporating him onto mirrors. Those drops are the breasts of the sky. This makes sense only to me. And that's the vision of damnation I really mean. It makes no sense to them, what I suggest. They will not do it. We are in the same hell for different reasons.

"I will be home, I calculate, soon after this letter. I can't wait."

Jeeping the Donner

" . . . the Kingdom of Heaven is like a mustard
seed which a man took and sowed in his
field. It is the smallest of all the seeds,
but when it has grown it is the biggest shrub
of all and becomes a tree so that the birds
of the air come and shelter in its branches."
—Matthew 13:31-2

There was a man who was a conscientious objector. He had refused to serve in the war. Not on religious grounds. His whole feeling for life said no. But that was not enough for the Courts so it was serve or go to jail. He chose jail and spent three years behind bars. Where he was treated worse by fellow prisoners than those guilty of violent crimes. When he was released he knew he could not live in his own country. His record was marked with a jail sentence and the reason was given. He could conceal it, but usually not for long. People asked him where he was during that period of time and he had to say. Because that's the way he was. Concealment was foreign to him. So before he left he got an old jeep to bum and work his way across the country. Because he loved its natural beauty and wanted to see with his naked eyes what he had seen only in photos.

That's the way he picked up a veteran of the war who was bumming across it also, but for a different reason, for bitterness. He was like some disease to people. He could feel their skin crawl at him. He had started talking the minute he climbed into the jeep and asked, "How far are you going?"

"Until I reach the water," had been the answer, "then you can have the jeep if you want." They were headed East and most of the country lay ahead.

Well, the hitchhiker started on a tear about "there's nowhere I can go that people don't look at me and get sick. So I get sick looking at them. Like I'm a killer and they're not. I've been shaved by bullets, and suntanned by napalm, and had my hair cut by chopper blades. Got my paycheck lobbed in by mortar shells. And used to lug my clothes around in a body bag. No mildew gets in those things. You could zipper God up in one and you wouldn't hear a peep."

They reached the crest of the Donner Pass and started down the incline. "Do you like this?" the man at the wheel asked, pointing to the scene.

"Yeah," said the hiker. "Seen B52s level stuff like it in ten minutes. You know what, you just couldn't breathe when those bombs started marching through the jungle. You ever see it?"

"No," said the man at the wheel. "You don't see things like that in jail." The hiker tensed. No fear, just wariness until he found out what crime.

"What'd you do?" the hiker asked.

"Three years," the driver said.

"I mean what for?" the hiker asked.

"Refusing to serve," the driver said.

"Just stop this thing!" the hiker said.

"Okay," the driver answered. So he pulled over on the shoulder of the road, just above the Donner Lake, shifted into first and waited for the hiker to get down. But the hiker sat there fighting for some kind of control.

"You let me get my ass shot off for you?" he said.

"I've been judged," the driver said. "And so have you. And we're paying the sentence. And you know what it is?" The hiker looked at the driver, surprised that he had a firm voice and seemed to know something.

So the hiker said, "Tell me."

"The sentence is you get it from everyone you meet," the driver said.

"Get what?" the hiker asked.

"As much punishment as they can give you," the driver said. "If it's a kid, kid punishment, if it's an adult, adult punishment."

"Yeah," said the hiker. "I could tell you some things."

"Then do it and leave," the driver said. "It will make you feel better, more at home here."

"What's with the here?" the hiker asked. He was calmer, the passion was settling in his eyes.

"Here's where people had to eat each other to stay alive. Down there. Soon as a body died it was food for the rest. Today we eat people alive."

"I'm eating you alive?" the hiker asked as his anger began to rise again.

"Yeah," the driver said, "the world's chewing on you and you're chewing on me. And I'm just giving you a ride. You learn that in prison."

They were both looking at each other now. And words seem to have run out. Then the hiker broke in, "Okay, I owe you some time. Tell me about prison from here to the bottom of the hill. Maybe you got an ass too."

So the driver shifted into first, ran the shoulder of the road to pick up speed, then headed down the long slope with the lake gradually disappearing as they got closer to it. "I've been shaved by switchblades," he said, "made from tomato cans. And my tan was from scalding steam out of pipes in the kitchen. And my hair got pulled out. But it's better than rape. And my paycheck I couldn't cash when I got out. No one would touch it. And that's all I want to say. Except one thing more. I would have died if I saw those B52s wipe out those forests. And I would have gone to hell if I saw them hit a human being."

They were at the bottom of the slope. A barbecue ranch was just off the road, so the driver pulled into the gravel area and up to the totem pole entrance.

"The cowboys were eskimos," the hiker said.

"With credit cards," the driver added.

"What do you do when you hit the sea?" the hiker asked.

"I go someplace where there's no war," the driver said.

"There's no place there's no war," the hiker said. And they couldn't say anything for a minute more.

Then the hiker said, "I could use a jeep."

And the driver said, "You can have it when I reach the water."

"Okay," the hiker said. "First let me buy you an eskimo steak."

"Be sure the eskimo's dead," the driver said. Then they both began to sob and laugh at the same time. And people coming out of the barbecue place saw them and gave them a wide berth. For some reason they didn't look right.

Old Story

I give you a heart wise and shrewd
as none before you has had and none
will have after you.
        —I Kings 3:12

There was an old man who knew vines the way a saint knows a soul. In the mezzogiorno, a place of dry soil and scarce water. He had given most of his land away to his sons but kept a difficult piece near the juncture of two hill roads. It was easier to walk down and up one of them from the village to the plot than do the sidehill pathways. His sons' vineyards stretched above him, around the shoulders of the rock where the village was, down a slope, then up a high one to some olive groves that belonged to in-laws. There wasn't an inch of the area that didn't yield something, the highest points forage for goats and sheep, the lowest, near the streams, for vegetable gardens, then the low cliffs down to the beach and sea where often seaweed could be harvested at certain tides. There were some waterfalls off those cliffs onto the beach and people had made pools below them where they stored fresh water fish. No one went out to sea from the village, there was really no port, though boats could land easily enough. To climb the cliffs was also easy given the paths carved out by centuries of use.

The old man loved the way everything yielded fruit under the labor of hands. The dry wine of the area was the very best, not a large yield, but always sold before it was grown. He knew wine making as well as growing, but his sons were better at the making than he.

There was a Don in the area, an arrogant man with an arrogant family, he took his rents, but knew a delicate balance had to be kept. If people worked and willingly, the area was rich. If they worked but unwillingly, the area was poor and his window drapes got tattered. But recently the Don had allowed drugs to come on shore in his region and enter the country through his village. He knew this was temporary, entry points had to keep shifting. But here could be fast money and new friends made and a future freed from the soil.

The old man saw this as did everyone else. And he saw lesser things, namely, that his plot of vines was a place for lovers by night. They could get to it as easily as he along the road, the soil was soft and warm in among the plants, the wall was low and the rows wide. He cleaned up after them, the condoms, the panties, it was a bit irritating, but then who cleans up after love? On occasion he would find a wallet. He would return it by putting it in the poor box in the church. The box had a wide gullet and the sacristan was an old man like himself who loved life despite appearances and would go to the one named inside and say the wallet was found in church. Nobody was fooled.

One day, the old man saw the raked soil had been ploughed by someone's shoulders and head, and the ploughing led to the wall on the sea side, and just below the wall there was a wallet. It was of the youngest son of the Don, the old man saw as he looked inside. The youngest raped people. "This is not rape," he thought, "this is death." He got over the wall slowly and onto the hard dirt of the road. There was an earring to pick up in the middle. He walked to the clumped grass on the other side and saw the trail of shoulders and head imprinted lightly in the grass the fifty yards to the cliff edge and the trails down. He looked over and saw the body of the youngest son of the Don lying in the sand where he had come to rest. A woman had brought him to the vineyard. Some man or men had finished him off. Those people had dragged him and dropped him over the edge.

The old man went back to his vineyard, took his wooden-toothed rake and restored all the lines of the place. Then he climbed the hill slowly and sat in the church. Widowed men sometimes did this, they were forgiven their faith when the women died first. He could not drop the wallet in the poorbox. If he did, his friend would get killed. No one tells a Don his son is dead without coming to grief. Hasty, hasty, he thought, any man who knew what he was doing would have tidied up. So it wasn't a man who helped, it was a woman. Two women maybe. Women do not kill.

He looked up at the Virgin over the altar. She came from Greece a thousand years ago and was darkened with candle soot. Her face was scarcely visible, no more than that of the child she held as she looked out at the benches. This had been his wife's icon. As she had been his more than the earth on his hands in which he held the wallet. So what women? A mother and a daughter? A knowlege rose in him. It is inside the Don's family, he thought. But whoever walks in with this wallet will get the blame. There will be passion, and a killing, and a profound regret about a crazed old man, which nobody will believe, especially not the police who will, nonetheless, accept the Don's explanation, the hatred of a peasant for the Don came out on a son making love to a woman in the dark of a vineyard. No, he thought, too clever. The women are in fear. They acted out of passion and are ready to kill themselves if more than the body is found. They are hoping in a mystery or they know there is some drug trouble and revenge is a possible motive.

"I have to see them, see which one, or someone innocent gets killed." He said this to the icon, but he said it to her who had never really left him. He went to his room in the house his sons now owned and took a potted vine he had been experimenting with, one that could enrich the yield of the vineyards because it could grow in tougher places. The pot recreated the tough place, it was heavy, so he climbed to the Don's villa slowly, and the Don's men could watch him enough to let him pass in unchallenged and ask for the Don. The Don came and the old man asked if he could see the Don's wife, he had a plant she asked him to grow and here was his first result. The Don was most interested and got all the information first, but was a little puzzled at his wife's interest. Yet the old man was almost a god with green things in the area so he told the old man sit, he would send her to the patio, that might be a better place for seeing a plant.

When the wife came, she had exactly the stillness and unblinking look the old man expected. He spoke, "Your daughter asked me last evening to bring this vine for you to see. She was with your son, and they saw this on the balcony of my home. She had seen it growing and loved the shape of it." The woman in front of him turned very pale. "They are like friends, your son and your daughter, she is very kind." The woman was without a word. Like someone for whom there was neither life nor death. "I have seen them often go by me to the cliff, then go down to the beach." The woman sat on the edge of the well that was just behind her in the patio. There was a small roof over it, and a wheel and rope for the bucket. The old man saw her as in a roadside shrine. "She is like his child," he continued, "it is wonderful the way she learns from him." The woman in front of him was now white with rage. "I have had to make this vine grow in very harsh soil," he said to her. "If you will look, you will see I have even used trash to harm the soil." He raised the pot up from where he had held it, low to his body, raised it up into his arms as one raises a heavy child.

She stood, looking at his face, not the plant. Then she looked down into the pot he held close and she saw the edge of the wallet showing above some other debris, rocks, and the harshest soil of the area. "I could leave this with you and have you watch it grow. You could see for yourself how strong it is. It has a future I will not see."

"Leave it," she said.

Then he, "I would be pleased. It will be safe here. In my vineyard no."

"What do you mean?" she asked.

"People come and go who are strangers now. I have heard men quarreling there. Some damage has been done to the vines that lovers never do. I wonder should the Don know there are strangers quarreling here. Men's wallets must contain great wealth for them to be so violent."

The woman flashed a look at him. "I shall tell the Don you told me," she said. Her look at him was unblinking. "I must hurry now," she said. "Goodbye."

"Goodbye," he said. The wallet was found with the body the next day when the son was missed. It was fat with money when the Don opened it. Foreign money. A message from outside. It meant war.

The Power of Carrion

Oh, come to the water all you who are thirsty;
though you have no money, come! Buy corn without
money, and eat, and, at no cost, wine and milk.
Why spend money on what is not bread,
your wages on what fails to satisfy?
—Isaiah 55:1-2

There was a woman who wanted power and wanted it badly. She had lived long enough as a plaything for other people. Power was money and she went after it. She soon discovered she was shrewd at the stock market. The little she started with had become a lot. She quit her steady job and spent the day at her broker's where she watched the board. And in the evening she analyzed her results and studied companies and products so she could spot trends and move with or against them. It became a fascination with her. She was making brilliant decisions and as she gained wealth her decisions became more profitable.

She began to enjoy dressing elegantly for her day at the broker's. And she bought extra comfortable furniture for her evenings studying. She had enough money for a cabin in the mountains complete with computer link to foreign markets so her weekends had hours of fresh air as well as fresh triumphs. In fact she had forgotten her search for power in the thrill of the chase.

But once she got into the millions people began to home in on her. She was being watched for every decision she made. So she became more discreet. People with projects began to speak to her on the way in and way out of her broker's office. Then letters started coming, requests for lunches, for dinners. She avoided all this to nurture her growing genius at the market. She had to be watchful every minute or she'd lose control of the board. So she bought a special computer link-up of her own, moved it into her apartment with an extra screen for the bedroom and one for the bathroom and one for the kitchen. Stock prices were showing almost every place in the house. No matter what direction she went, she could see the changes occurring. And she moved about a great deal, cooking, showering, dressing in her wonderful loose clothing for the house, exercising on her several machines, talking on the telephone. She even had a small screen put in her BMW for her drive out to the country where her cabin was now outfitted as was her apartment. And her international speculation was as successful as her national, and she was approaching a hundred million in assets and the ten years she had spent at amassing it seemed like nothing. And she had forgotten power for the pleasure at getting it.

But at a hundred million the power became utterly clear to her. When she spoke over the phone her authority was absolute. She never got an argument, only compliance. And quality things showed up at the snap of her fingers, a new car, new clothing, lawyers and their advice, even the IRS people treated her like a sacrament because she was purposefully paying exactly what taxes she had to so as not to be distracted from the pleasure of her genius for guessing the market. And foundations looking for money treated her as Sheba's Queen, religious ones included. And even seducers were aware of her power and knew her wrath could buy ruin for them, all legal, but ruin nonetheless.

"Perfect," she thought. "Power. But there's another step." So in several swift moves she gave her huge fortune away, to land preservation groups, and cut herself down to a nearly bare apartment, a wreck of a car, stone washed jeans and sweaters, and went back to her broker's office and watched the board, made judgments, but did no buying or selling. People began to offer her fortunes for counsel. Then she realized that she could affect the whole board with what she said. So she said to them, "I'll stand on this chair every day at 11AM and tell you what I think." Well, no one could get in the place at 11, it was jammed. She interpreted the general movements of the market and was mostly right.

She couldn't pay for anything. Her checks in restaurants disappeared. Cabs showed up practically in her coat pockets. She never heard from her landlord. Then finally the call came from the government, from Treasury, and she was offerred a top post. Now power and pleasure were perfectly synonymous. She loved every minute of her genius, every result it produced, she loved having absolutely nothing and absolutely everything. What thrilled her most was her power over human life. She saw the reaches of economics. And she knew she could do a lot of harm before anyone spotted it, and she could do a lot of good before anyone spotted it. And that was true at every minute of the financial day and financial night.

So she said absolutely no to Treasury. And she stopped her morning conferences. And she changed apartments and lead a life no one could track. And she felt a sense of power beyond anything she had ever known. She felt untouchable. By anybody, by anything. Even sickness, even old age, even death. Because she knew she could cancel herself at any moment. She had a magnificent pill only super spies were allowed to have, or rather were required to have. But the pill was from outside her. Her will was within. She could starve herself and defeat sickness, old age, and death that way.

So she got some hiking gear, some maps, went to the Grand Canyon, and without anyone's notice, she descended the trail to the Tonto Platform, then went eastward off the trail until she came to a promontory overlooking the river a few thousand feet below. She sat, back to a rock where no one could see her, but from which she could see everything. And she prepared for this ultimate test. She drank the last water from her canteen. Ate her last bit of fruit. Drew herself up in the lotus position and waited for the fierce assaults that would come, the hunger, the dehydration, the panic. If she couldn't take it by her own inward power, she would use that pill, or tumble forward into the river far below and disappear into its muddy water.

It was then she noticed a hawk, at eye level with her, but out over the canyon and watching her as it rode an updraft brilliantly, opening and closing its wings like a fan. it began to drift in towards her. "It thinks I'm carrion," the woman thought. She stilled herself even more so she would seem freshly dead to the bird.

As it came closer she sensed her breasts begin to swell and pleasure began to spread through her pelvis. She realized she was being aroused by this death she was pretending so as to lure the hawk in close. Soon she was trembling all over, but managed to be silent enough to draw the hawk to within a few feet of her, it turning its head from side to side so she could see its magnificent, unblinking eye. Something that would never touch her alive would touch her dead. The spasms passed and gave way to echoing pleasure along every nerve of her body. Still she did not move. And the hawk landed on a rock just next to her knee which was out in the lotus position. Its eye was staring at her like a camera. A gust of wind lifted it lightly so it spread its wings to stay in place and the wing feathers brushed across her and she felt their silken delicacy. She had never felt such power in her life.

The hawk moved along the rock until it was next to her face, she knew it, and knew the instant its beak went for her eye, and she jerked her head back so the hawk face grazed by her like a cheek to cheek kiss, but it was no kiss, the hawk wanted the delicious eye. It beat into the air instantly, hitting her several times with those same silken feathers, then plummeted down out of reach, then soared back up past her on a thermal current and floated again at eye level a safe distance out.

"That's my only real power," she thought as she looked at it, "the power of carrion." So she stood up and the hawk dove away. She took two steps to the edge of the plateau, spread her arms to dive after the hawk, but felt the nakedness of her arms and lowered them slowly. "No," she thought, "my only power is not to be a fool."

She stepped back and leaned against the warm rock until all light was gone. Then, when the moon showed in the east she found her way back to the marked trail and by moonlight climbed back up to the rim to go home.

Fire Break

There came a mighty wind . . . But the Lord was
not in the wind. After the wind came an earth-
quake. But the Lord was not in the earthquake.
After the earthquake came a fire. But the Lord
was not in the fire. And after the fire there
came the sound of a gentle breeze
—1 Kings 19:11-12

A man was camping in the Sierras. He was alone on a kind of retreat. He had a Bible with him and a flora and fauna book. Plus enough to eat for a week. He found a ledge out from the campground a good distance where he could set up his tent, a ledge that dropped on three sides down to a fine creek with dam pools made by rocks that had fallen over the centuries. He could hang his food in a tree back from the ledge and creek, so if a bear wanted to eat him as well as the food he could jump it thirty or forty feet into one of the pools.

He sat one evening and watched the light thicken. There must have been a lot of dust in the air because the light flared into beautiful bands of color. When it was dark he crawled into his one man tent near the edge of the drop and went to sleep to the creaking of the wind in the woods.

It was the wind that woke him, a warm wind moving the way heat does. It was not easy to breathe. "There's a fire behind me," he thought. He got out of his tent pronto. The stars were obscured. Then his nostrils picked up the scent of smoke. He knew he was in a natural firebreak so he was not too worried. He had the cliff below and the water to protect him. Maybe the fire would leap right over. But it could suck all the oxygen out of the air. "So, wait," he thought, "see which way it goes."

There was a glow to the East. He spotted it just above the trees. "That's close," he thought, "that's from a careless camper, not heat lightning. Somebody's running scared." The woods began to come alive. He heard running animals. And it wasn't long before he could see some vague shapes come to the edge of the ravine, look for a path down, then start sending gravel and rocks skittering ahead into the water, then themselves splash in and go up into the brush and trees on the other side. In fact two bear shapes came onto his small promontory, sniffed his presence, then turned and made a noisy slide down to the water. And deer began to show. They were not good at getting down into ravines so they had to run along the ridge for some distance before they could crash down into the creek and then put it swiftly behind them. Then there was another bear who got tangled in the man's tent as it tried to find a way down. With one swipe it sent the tent flying then turned and went upstream for a better escape.

"Now," thought the man, "now, down into that stream. I'll get nowhere running in this dark." So he moved to his left where he knew he could slide down the cliff face. It took him ten minutes to make it and hunker then under a hang of rocks up to his knees in one of those pools the falling rocks had formed. It was cold water, a miracle of cold water, wherever it came from, snow melt from well to the north. The sky was glowing now overhead, and the hot wind was picking up. So he got out some bandannas to wet and put over his head and mouth so he wouldn't breathe the heated air. He heard some plops and in the light from the oncoming fire he saw there were two or three salmon locked in that pool. The water had dropped and left them stranded. Then some animals crowded in under rock faces near him, the slower creatures like himself.

Now smoke began to curl down toward him and a hellfire glow began to fill the ravine. "Not much of a wind, thank god, maybe the fire won't leap the ravine." He could hear it roaring closer. Then he felt something climb his arm and sit on his shoulder. It was a squirrel. Getting in under the rock as far as it could. He could feel its wild heartbeat through his own jacket. Only his shoulders were above water and his bandanna shrouded head and face. Then there was another squirrel, then another, and this one sank its claws into his head to hold on. So the man simply lowered himself under the water and the squirrels leaped for a nearby rock. As the man went under he could feel the salmon shapes brush by his hands as they raced around their prison for safety.

Then a big bird landed out in front of him, it had broken its wing somehow and had been hopping through the woods. It was a buzzard. It saw the man, saw the fire, saw the man was less of a danger and edged in toward him along some rocks as sparks began to fall into the water hissing. Then the man sensed the fire was very close overhead, the smoke itself was now lighted like garish neon, and the animals who had been able to flee were now past him and his squirrel companions. The roar was incredible. And the heat. The man was breathing with the bandanna over his face, then dipping in the water, then breathing. But the wind was still low, miracle of miracles, so the fire stopped just over his head and did not leap the ravine. So the woods across from him were spared.

It was several hours before the real burning died down. And the heat began to go out of the air. The water had warmed, but the level stayed. And then daylight replaced the neon light of the fire. And the man looked out ahead of him at the saved greenery, then up and down the ravine. There were a lot of animal bodies. Some had jumped in the dark and killed themselves on the rocks. And the water kept flowing by them. Overhead the kindred of the buzzards began to show. They would clean the stream. The broken-winged buzzard in front of him now flapped toward something it could eat. The squirrels were gone. He could see three salmon under the lip of a rock, waving their delicate tails as if to fan themselves cool. And the man felt life coming back into his hands as if someone were counting bills into them and saying the count out loud.

Then he noticed a book lying face down and wet over one of the rocks. His Bible. The bear had sent it flying with his tent a few hours before. He came out from under the rock face stiff from crouching. There was still a flickering scene behind him. And ashes were drifting now, still on the light, miraculously light wind. "That's what I'd be," he thought, "ashes." He looked down at the water, the mindless water, that had saved him from the mindless fire. And he leaned and picked up his soggy Bible. It would never know what saved it.

Animals were coming back to the stream driven by thirst, and birds, small, large. There was sound, movement, the old life. "Those ashes will sprout greenery in two weeks," he thought. He put the Bible in his pocket, crossed the rocks of the stream and climbed to the spared forest and walked out. Until he met some rangers who said he was lucky and offerred him some water. He took a mouthful, and as he did, a feeling of thanksgiving flooded through him. "It was more than luck," he said.

20th Sunday, Ordinary Time

A Heathen Place

God imprisoned all men in their own disobedience
only to show mercy to all mankind.
—Romans 11:32

A woman married a preacher. He was high energy and the Book was his rule. She loved him and this combination of heaven and earth, like chinaware, it felt right, it poured right, it sat right, it looked right. But she was wrong. She found soon she was for respectability, Wednesdays at home, Sundays in church, gone the rest of the week to comfort the faithful. The faithful women. If she broke with him, she broke from the church, they all knew his whereabouts. They put up with the shadows to get the marvelous light.

Not she. She stood up in church one Sunday, after his sermon, before the hymn, and said, "You want to see someone disappear? I mean disappear right before your eyes? I mean like Jesus after Easter? Not straight up and not straight down but straight out! And what Jesus didn't say I'm going to say, you know what? 'Tie your shoes,' he said. And when they did, he said, 'Now zip your flies, zip your flies,' and when they did, you know what he said? He said, 'tuck your shirt and buckle your belt and fix your hair.' Do you know why, why he said that? Do you? 'Then put some money, put some money, in the ashtray, on the bureau,' and they did. Then what he said, do you know? Do you know? Just before he asked them out, to the desert, just before, 'Women have to live,' he said, 'women have to live, and after what you give them comes the money,'cause you are gone between, you are gone for something else, and money is a floor to walk on, money is a wall, and money is a way to eat and keep the bosom heavy and keep the belly round and keep the muscles moving. Then what he said, do you know? 'Come on, leave them be!' and do you know that nothing happened in that room, that no one moved and he said, 'Come on,'

181

once again, 'I'm going,' and no one moved. 'I'm gone,' he said, 'I'm gone,' and out the door he went and slammed it, slammed it, and they heard his sounds like winds before a storm, and they said, 'He's gone, he's gone. Thank God! Thank God!' Then went their trousers down and went their shirts and shorts, then went their shoes and there were sounds but not like winds until they heard a knock, big knock, and a big voice, big voice, 'You coming?' And they laughed, they laughed, 'Yes! Yes! they said, 'We know now what you mean and we believe!'"

She stopped. "So what am I?" she said. "If I go through that door? But you know what? There's no one there!"

"O, Jesus," groaned a woman's voice, "you are there and falling straight and never stop!"

"They are what they are!" another said.

"You go," a third voice said, "you go and leave us."

"He's out there and he'll do it to you too," a fourth voice said, and there was a gasp. "He's a man," the voice continued, "and the man takes over. And it's heaven if you just don't mind." There was a shock. "And he rises from the dead that way." People turned and looked and she who spoke was there, at the organ bench in back. "Then he dies and gets confused."

"Stop it!" shouted the preacher who had heard enough. "You crucify the Lord again!"

"It's what he wants," another woman shouted. "It makes him feel like God; and he don't mind. He gets us all that way, gets us all believing."

"Nothing like that here!" shouted the preacher, and he was waving the Book at his woman.

"Jesus never read it," said a fifth woman from the side. "He never read that book."

"He said things when she grabbed him," said a sixth. "He was moving fast and she grabbed him and he said things she remembered."

"This is a heathen place!" the preacher shouted and he slammed the Book down on the floor before the pulpit, like Moses with the tablets on the Mount. He was livid with rage. He moved out from behind the pulpit and stood in the center looking down at them from the top step. "If you don't know you're a sinner, you don't know you've been saved," he shouted.

"It ain't no sin!" a voice said loud enough just behind his roar. It was a young woman who ducked behind her hand. And it took the breath out of the preacher. Enough to let the preacher's wife begin again. "O, it is if you're not a bumble bee! If you're not pots and pans it is! If you're not a brood mare! He was just for one! And she was just for him! And she hurt in her belly from all those men. And he never hurt her more! She didn't grab his body. She didn't grab his soul. She grabbed the cross and threw it, she threw it in the dump, she grabbed the thorns and ripped them like a rag, and she threw those nails like knives so they stuck in a rock and shook their asses, and she stomped on that whip like she was killing snakes and she said, 'Dumb! Dumb! All of you are dumb!' Then, 'Go,' she said, 'go do some good, and leave this stuff, I'm not going with you, you broke me, not yourself, look at your poor face! Go do some good with it.' That's what she said, and he said, 'Go tell them I came back,' and, 'No,' she said, 'no, you go tell them for yourself.' And he said, 'What are you to do?' and she said, 'just what I have been doing, clean up after and find someplace to sit. Then I'm going on my own.' 'I'm dead,' he said, 'without you.' 'Right.' she said. 'Right, and don't forget it!' And she cleaned up and left."

There was a great big laugh broke out from a great big man. "O, write this down," he said, "write it down, the Book is new and it's a lark!" Another man laughed, and another, "Love it, love it, I'm high as Jesus, keep it up, keep it up."

But a rage of women and men broke in on this, "Send them out, out, out! We want Jesus in the Book! Someone speak for him, someone clean get up and speak!" When that last was heard, "Someone clean get up and speak," there was a silence as if someone flipped a switch. And it lasted for a time.

The preacher's wife walked to the door. It was with dignity. And the door closed behind her with a sound of dignity. And the preacher was without a voice. So the organist turned and began in the softest notes a hymn in the slowest time until a hum began at JESUS TAKE MY HAND but no one dared the words.

Foxy Lady

*' . . . whatever you bind on earth shall
be considered bound in heaven,whatever
you loose on earth shall be considered
loosed in heaven.'*
—Matthew 16:19:20

There was a woman who loved beast fables. Medieval ones. Ones that were carved in stone as well as written in illuminated manuscripts. After college, she traveled and studied and got her doctoral degree. Her major work was on the beasts who were the companions of saints. The cats of the Irish hermits. The greyhounds of the mendicants. The hawks of the desert fathers who would not hunt for their masters but flew beautifully against the sky and made them ripple with spiritual joy. There were donkeys that made choices and fish that jumped in fires and deer that stabbed the heart with beauty and gentleness and led saints to grottoes high in the hills where they could pray apart from temptation.

This world absorbed her completely, she never married. She was in her forties and had barely scratched her subject, so she thought, when she was named executor of an estate. Her stepfather's. He had married her mother after she left for college and both had moved to the desert since his lungs had been harmed in the war and were acting up, a plane crash and the searing heat of flames had done the harm. He had pulled two men out before the wreck exploded. Her mother loved him because he thought nothing of giving. Oddly, she had died before him. An embolism. His grief was almost too great for him to contain. During that time, the stepdaughter had written him long and consoling letters, not directly consoling, indirectly, telling him of her researches and the charming texts and sculptures she had found and the whole world of miracle and transformation they represented.

The children of his first wife were unlike him. They thought nothing of taking. A curious switch from their father, but then again maybe not. He was very wealthy. For reasons of luck, primarily, he had hit a huge lottery, millions, just before moving to the desert, had bought stocks in electronics which doubled, tripled, quadrupled, which left him and her mother laughing, they needed so little of it. So they let it build for their offspring. Now he was dead and the stepdaughter had been named executor and her stepbrothers and sisters were furious! She was to keep the estate intact, give certain percentages out each year to family and charity, then name another executor at the end of her life.

She scarcely recognised the attempt made then to kill her. Her stepbrother had asked her over to his jewelry shop on the east side to talk about the will and her role. He said come after hours, there would be a closed sign on the door, but just walk in, he'd be in back working on some old moon phase watches he was remaking for an exhibition. So she opened the door and closed it, turned, and an attack dog flew at her, literally, through the air, right for her throat. Some miracle of fear took the sinew out of her knees so the dog's snapping jaw went right by her, hit the glass of the door. The dog stunned itself, but had grazed her cheek, cutting it some. She stiffened straight, did a spin, and was out the door, pulling it shut behind her as the dog hit the glass again to come after her. Her stepbrother appeared, grabbed and leashed the animal, then opened the door and pulled her gently in. She said, "No, no, some other time, I'm too shaken, I'll just go home and pull myself together, what was the dog doing loose?" He explained it was his way of preventing robberies. Robbers sensed the presence of attack dogs. He had gone out into the alley to get rid of some trash just as she came in and had forgotten to leash the dog. He kept insisting she sit and she kept wanting to go then he insisted on taking her home in a cab, just let him secure the store and the dog. The delay was elaborate and she did not notice the blood on her cheek nor did he bring it to her attention more than to say let me wipe some saliva off your face, which he did roughly with a comforting kind of laugh. Finally, she said, "I'm going. I'm going alone. I'll be in touch shortly," and she practically pulled herself out of his hands.

She told the cabbie, "Emergency Room, Metropolitan Hospital. A dog has bitten me." It was a rabid dog, tests proved. And she went through hell with rabies shots. Animal Rescue went for the culprit, but it was not the same animal, it was a tame, clean animal. So the Police were puzzled. But she was not. She knew her stepfather had put her in the wrong position, though his motives were good. So she refused the executorship, she refused her part of the inheritance, and threw the whole estate into the Court for her stepfamily to quarrel about. The dark side of the bestiary came out. They were at each others' throats. The will would eventually be broken, but it would cost a fortune and take years, so the members of the family now recognised this and came back to her and begged her to reassume executorship, they would ask the courts to allow it if she would consent. Actual money was better to them than rainbow gold.

The woman remembered the attack dog, then thought how much she wanted them to devour each other and the Courts to devour that money. She thought of the saint and the famished wolf. The saint who knew how to bare his neck and become a wolf so his fellow would look for food elsewhere than on his stringy frame. And how the wolf began to lick the saint's face, and lick and lick until it seemed to be satisfied. And the saint felt his own sweat seep into his own mouth. It was honey, rich, luscious honey. The wolf would not leave him. So he was safe from others, and warm at night with the wolf curled up beside him.

"Fat chance," she thought. "I'm sweating bills." Then she said aloud, "On one condition." They asked what it was. "That you allow me immediately to name my stepbrother executor and then I resign and have no part in the estate." There was a cunning silence.

"No," her stepbrother said, "I will refuse it." There was another cunning silence.

"Then I'll make another condition," she said. "If I die anything but a normal death, including a normal accident, the whole estate goes to charity."

They said yes, and she knew they were all killers for sure. No one could ever be held to that kind of agreement. Then she recognised what they were really after. She would have discretion. She could be worked on to give each more than the dole. There were wealths of strategy, crises, mercies, blackmails, that could be used on her, but not on any one of them. This bestiary would last the rest of her life if she said yes.

"Yes," she said. "But I want to tell you a story first. It's about a fox. A red fox with beautiful fur. He knew everyone was after him for that fur. He had been chased so often he could hide in someone's pocket. He often ended up chasing them when they didn't know it. He hid in the smoke house one day, behind the barn, hid with the hanging hams and smoked bacon and curing beef and strings of sausage. No dog would ever smell fox in that heaven for noses. But one did. And set up a hue and a cry that brought the hunt right to the smoke house door. The dogs would pour into that place if the door was opened. They would ravage the food chasing the fox corner to corner if they spotted him or even if they didn't. The thing to do was corral the dogs then send someone in. But the fox would be out and gone through the hole he had entered and the hunt might have to go on forever. No fox, no dogs, no hunt, no life.

So they corraled the dogs, the fox could hear them, and see them through a crack. Then someone came to the door and opened it, but did not come in, stepped aside instead. The lane was free all the way to the woods for a dash. He knew he could make that dash and lose them all. But that was no life for him either, it was too dull. So he looked around, saw a small smoked ham hanging on a string. He bit it loose. He curled his beautiful tail, perked his ears, held the ham in his mouth, and in a gentle trot came out the door and headed for the woods. There was absolute astonishment. They watched him in fascination. Not the dogs, though, who hit the barriers like storm waves. He trotted over to the corral and shoved the ham through the wickets. The dogs were seething like piranha after him. But some seethed after the ham. Then he trotted to the edge of the woods where he stopped and barked once. Nothing. He barked again. Nothing. Then the handlers woke up. They opened the gate, the dogs spewed out, the fox flicked into the brush, the horses reared and life began all over. But some dogs stayed for the ham and the smokehouse. They ate themselves to death. The others went after the fox. They are alive to this day."

She stood up and went to the door and said, "Your choice," and she left.

Means and Ends

I used to say, 'I will not think about him.
I will not speak in his name anymore.' Then
there seemed to be a fire burning in my
heart, imprisoned in my bones. The effort to
restrain it wearied me, I could not bear it.
—Jeremiah 20:9

A man was in Foreign Service, a cultural attaché in South America, a country in the Andes, and it was his task to foster peace groups within the country to provide an alternative to the war groups. He was a convinced pacifist himself, but career had made him keep his mouth shut during Vietnam. He was not drafted. He was serving in Europe during the time. There his job was to receive peace groups, show tremendous sympathy, then promise to report objections to higher ups. He was really a lackey and he knew it. He spent a lot of nights in bitterness about himself. There was something noble about human rights. No nation or institution he knew had ever respected them fully. That kept him working for a government which held those rights in theory and harmed them in practice, but against hoodlums too, he thought. Then the bitterness of the end justifying the means would sit in his mouth like the aftertaste of vinegar.

That was over but this one against guerrillas was not. The bitterness of this war was that it was between right wing and left wing gospel. He was to foster conservative church groups against liberal ones. What broke him was the day he had to escort an American conservative missionary back to the States for sick leave. The man had been working in the mountain villages. The local government was touchy about all clergy working up there so it seemed best to send the man home in the company of a US government official rather than in the company of a coreligionist. He was told at the Embassy, "This job requires absolute confidentiality. You will have to

188

cross into Peru, then up to Canada, then down to the States. You will not speak to this man at all. He has been instructed not to speak to you. He will act ill and you will tend him as such."

"Act ill?" the attache said, "he is ill!"

"So far as you are concerned, yes," they told him.

"What are you having me do?" he asked them.

"Your duty to your country," they said.

When he met the man he knew immediately he was dealing with a butcher. This was the one who provoked slaughters blamed on guerrillas. So the government could cry horror. "He's ours," the attache thought. The meeting point was the bus terminal for the airport. "And I'm a pawn. Everyone has me down as a patsy, so this is a likely story, not some smelly skunk. And this guy will kill me if he has to. He didn't need to be told he could. Then the blame lands on me. My fingerprints change. And he goes home as me. In fact, that's it! My duty is to die and not know the reason."

They were in line to get on and he felt the man lean on him as he had been told to. The man was in against the side of the bus. "Should be any second now," the attache thought, the fear rising in his throat. "I will know from this man's grip. He'll see before I do."

But not so, the attache saw first, some men in Indian wool ponchos step out from under the arcade. He grabbed the clergyman and spun him as a dancer spins a partner so he was against the bus and the clergyman out, and then he dropped to the ground the next instant. The automatic fire caught everyone standing. Lethal fire. The clergyman was riddled. It was over the instant it began. The attache feared something more violent, an explosion of fuel, so he rolled like a downhill log under the bus and came up running away from it on the other side. It blew and scattered people like smashed glass and created the chaos needed by the gunmen to escape.

"I have to know he's dead," the attache thought, so he veered back, still running, toward the bus, got on the murderous side of it and saw his companion on fire lying where he had fallen. "That's me," he thought. "Maybe the two of us were set ups. A triple cross." He felt the exhilaration of being smart. Then the fear again. Someone needed his name and his identity. To get someone out. A nice, fat, drug running General, how about? "There's a shot waiting for me yet. The one who loves villas. Miami in return for names. And he gets to keep his Swiss account. But if they see us together? Nobody makes a mistake."

The attache couldn't go back to the Embassy. He had to verify his reading of the situation. In two days time, there would be a Mass in the Cathedral, the feast of the national saint, the General and everyone would be there, have to be, unless the plans were to be carried out immediately, he'd see, if the General was not there, that he himself would have no identity.

The victims of the attack were now burned beyond recognition. He was still standing on the hell side of the bus with all these thoughts racing through his mind. He made himself as neat as he could, walked across the square, down the street to a Dominican monastery. He needed an excuse to get hold of a Dominican habit, the gown the Dominicans wore. Ah, he was giving a lecture on religious traditions in the formation of the New World. He needed illustrations, ones he could perhaps wear, Franciscan, Augustinian, Dominican, could the convent lend him one for a week. Most willingly. In fact someone had just left the order, a novice, and the new habit would probably fit him. "Now, disappear for a few days," he thought, "then reappear, at the Mass, as a Dominican, in the sanctuary, and confront that General if he's there."

He went to a small hotel, got a room, and waited for the evening paper. Sure enough: American Attache Killed In Terrorist Attack. Victims all burned beyond recognition. "So, he's going home in my casket," the attache thought. "US jet, oh shit! He couldn't move otherwise. Well, he won't." The attache stayed in his room the next day. Except to step out and buy some fruit off vendors and a razor off kids. The day after, he bundled his Dominican habit under his arm, left the hotel, went into the Dominican Church down the street from the Cathedral, changed in the confessional box, and came out as a normal, natural Dominican. He went to the Cathedral and got in the procession of clergy as it came down the aisle. Only the Bishop and his chaplains were vested for the Mass. The clergy stationed themselves in the choir stalls to the left and right of the altar, the pulpit, and the Bishop's throne. The Generals and civilian officials sat in front rows, then the diplomatic corps and the people behind. The choir in the balcony were to sing two Bach pieces that day. The ceremony was formal, the Bishop spoke, but spoke of the hereafter, not the here. And then sat while one of the Bach pieces was sung.

Just at the end the attache in his Dominican habit rose, stepped over his neighbors' feet in the choir stalls, entered the sanctuary space, bowed to the Bishop gently, then walked to the microphone for lectors and stood as if to make an announcement. It happened so easily no one really clicked that something was out of the ordinary. The instant the music stopped, the attache began in his best Spanish, "A miracle. A miracle has happened. The gift of our patron saint. I was dead two days ago. My body was riddled with bullets and burned beyond recognition. But look at me now, alive. I was an American before I died. I worked at the Embassy here. My old body is going home on a plane tomorrow. My new body is here. To show you. So you will have hope. The dead are really the living. The living are really the dead. May our saint be praised. And our beloved Bishop. And our beloved General who keeps death from our door. May he never leave us to the forces of death."

People had recovered. They recognised the attache from the photo in the paper. Two priests had risen at a signal from the Bishop and they took the attache's arm, gently, and motioned toward the sacristy. He kissed them one after the other, turned with them and moved in the right direction. He had been seen absolutely. Inside, he faced the two priests, they were pale with fear, they smelled the evil going on, they turned to go out into the sanctuary where it was safe. The outer door would open any second and they preferred not to see who came through it. The Police came through it just as the priests' heels vanished. With some quick strides the Police had the attache muffled and dragged out and gone.

He would go home. Go home a crazy man. The effects of a brush with death were too much for him. He might never mend.

Parlor Game

Love is the one thing that cannot hurt
your neighbor; that is why it is the
answer to every one of the commandments.
—Romans 13:10

There was a woman who loved the truth. She sought it fiercely. Her fierceness had cost her her marriage. He was a loveable slob but he kept things from her or waved things away as not really important. Like a couple of affairs at work. She had faced him with it, shape up or ship out, and he had shipped out saying, "You're making too much of too little." She was a lawyer and used to the opposite in court where people made too little out of too much.

The children were having a fight in the living room. She was in the den checking some legal briefs. Her daughter was nine and her son seven and he had arranged the parlor into a football field and had just scored a touchdown, he thought, despite her daughter's brilliant goal line tackle, and they were arguing whether it was six points or first and goal at the edge of the Persian rug. The Persian cat was crouched in terror up on the fireplace mantle and had already knocked a belleek tea cup and saucer smash down on the bricks.

Mother came in waving a legal pad and gave each a tap on the head so they backed off and let the pillow drop which was the football. "Don't you have any sense of peace?" she said to them. "Do you have to turn a game into a fight?"

"Well, she cheats!" the seven year old said. "She keeps changing the goal line! It's outside the window now!"

"A lie!" the nine year old said. "You're just mad 'cause I clotheslined you and you went backwards. You have to score with your head, not your feet. And the ball has to be over the line!"

"What are you talking about?" the mother said. "You from the planet Mars?"

"Don't you know anything?" the nine year old said to her mother. "Do I have to explain the whole game to you too?"

"You make up a whole game every time we play," the seven year old said to his sister. "If I win, I lose with you."

"Not so," said the nine year old. "You don't listen anyway. You're like my frog. You just jump and hit anything."

"You were the one who left the toilet cover up so it jumped in," the seven year old said.

"Yes, but you flushed it just so you could laugh," said the nine year old.

"It's better off in the sewer," said the seven year old.

The mother cut in, "You people will fight about anything. Why don't you just respect the truth. Where's the goal line?" The two got very silent and they even started to edge toward one another. "Did you deliberately flush the frog down the toilet?" she said looking at her son. He said nothing and was now standing in front of his sister as if she were a pole he had to lean against. "Why don't you like each other?" the mother continued. The sister now had part of her brother's loose T-shirt bunched in her fist and she was looking away from her mother toward the cat on the mantle.

The cat jumped and made a thud which startled the mother a bit so she broke her stern stare at her children and gave a quick look, spotted the broken tea cup and saucer, gave a groan, "My best stuff!" and went over to look at the fragments to see if they could be glued. They couldn't. So she looked back at her children and said in a hurt voice, "Do you have to break beautiful things?" The boy turned in to his sister the way one turns in to a pillow, and she had his T-shirt bunched in both hands as if she were holding a life preserver.

"The cat did," the nine year old said.

"But you made the cat do it!" the mother said.

"Did not," the little boy said, muffled against his sister's belly. The mother felt a quick anger rise in her at this resistence.

"You did," the boy said, "who wants a cat!"

"I do," the mother said, "it's a rare kind and costs a lot." As she spoke she saw the two children almost stuck together with glue. And for the first time in her life as a mother she felt outside them. And it terrified her. She backed a few steps and sat slowly into a chair and the blood rose into her face. "I'm sorry," she said. But they didn't know what she meant. "Where's the goal line?" she said. But they still didn't move. "Do you want another frog?" she said to her daughter. There was no answer. So she got up and went to them and put both arms around them as she knelt and said, "I feel an emptiness too. But I can't live with lies. I have to do the best I can alone. I never knew where the goal line was with your father."

"I tackled him before he got there," the girl said.

"Me too," the boy said. "I would get him so he had to kick and she would run the kick back a hundred yards and the cat used to chase her and claw the ball, crazy cat."

"You know I've asked him to come and see you more often," the woman said. "And you know I'm missing something too. My heart can be as empty as yours. There are some games where the rules keep changing. But I don't want them to change between us. I want this house to be a house of love or a house of forgiveness, whichever we need most."

"You forgive Daddy?" the nine year old asked in the smallest possible voice. The woman stopped, almost stopped breathing.

"No," she said. "No, I haven't." And she let them go and sat on the floor in front of them. "It hurts me too much." She looked at them, then said more. "I guess I change the goal line too. What if I call him and tell him about this?" They said nothing, but their faces were alive with something and they sat in against her. "But we do have to live with broken things," she said, "no matter whose fault it is. Now, where's the goal line?" The two pointed to the edge of the Persian rug. "Did you flush the frog down the drain?" she asked further. The boy squirmed with delight. "Do you want another frog?" the woman said to her girl.

"A parrot," said the girl.

"Yuk," said the boy and rolled against the woman.

"You forgive me?" the woman asked. And they were speechless. They hung on to her like a football.

24th Sunday, Ordinary Time

Cool Judgments

*The life and death of each of us
has its influence on others . . .*
—Romans 14:7

A woman loved watching birds. Not to know their names. She was an actuary and knew too many names. She loved the experience of sight, a red-winged blackbird clinging sideways to a cattail in a swamp and making its grackling sound. There was the shadow of the stalk in the water, the ripple of the water under the wind that swayed the bird, the hot eye of the sun that burned into nothing with its magnifying glass. She saw the skeletons of things too, breast bones, wing bones. And she saw the furies of self-defense, hawks under attack for raiding nests of the smaller birds, or the futile flappings of fish in the talons of the osprey now making a comeback since insecticides were outlawed near the wetlands. She was willing to feed the mosquitoes some, the ones who found where she hadn't smeared on repellant. Nature was savage, not malevolent.

Her job dealt with malevolence. She judged insurance rates offerred to security forces. Particularly to police. Much depended on the areas. She had to make actuarial decisions that bordered on racism, sexism, bigotries, the way fliers had to use the Ptolemaic system by which to navigate at night. It was often the bitter business of knowing what sorts of families a dead cop might have and how close to survival to keep the payments and still make a profit. Private security forces were even tougher to judge. A question of training, most often poor, they got themselves into trouble with dumb moves or heroics. They were often with grown families, retirees, so the risk of insurance was less. But the change in criminal weaponry had transformed the field. Submachine guns against slow firing revolvers. Police had been killed while reloading. She had been tapped by the Government too, to make judgments about Secret Service compensations, what were acceptable levels. So she had to know the criminal mind, the terrorist mind, the anarchist mind, the mind of passion, all in order to fix certain insurance rates and maintain a margin of profit.

The only balance she had was bird watching. Her husband and she led separate lives. He was an entymologist for the UN, spending most of his time overseas. They were very good friends, like literary club friends, he lived in his head and loved it, felt no call to bed or breeding. He was a specialist in butterflies as well as pollinating insects. He had been her entry into bird watching. But she had never introduced him to death watching. Which one day turned out to be.

She was standing on a hummock in a salt marsh, just at the edge of a tidal creek, a fairly large one where it met the sea, the muck was magnificent, with little holes in it like the holes in a pancake when one side was done and it was time to flip. The terns would come and pluck delicious things from that mud, and smaller birds would work in the sea grass on insects and seed. The rustle of the grass was beautiful and the play of shadows. She saw some cotton cloth floating on the incoming tide, it looked like a tank top. It was out of her reach, probably from a beach a few miles up. But then she saw some shorts floating. She could tell they were ripped. They were small. Woman small. She couldn't walk on water, she couldn't walk on mud, some shipboard shenanigans maybe, power boat stuff and home in a raincoat.

Then she saw the body. An arm out in the flow. It was caught in the sea grass to the inside of it. The woman slipped her shoes, rolled her slacks, and stepped off the hummock into the mud, down into it three or four inches before it held. "Never make it walking," she thought, so she slipped clothed into the water, went belly down floating, then hand walked along the bottom until she came to what was a young girl dead now for some days. The body was swollen. She had risen and fallen with the tide, a hand and leg caught in the grass. So the woman returned to her hummock, then retraced her step the mile back through the swamp to her car which had a phone and called in her find. "Bring a canoe," she asked the police.

There were a few hours of painful cooperation, painful for everyone. When she left, a policeman actually tried to comfort her, but he knew he was comforting himself, "Those bastards should be fried." It was a rape murder, the girl was ten.

A week later the woman answered a phone call from the mother of the slain girl. She wanted to know anything that would humanize this terrible thing, what had her daughter looked like, was there anything peaceful, the husband had identified the daughter, the casket had been closed. The woman listening realized there was a growing hysteria in the mother's voice. She couldn't interrupt. "I would like to torture him to death," she said without a break from her question to allow an answer. "I would torture him, torture him, torture him, I wouldn't let him die." The voice seemed to distance itself then another voice came on the line, it was the husband, and he said, "I'm sorry, she really did just want to talk to you, but every time she breaks and you heard, she just does, maybe later when she's . . ."

"No, now," said the actuary back over the phone, "put her back on, say I asked."

"Okay," the husband said, and there was some fear in his voice.

"Yes," said the mother in the coldest warmest voice the actuary had ever heard.

"She was floating gently on the tide," the actuary said, "I remember now. The water was clear and rippling and she was above the mud but I could see she had left the imprint of her body on it. It was her hair that held her to the sea grass more than her limbs and she was face down. And below her I saw a horseshoe crab moving through the depression she had left and there were some minnows feeding. And she seemed to sway gently with the small waves coming in and receding, the waves went around her into the grass and then made little sucking sounds against the hummocks. And there was light on her. And the earth seemed to be reaching to take her back to itself and it would have if we had not found her. We know the violence on her is from somewhere else. And I am sick too, my dear mother. My job is judging violence, but this is beyond violence, this is sacrilege and my heart is broken for you." There was silence on the other end. "Are you there?" the actuary asked.

There was a sob. "If only someone else had been there!" was what she could pick up. She meant God. The God of the innocent.

"I can't tell you anything more except that marsh was kind to her where a human being was not."

"We must find him, we must torture him," the mother said.

"Stop, please, stop," the actuary said, "you torture yourself. And soon you will torture those around you, please, make something where people can be healed, I don't know how, but don't add another ounce to the horror, please, we cannot do it as you, you are the mother."

"Don't ask me," the mother said, again in the coldest warmest the actuary had ever heard. "When it comes your turn you will not say what you just said to me. I hope you know someday!" And the phone crashed down.

"You never kill just one," the woman thought. So she called back on the phone. The husband answered. "I want to talk to the dead woman," she said. The husband hesitated. "Put her on or I'll come down there." The mother came and just breathed. "You wished death on me," the actuary said. "You stink!" and she slammed the phone down in her turn. "Grief is no excuse," she exploded between her teeth.

It was impossible for her now to make cool judgments. She had to add a clause to a contract about officers who were killed but later proven to have been corrupt in some way. Were the families to be compensated the same or less or not at all? The telephone rang again as she knew it would. There was silence again, nearly strangling itself.

"I wanted someone to share this with," the mother said. "No one is enough but you."

"I want you to come with me," the actuary said. "I will lead you out there. We will take off our shoes when the tide is right and we will walk that mud then swim that water to the place. It is innocent of what was done. We will leave death there, my dear mother, we will leave it there. And if he were to come, if he were to come, we would not kill him. We do not believe in him, we do not believe in his ways. We believe in her, we believe in her ways. I can judge death, I have to, but I can't work it!"

"Ohhhh," the mother said, "Ohhhh!" Then nothing. Then, "I will come," she said. "The two of us alone."

"When you want," the actuary said.

"No, when you are free," the mother answered. "You have your work."

Gray's Anatomy

. . . if living in this body means
doing work which is having good results—
I do not know what I should choose
. . . for me to stay alive in this body
is a more urgent need.
　　　　　—Philippians 1:22,24

There was a woman who loved working a computer, but hated doing it for money. Teaching the ABC's of it was not much better, though she got a feeling of some worth. So she took the job when it was offered of running the organ donor computer in a hospital, the one used by all the major transplant hospitals. The system had already been set up and the programs already worked out, there wasn't much challenge to that side of it. But there was this powerful sense of worth to taking a case through to the finish.

Accident victim flashes on screen. Male. 35 years old. Head injuries. A matter of hours. Torso intact. Widow willing to release. A rapid run through heart, liver, kidney. A choice to make. Children out, some women. Here, male, 45, kidney needed, may be compatible, send forwarding info to hospital X, notify hospital Y, kidney available soon. Alert ambulance, helicopter, airplane service. Police in two locales to clear roads. Store info on top of screen, flashing print until moment of death. Other accident victims show. An eye needed here, a heart there. Then volunteers. People who know someone needs a kidney, member of family.

She recorded in her file the number of successes and failures. Often it took months before she knew, a computer contact with hospital X. She got so when she left work she looked at people as walking spare parts. Like the Gray's Anatomy dummy she had learned from in high school. Pieces could be taken off to reveal pieces underneath. She began to notice how some people had marvelous cheekbones but funny noses. Or vice versa.

But she never thought of herself as a tool bag of spare parts until one day someone ran a light when she was crossing the street on foot and took a button right off her coat. Just outside the hospital. She ran after that van truck like fury right down the middle of the street with cars honking behind her and heaved her handbag at it which fell short and scattered her things all over the street. She picked them up like a threatened lion picking up its cubs, damned if she'd move for the honking traffic until she had it all stored back in her purse and had shouted down the cabbie who kept nudging her with his fender. She got on the sidewalk all steamed with sweat and rage ready to face charging bulls if she had to.

There was an old guy standing there with her button. "It hit me in the face," he said. "I was looking at you cross and it hit me in the face. Another inch and *you* would have hit me in the face. Be better than a button, but we'd both be beef stew. What the hell! You okay now? You want this button?"

She couldn't say a word. A love for herself poured through her like heated blood. She looked at the frayed sprouts of thread on her suitcoat where the leather button had been. She saw her own breasts up and down, in and out, and sweat showing her nipples through the blouse. She saw her hands, the marvelous muscles and veins, the quick fingers that made her computers act their lightning. They were not parts. Break the whole and there are no parts. She looked at the old guy.

"I'm a vet," he said. "Shot full of holes, so I taught until I couldn't. So I walk to keep the knots loose. You want to hear a steel band? Just walk me somewhere."

"Somebody nearly killed me," she said to him. Her love was turning back to anger.

"I saw," he said. "I know the name of the van and got the three last numbers on its plate. You can nail the bastard. If he can be nailed. That kind runs over his own mother and sues her for damaging the tires."

"So I just stand here getting wisecracks from an old goat," she burst out. "An old goat who's got nothing to lose but a lot of shrapnel!" She was practically spitting the tears off her face.

The man moved and simply put his hands on her stiff self. "I've got more love to give than you can take, lady," he said. "Right now all you got is body. That guy ran over your soul. And this is mouth to mouth from me. Don't you let him turn you into a fury. The way you chased him, the way you fought that street for your pocketbook, that's heroics, that's for kids."

"Then what's for me?" she said still stiff in his hold.

"You're not him, that's what for you. You're not some mindless bastard. Feel this life in you. He hasn't got that. God only knows what else you've got he hasn't. He's the dead man."

"Let me go," she said.

"Sorry," he said. "I'm old school. We used to hold the guys that got scared. Like we gave them another body. You just get a cage to rattle with me."

"I didn't mean it that way," she said. "I mean I don't need another body. I need this one." And she practically broke on those words. Which made her put two hands out on the man in turn. So she could feel his bony shoulders. "You are a cage," she said. "You should eat potatoes."

"Eating days are over," he said. She kept her hands on him aware she had heard something but not understood. "Yours aren't," he said further. "And you can be eaten. Some man. Some baby. Some friend. So that's what stays with you from this. Not an empty headed bastard or a wild fury. I lost guys to that wild fury. I had to haul them back in pieces so something would go home."

"I'm sorry I said what I said to you," she said. "I just didn't think you knew anything. Except it was my button."

"I know it's your body too," he said. "Great body. I couldn't give mine away. I was just in that hospital to see if they wanted an eye or something, maybe the whole thing for a young doc to work on. Find out what's connected to what. But nothing's right, so they won't even take it for a lab. Try the manure pile next, I guess."

"What is it with you?" she said.

"O, I got about a week, then something will go, one of those snap things. I thought I'd see if I couldn't do something from a pickle jar instead of the fiery furnace down below. Can't do it. So I come out here and see you and get a button in the face. And I know fear. And I know fury. So I said I'll stroke you a bit until you saw."

"Saw what?" she said.

"If you don't get killed, you have more life than you had before. And people smell it on you. And they'll want you like food. If you don't go nuts or pity yourself. So don't. You want the button?" And he reached it toward her.

"Yes," she said. "I'll sew it on when I get home."

"No, wait a few days," he said. "You got 'em. A while ago you didn't. Goodbye, lady."

"Goodbye," she said, and straightened his lapel before she let go.

26th Sunday, Ordinary Time

Power Plays

You object: "What the Lord does is unjust!"
Listen, you House of Israel: is
what I do unjust? Is it not what you do
that is unjust?
—Ezekiel 18:25

A man had a choice between his wife and his work. He chose his work.
But he didn't tell his wife. She was so focused on herself she didn't notice.
He was a think-tank man and there were a lot of crises he was paid to think
about. But there was one they didn't have to pay him to do. It concerned a
woman who ran a country from behind the throne, so to speak. It was an
Arab country, oil country, that was what was so strange, and she wasn't
Arab but western. And she wasn't kept either. A wealthy woman, part of
a merchant family that had billions, but enamored of a Sheik and the utter
lawlessness there could be within a strict religious system. And he was in-
fatuated with her, crazy in love, though he presented a picture of complete
control. His ministers lived in fear of the moment when she would sway
his decisions against the best interests of the country. They would have to
become violent and if they missed, they would be the victims. But so far,
her counsel was shrewd and correct. And invisible.

Except to the think-tank man. Whose information about her came from
many sources, public and private, business and government. Something
was brewing. There were signs of fanatical religiosity. It couldn't be that
she was making him fundamentalist. That would realign the country and
cut her out completely. Unless she was making him fanatic to undercut
other fanatics. What a switch that would be! To defeat fanaticism with
fanaticism and attach the oil more firmly to the West even if she disappeared for it. She couldn't be that calculating, that altruistic, not for oil con-
sumers in a mindless Europe or USA or Japan. Maybe she needed the one

whiff of pure power even as it killed her. He could come home late at night with a head abuzz with such speculations. His wife could smell that he had not been drinking. She had an incredible sense of smell, for physical things, though, not emotional. If he had had a beer and she was in the kitchen when he walked in the door she knew it. She would launch into books and phone calls and projects the minute he showed. She had the absolute conviction that he would be nourished by every word she said. And he'd go to bed while she worked for some more hours on projects due the next day. She was a researcher for Public Broadcasting.

Meantime that other woman possessed his mind. There was a drop in her country's price of oil, then a drop in production. Then a gradual cancellation of contracts to Western builders. Foreign workers were sent home. Just enough oil was produced to buy needed imports like food and medicine. The country seemed headed back into the last century. There were pictures of the woman visiting family in Belgium. A very modest looking but very beautiful woman. In fact, even in a newspaper photo one could see how fascinating she was physically. So what was it? Was she taking that country back into the last century, or did she see something about the future she was readying the country for? The Sheik lived only in the present. So did his ministers. Where he got his steel courage to go fanatic had to come from her. Where did she get it?

When he reached that question, the man spotted something in the paper which told him. She had been dumped by someone. Unbelievable. By a man who became a missionary in the Congo. Unbelievable. A medical missionary, someone in on the AIDS disaster that was cutting the heart out of the same Congo. So she was after revenge. She couldn't capture a Pope or a Geneva Bishop so this was the way, get an Arab who was God to his people and make him beg her. For what? For beauty. For the satisfactions of beauty. For paradise. But not know he was begging. Because people kill beauty when they have to beg for it. So he had to be made to think it was his power that fascinated her. But why ruin a whole nation? And why keep showing up in Europe apparently not doing anything but making the papers constantly in discreet and beautiful clothing?

Ah! It was seduction! These papers got to the Congo! She was doing two things. Ruining a Sheik, a religion, to see if she couldn't win back the lost man. And if she did, would she then have the last great moment to say to him, "Now I say no to you?" And that would be the moment of absolute freedom, freedom even from her own beauty. Yet she would still have the whole world thirsting for her. And maybe even God.

He woke up with these thoughts running through his head. His wife was up, not dressed yet, on the phone, to a camera crew, talking softly not to wake him. She would never know what power she could have over him. Not through body. She didn't know she had one. Fine one. She didn't know he was fascinated with mind. Not trivial mind. As she had made hers to be. The woman behind the throne in the sheikdom had taken on the whole of existence and was about to win. Who cares if it was only for a short time. His wife put the phone down, then jumped as if shocked when it rang the second it hit the cradle.

She picked it up and listened a minute to someone, then said softly, "Well, he isn't awake yet and I don't want to call him." His eyes were half open, but he didn't want to let her know he was awake. "I'm afraid I don't know who you are," his wife said. There was a suspicion about her voice he had never heard. The voice on the other end of the phone went on for some minutes and his wife was stock still listening, something very unlike her. She usually got into the middle of anyone's sentences. "Well, I'll tell him," she said, "but I'm not sure I understand. What sheikdom did you say?" Then after a reply, "And your name?" Then, "And you are the sheik's wife? No, not wife? His woman? He's yours, you are not his? I'm confused. What has this to do with my husband? He knows you? He knows you well? Intimately?" His wife's whole naked body was tense. Athletic tense, all her muscles showing. "You will do what to him?" "If he doesn't do what?" "But that will ruin him. He has to be trusted." "You'll tell what?" "That will ruin you!" "Why won't it?" "To save what?" "Listen, you're crazy." "Listen, you go jump in your Persian Gulf!" "That's it, I'm hanging up!" And his wife did, with a slam.

Which let him seem to wake up. But he knew all the unheard conversation. What a brilliant move it was to compromise him out of being taken seriously by anyone he gave advice to. She was going to say she had had an affair with him. In Europe where he often went also. For the sake of her new country. So everything he said would look owned. She would win. Only for a short time before someone else caught on to her revenge. He smiled at the absolute brilliance of how she had tracked him down. If you listen for someone, they can listen for you. His wife only saw the smile. She was furious.

"Behind my back?" she said to him. "Was that the work?" "Is that the way you get your info?" "Something about me not enough?" The smile was still plastered on his face and the covers were still up under his chin. For the first time in a long time she was facing him about themselves and her naked body was like an old time juke box, what with the early light of the sun through the venetian blinds crossing it with bars and bubbles made by the shaking leaves outside.

"It's funny, isn't it!" she said. "Well, you can take your goddam work!" But she was too refined to say shove it. The door buzzer rang. The camera crew to pick her up. She looked down at herself. Then at him with the grin still on his face. "You're finished," she said. "Be out when I get back!" She started for the door, then realized again she was naked and turned back and saw him still grinning. So she leaped at him in the bed and he ducked under the down comforter and she began to belt him through it, riding him like a steer as he wriggled and laughed as she got more furious and began to dig under the clothes to get at him. "You bastard!" she said. "You bastard!"

Finally they were both trapped in a tangle of bed clothes but she had his hair in one hand and he had his hand on her wrist. And he said only one thing to her. "She must think you're real dumb." She let his hair go. And she thought a minute. And she looked at him, then said, "Right. Real dumb." There was an emptiness between them they could both feel. The buzzer sounded again. And the phone rang. Then the buzzer. Then the phone. But the emptiness was more powerful. They couldn't move.

The Divine She

Fill your minds with everything that is true,
everything that is noble, everything that is
good and pure, everything we love and honor
. . . then the God of peace will be with you.
—Philippians 4:8-9

An architect was watching a building about to be imploded. It was his design, a prize winner years back, still referred to in books on glass buildings, but only twenty-five stories in height where the new owners wanted eighty, plus other buildings alongside in the space left open by the original one. That original had stood free in its lightly coppered glass sheath and acted like a Stonehenge monolith for people, something mystical, like the marker on a sun dial, or an Easter Island statue that stood praying skyward. It was basically an insurance building on the inside, but not outside.

The architect loved his own creation, but the way a parent loves an adult child, one that achieved its own maturity. During his long fight to save it he often felt that if he lost he would like to go down also. Not out of self-pity. But because he could not get beauty built anymore. He had designs, but commissions came for functional spaces, not aesthetic, or for decorated space, things that looked like Victorian dressers.

His feet shook with the sidewalk as the interior detonations began. The implosion was perfect, the structure caved in on itself in the seconds calculated and his praying form was finished. A spectacular sight to the large Sunday morning crowd. He made himself wait until the dust cleared then looked carefully at the jagged mass of snapped steel and shards of glass, all the bits and pieces of ceiling and floor. He raised his camera and took a snapshot, then turned and left. He was at a point of despair.

The wreckage looked like his life. His work to create beauty had made him ugly, ugly enough to drive away two wives and the five children he had with them, and the children looked on him as an eccentric who should be left to his own edges. But it took a terrific asceticism for him to do things with the perfection those things demanded. Nobody understood that, a form developing in one's mind, in one's imagination, could be unyielding in its demands. He had nearly ruined himself on several forms. This one behind him, he had wanted that deep prayerful aspect, the unnamed mysticism, and he had had to conceal it so the insurance people noticed only the solidity aspect. But people saw right away, he stood on corners opposite often enough to catch the look on their faces mornings and evenings and even summer noondays when the sun was a ball of fire on one of the sides, up top, like a welder's spot. "Beauty is the savage God," he thought, "savage. And it doesn't drive you to suicide. It leaves you alive. It breaks what you made right in front of you. Then tempts you again, the next one! the next one! you will see! it will stun us both!"

He felt some high heel sounds keeping pace with him, just to his right, a little behind, why he should notice he didn't know, except he recognised people by the sound of their shoes. He had built the foyer in the copper building to echo the beauty of his first wife's walk. The walk he heard. He stopped and turned and she came up to him, looked and said, "I'm sorry. I didn't know if you could watch. I didn't know if I could either." He moved his hands helplessly to say he couldn't speak. But he looked at her and there was no wall between them. There had been when they broke. His second wife had left because she didn't want to be a draughtman's ruler anymore.

"You create great beauty," the first wife said, "you always have." She had said that to him often before, but this time she did not add the bitter rider, "Then why are you such a wretch?" And he sensed the rider was missing.

"This is good of you," he said. "I knew your walk."

"A little heavier," she said.

"Yes," he said. He reached out quietly and put his arm in hers and they began to move. "I was not big enough for beauty," he said. "I know others who were. I am not big enough for it now."

"You live alone?" she asked.

"Yes. It's better," he said. "I should have been alone from the start. Or said no to this."

"Well," she said, "there are some people who serve. I am not one. As you know. Maybe you weren't lucky."

"I couldn't stand that type," he said. "You know it. And I'm impossible for someone like you."

"What will you do when the beauty is all blown down and you can't make anything anymore?" she asked. There was real concern in her voice. She went on, "Your families have little room for you, they are making their own lives."

"I don't know," he said. He came to a stop. "I'll just stand in the streets and shake my fist. And whoever it is will know what I'm saying!"

She turned to face him. "How can gods do this? How can they get you to spend yourself? Then leave you empty of both a future and a past?" He knew she was talking also about the two of them and their failed life together. He just stuttered for a second, then silence. "We seem to be just the packing cases," she said.

"That is what I am now, I guess," he said. "The Pieta is on display and I'm in the Jersey dumps."

"I think you should just design," she said, "design for publication. I have talked to my husband and he will pay the price of publication if no house will take it. And if you have to live on slim means, do it."

"You want me to live with that she, don't you, the she who is like me, who gives up being human to force us to do something divine." He said this in a light enough voice so she knew he was beyond bitterness and into the drama. There was even a small smile on his face. "You want a celestial confrontation."

"Not really," she said, "and if there is one I hope the divine she loses. What I saw this morning was the divine she winning. And even she must regret it now."

"You mean I have something on her?" he asked.

"Yes," his first wife said.

"She might drive me crazy," he said, still in that lighter voice.

"You're crazy already," his first wife said and she also smiled. They started walking again.

"You've wanted to say this to me. The building gave you the chance." Again he spoke in an open tone.

"The chance, yes," she said. "But only. I have seen recently the work of a sculptress who broke with everything to do her work, with family, with religion, with propriety, and when the power to create left her, she was truly crazed, and spent her thirty later years locked up. Beauty was a man who left her for another woman." What she said shook him the way the sidewalk had that morning.

"You are saying . . ." He couldn't finish.

"You would have been locked up a long time ago," she said, "if you hadn't kept answering. And I fear you will not listen any more. I've seen photos of that woman in the Swiss asylum. She was as beautiful as you when she was young. But there she was as wretched looking as you could be."

"I'm locked up either way," he said.

"You can't say that," she said, and there was fear in her voice as she faced him, fear that her insight was lost.

"No, I can't," he said, "that was small." Then, "You lost to her."

"She is cruel," his first wife said, "but she is not a killer. And you are better off with her."

"She cannot create for herself," the man said.

"No," his first wife said, almost explosively, "no she cannot. But you will only respond to her. To no one else. And if she destroys what you make, the judgment will be on her, not on you."

"Who will make that judgment?" he asked.

"I will," she said, and said it again almost explosively.

"I see a geometric group," he said. "Again all glass, but of different colors, they will change with the changes of light, but all subtly so you have to watch. And they will be like aurora at night, again subtly. Office space and living space and mercantile space. With a look of tremendous fragility. Inside, the sounds will be like wind chimes in the various spaces. The flooring will be xylophonic but scarcely noticeable." He paused. "I don't know if I can pay the price to do it." He paused again. The alternative showed between them. She shook her head no, lightly, side to side, no, please. He backed away from her then. He was shaking. But kept looking at her. So when he turned she knew she would see him later in front of something he had made. Or behind something he had not.

28th Sunday, Ordinary Time

Sour Pickles/
Heavenly Hash

. . . it was good of you to share
with me in my hardships.
—Philippians 4:14

A man belonged to a club that had just been forced to admit women. The force was moral, not legal, they had swallowed hard and voted yes, though he had voted no. They asked him why, his fellow club members, his opposition was no secret. "I am an obstetrician," he said, "you know that. I am married with four daughters. One is a lawyer. One is a doctor. One is a stunt pilot. One is an archeologist. And my wife has just finished a doctorate in fine arts. The children are not married and home is like a spy novel. This is the only place I can come and get relief, relief is spelled silence, nada, nihil. Some days at home I talk with a high voice and don't even know it. Here I can be a bass if I have to talk."

One day after lunch he was sitting in a reading bay with Le Monde open to the international section. He loved French, loved to keep up with reading it. So last week's news was not stale to him He could hear the women's heels in the marble foyer, then on the parquet floor, then the muffling by the rug, then the raprap again, muffle, then the soprano excuse-me's, then the rustle of nylons and linens, the high throat clearings, then the process again.

One process happened just opposite him. And he burned, not with anger, but with disappointment. He lowered the paper even though he knew there were tears in his eyes. He was looking at her and she was a blur. She was looking at him and he was only too clear.

213

"You lose your dog?" she asked softly. He nodded like a kid at the back door facing his friend's mother who was ready to cure the pain with a piece of pie.

"Named Spot," the obstetrician said. "He chased trucks. Still is, somewhere."

"I chase trucks," she said.

"Ever catch 'em?" he asked.

"Nope," she said, "the fun'd be gone."

"Spot wasn't funning," he said, "trucks were bad and had to go."

"Dumb dog," she said.

"Yup," he said again, "it's why I liked him. Most times I was smarter."

"Sometimes not?" she asked.

"Sometimes not," he said. "He knew things with his nose. Found my kid brother one day."

"Where?" she asked.

"In an ice box," he said.

"I couldn't have either," she said.

"What can you?" he asked.

"Where to find a virus," she said.

"Neat," he said, "I'm an obstetrician. Viruses frighten me."

"Not that kind," the woman said. "Computer kind."

"Man made?" he asked.

"Person made," she said, "women make them too."

"Cost people money," he said.

"More," she said. "Lives." His eyes were cleared. "Government," she continued. "Defense discs." Then she stopped and he knew she had said enough.

"I had one this morning," he said. "Birth canal infection. We all use gloves, you know I'm sure. But I could feel tragedy. Head in my hand. I couldn't see after. For a while."

"You couldn't see me either," she said.

"Can now," he said. "A black eye and crimped ears. A bull terrier. Spot."

She looked down at her newspaper. She had thought the conversation was growing. He sat with Le Monde in his lap for a while, then said, "Married to a man you love. Maybe two children. Boys, I think. Natural childbirth. He's maybe not as smart as you, but deep in feeling, and savvy about things. Maybe a teacher. Maybe a writer. And he loves the fine mind in you. And is not afraid of it."

"Three boys," she said. "A set of twins. Yes to the rest. He's a writer."

"Women are a powerful force to me," the man said. "They fill space. Not sex. Space. I can't count the births I've been at. I've trained midwives. I've been in third world places. So dirty they would infect God. Always, women fill space. When I have to sew one up I don't want to leave a mark, but I must. So that's why I said no. You fill this space. And this Le Monde means nothing."

"Men don't fill space?" she asked.

"No," he said, "they divide it and conquer it. You know that. You enter a man's space and you know it."

"You do indeed!" she said. "What's the point of this?"

"There isn't any," he said, "except no one sees my birth process."

"You don't give birth," the woman said.

"A man would see the metaphor," he said.

"A man might laugh," she said.

Now he looked at his paper, smoothed it a bit, folded it back so it was only one page. "My husband wouldn't," she said. She almost spoke to herself. "The books he writes are the last week of a pregnancy for a whole year. He needs the sour pickles and heavenly hash."

"I could be with him," the obstetrician said.

"But without me," the woman said.

"Just for an hour," he said.

"It's amazing," she said. "I feel you want to be a woman for an hour. That's why this. With other women you'd be nothing."

"Right," he said, "right. I have a wife and four daughters. If I lost an ounce of one of them I'd die, and want to die."

"You think women cancel women out?" she asked, "that men don't cancel men?"

"Everybody cancels everybody," he said, "but some don't."

"Then tell me once," she said, "tell me once about your birth process. I have a virus on my desk and have to track it soon."

"I was with a friend who wanted to kill himself," the obstetrician said. "Last week. He's a psychiatrist. Depression specialist. Believes in talk as much as pills. He's been cleaning up after someone who used shock a lot. I nearly couldn't talk him out of it. I got a call in the middle to come and take a baby out of a woman in a coma for three months. She was brain dead but we kept her alive and she formed the rest of that baby. But we had to take it out, her body was failing. I took a chance and brought my friend with me and suited him up so he could watch. If he ever broke there . . . He didn't. He saw that living creature born out of a dead one. O, he knew all the technicalities. But he saw me weeping, I guess. I'm a sprinkler as you noticed. So he's okay. It was he saw too much frying someone had done. He'll take time away now. He's a lovely man."

"What about the woman?" the woman asked.

"I then turned off the machines," he said. "And I stood there until she ceased. I made her husband come in for that. She was intact, you know, the accident had caused nerve damage only. Her face was in perfect sleep."

"And the child?" the woman asked.

"Girl," he said. "The only one I ever felt float in my hands. The others have their own weight, no matter how premature. She had none. She sneezed herself awake. Lovely. Lovely. But a sorrowful name they gave her, Dolores, should be Ariel, or Lillian, something light.

"I'm a Lillian," the woman said. "It was my father's last name until he got beaten up too often by the boys, then changed it."

"I hope you don't get beaten up too often by the boys," he said.

"You promise?" she asked.

"I promise," he said.

"Well, I have to go chase a truck," she said, "they get lazy."

"Will I lose you too?" he asked.

"Not if it's for fun," she said. She clacked across the parquet, muffled across the rug, clacked across the marble, hit one soprano note goodbye, and there was peace.

Then another clack.

Needed Break

You will shine in the world like
bright stars because you are
offering it the word of life.
—Philemon 2:15

There was a woman who got on too many mailing lists and she hadn't done but one thing, send some money to Amnesty. Soon Bread For The World envelopes began to show up. "Well, okay," she thought, "I'm honored to be asked." Then liberal candidates for political office began to send. Then environmentalist causes. Then one day an insurance company with an offer of a job if she would do such and such. Then seed catalogues, clothing catalogues, book catalogues. Then lay away plans for funerals. She judged the seriousness of the envelopes by the amount of stampage on them. So someone had taken an original list and was selling it around.

"I wonder if I could get my name off these lists?" she thought. "No way," she answered herself. Her dead neighbor three years still got Museum invitations, concert invitations. She had been a culture fanatic. They never die. "I'm money," she said to herself one day at the mailbox downstairs in the apartment building where she lived. "I'm not," she said then quickly.

So she made a couple of phone calls to causes, their headquarters, and found they didn't do their own mailing, they paid someone with the list to do it. The office of that someone was right in her own city. So the woman took a morning out from work, she was in rare books at the university library, and went to the office that did the mailing. It was in an old warehouse redone near a railroad depot just off the docks. Most cargo was containerized so these fine warehouse spaces were filled with all kinds of landlubber industry. She saw the place she looked for, the office, with a HELP WANTED sign pasted to the door at eye level. "I wonder," she thought, "I've months of sick leave piled up. Yes. A month here and I'll know."

So she walked in looking for a job, not the master list her name was on. She knew machines and programs already and made the excuse that a huge budget cut at school had lopped off the lesser beings like herself. The budget was bound to be restored so she needed a few months. They saw she could catch on quickly so they hired her. And her education began. She was taught to spot the features of each name on lists that came in from the sources. And sources were paid. There were people sensitive to organ transplants, pro or con, and these were put on lists as disparate as Holy Cards or Health Spas. There were people sensitive to Bibles in bedrooms, pro and con, and they were parceled out to such things as Can Recycling lobbies or anti-prayer movements. After a time, she was put on a main machine console that had every name at its disposal plus all the signs that indicated what to send this person, what not, though she still had to exercise her judgment when a new request came in for a list. It wasn't automatic to send a sea otter preservation plea to fishermen or to folks who wanted to develop shore lines for condominiums. And you didn't send family planning materials to minority groups who might think you wanted them to disappear from the face of the earth.

What she was after, though, was her own name. She wanted to delete it from the master list. She couldn't leave it on there even for one good cause. The machine would instantly associate her with kindred causes all the way from Altzheimer's Research to Black Haarlem tulip bulbs. So she drew her name up. It took a long time because the master list was undifferentiated and appeared on the screen as a scroll. She couldn't believe how many names. And there were many with exactly her own name. So it was address that told her. Then, very deftly, she canceled out her name. The machine automatically closed the gap so there was no trace of her, though traces of many like her.

As she stared at the screen the space opened up again and letter by letter her name marched across and her address as well. Someone in the office was typing it in. And codes after it indicating what kind of a touch she was and for whom. She got up and walked among the other consoles in the office looking at what each of the operators was copying. There was a newspaper subscription list in front of one woman. For the New York Times. And the operator was thinking about each signal she placed after the first woman's name. The x meant send to no conservatives on any list. The + meant susceptible to charitable demands. The 0 after the + meant liberal charities, the heart string ones. The ? meant possibly radical causes but exercise judgment each time. The D meant democratic requests okay. And the - after the D meant careful on the kind of democrat. Then there was an M with an upward arrow beside it which indicated mail order catalogues for moderate to expensive in their prices. Then there was a Z indicating a high interest in travel. Then a sideways U, not a C, indicating that more research into this woman was needed.

So the woman who was being graded walked back to her own machine and waited until her name was moved up off the screen of the other woman. She got ready to cancel it. But then she thought, "It'd be like weeding out the world. My credit card people would be tapped. My life insurance people. My Blue Cross. I'm on everybody's list and I'm pegged." So she got up and went to the woman who had just typed her in, stood behind her and put two hands lightly on her shoulders and said, "Could you go back a name?"

The operator was surprised but could feel the easy hands on her shoulders. "Sure," she said, and scrolled back to the previous name.

"That's me," said the woman behind her.

"O, terrific!" said the operator. "What do you think? Should I add or subtract?"

"No, you did pretty well, there's no mystery to me. My New York Times tells all about me."

But the operator could feel a sadness in the two hands on her shoulders. And she could feel the other woman standing in against her. So she leaned her head back to look up and see someone sad. "It's just a list, you chuck in whatever comes. And we get paid," she said.

The woman behind her said, "Will you add some things?"

"Sure," said the operator.

"I love jazz, I love ragtime," the standing woman said.

"Let's see," the operator said, "I take out the sideways U and put in an asterisk *. Cultural stuff. What else?"

"I love men," the standing woman said.

"You got one?" said the operator.

"No," the standing woman said. "Had one but he's gone for someone younger."

"Okay," the operator said, "we put in a percent sign % for health foods and health literature and women's causes but not fringe ones. What else?"

"I love rare books," the standing woman said.

"That's under cultural. I'll double the asterisk **. That will include you under the rarer stuff. Some mailers ask for greater discrimination."

"I love beauty," the standing woman said.

"Well, we'd have to break that down," the operator said. "There's a bracket [ ] for cosmetics. There's an exclamation point ! for surgical possibilities. Art catalogues go under culture. But there's a dollar sign $ for wigs. That's funny, I always laugh at it. So. What?"

"Leave it at culture," the standing woman said.

"What else?" said the operator.

"I love God. Even though there isn't any," the standing woman said.

"Well," said the operator, "need to think about that one. Civil Liberties mailings, I guess. No, that's not right. Don't have anything for that. Maybe dating services. No, that's silly. Neither of us is younger. Sorry, can't help. Jeez, what'd fit that? You love someone who isn't! How about this. An and & sign. It's for monasteries who want to market jams and jellies and scented candles and liqueurs. Might be fun. Maybe the someone who isn't tastes good anyway. Okay? What else do you love?"

The standing woman just looked down at the screen and said, "That about exhausts me."

"Nice," said the operator and she hit the save button and send button and the whole thing appeared on the screen in isolation. Then she hit another button and the whole thing appeared in the list that slowly then scrolled upward and off the screen.

"I'm gone," said the standing woman as she rubbed the operator's shoulders lightly with her hands.

"But not forgotten," said the operator. "I wish I could talk to all those names. It's fun. After a while, everything fits. You want some coffee with me? I got this guy I want to talk about. God! Is he something. I have to hold him somehow. Okay?"

"Yes," said the standing woman, "yes, I need a break too."

Final Request

You must love the Lord your God with all your
heart, with all your soul, with all your mind
. . . you must love your neighbor as yourself.
On these two commandments hang the whole law,
and the prophets also.
—Matthew 22:37-40

A woman was asked to be an official witness to an execution. By a magazine. She was a free lance writer. And the authorities were willing. It was a woman who was to be electrocuted. First one in the state. She had been someone's mistress for years. When he went back to his family under threat from his wife, she had gone to the home, walked in the door and killed them all ruthlessly, first the one who opened it, she had a silencer on the gun, then the one who stepped into the hallway at hearing the funny sound and thump, then someone skipping down the stairs also to answer the door bell, then someone who looked out of the kitchen holding a casserole dish ready for the table, then one startled small human being who looked up from its place at dinner. Five up, five down. She put the gun on the dining room table and left the house closing the door behind her.

The lights on in the house at two in the morning plus unanswered phone calls raised the suspicion that brought the police and the terrible night long watch by the neighborhood, the search of memories for any kind of oddity, the check of the gun for fingerprints. All of it not necessary because the killer came in to a nearby police station and surrendered herself. She was not a young woman. But she was powerful, like a Medea who could give you a choice of her love or her hate and you had to know she meant it.

She was a defector from Eastern Europe who knew a lot about embassy espionage. He was a handler who got information then blended informers into society where they were to live happily. He had handled her too closely. And she had wanted to blend into him. But his wife was not weak. She too could offer choices. And one was the loss of his career. Government knew and had a lot to lose if the wife went public, about his doings on certain highly embarrassing occasions.

The mistress was killing the whole world she had defected to when she murdered her handler and his family. She herself had asked for the death penalty. It was the only thing she said to anyone. Except to the writer. And on the evening of the execution. Many wanted to see her. She chose the writer because she would also be a witness.

"You will have to pay a price for this," were her first words to the writer. "You will have to watch a body jerk in death." The writer started to speak. The prisoner raised her hands. "You will not ask me the right questions. I will talk. Or I will not." Her words were not harsh. "As it jerks in death you will know what revenge is. Maybe not your own. But someone's. What you hold precious will be revenging itself. And you will be free to feel what you feel. And you will be purged. Then you will turn and know someone will clean up after it. Or you will be free not to feel. When you are free not to feel, the whole world is laid bare for you. It will never reach you again. Not with volts. Not with love. Not with reason either. So you will tell them that is where I am. If more of him were in that house I would have removed them as well. All is connected. One can only disconnect a little. You will be. And the man who pulls down the switch. The group of you who watch. You are paid. And the people at the gate who cheer. Now no more."

She stood up and moved her head to the writer to leave. "I will say nothing like it," said the writer to the prisoner. "I think I will go out and lie about you. Say the opposite of what you just said. How you see the coming volts as his last orgasm in you. That you were so hungry to live you tried to bite through my dress to my breasts." She paused. The prisoner began to smile a cold, cold smile.

"Then I will kill you for a long time to come," she said. "And I do not even know you."

"You are a master at death," the writer said, "yes, I have to say what you said if I am ever to be rid of you."

"So you see," the prisoner said, "you have to cooperate. I die or you do after what I said."

"You did not learn this with five shots," the writer said. The two were glued together like tongues to ice.

"You learn it in any feeling. You learn it with a man between your legs or a baby or a menstrual flow."

"Ah," the writer gasped, "ah, no! Too simple!" She turned her head. "Too simple for slaughter. Then for suicide."

"You are too simple," the prisoner said. "Sit and I will tell you."

"Not sitting," the writer said, "sitting is death tonight."

"You will be purged," the prisoner said. The writer stared at her. "You had better be," the prisoner continued, "or you will do some killing of your own." The writer shook her head. Her throat was frozen. The prisoner was thinking, thinking into the writer. "You do not want me to die," she said, "you want me to live maybe, live until feelings come back and then I go mad with remorse. No?" The writer shook her head again. "You want me to live and find some redemption. Some priest who will save my soul. And give me penances for jail. No?" The writer still could say nothing. "You want me just to live. Live here. In nothing. Until the end. No?" Still nothing from the writer who stood as if she were before a judge. She started to speak but just sounds came. Her face was flushed.

"You do not love women?" the prisoner continued. She was watching the writer now almost without blinking. She could see the answer no on the writer's face. "So this is not the ultimate in sex?" No was on the writer's face. The prisoner looked up slowly toward the ceiling. "I will not share him with anyone. You built a weakness into him. I will not let you reach that weakness ever again. And I have made you choose to be a killer. I am now rid of you." She looked down again slowly.

The writer was able to say a word. "God," she said.

"O, yes," the prisoner said, "yes. God gives us this to play with." She raised her hands and ran them down the length of her beautiful body. The prison gown could not hide it.

"May I?" the writer asked.

"May you what?" the prisoner said.

"Touch you," she said. The prisoner stepped around her chair and began to move toward the writer. The guards watching through the glass got ready to enter and intervene. The writer put her hands on the prisoner's shoulders then let them fall to her breasts, then to her hips, then drew them back across her stomach and slowly up to her face which she enclosed in both hands for a moment. Then she let them drop to her own sides. "I do not believe you," she said to the prisoner, "you will never escape this."

"You love me," the prisoner said.

"Yes," the writer said.

"Now," the prisoner said, "if I have fooled you . . . do you see? . . . you will have to kill me . . . or be the evil . . . yourself."

The writer was suspended in space as though waiting for gravity. "Evil how?" she said.

"You are the lie," the prisoner said.

The writer walked back to the other side of the table. "But you haven't fooled me," she said.

The prisoner stood absolutely immobile, then said, "Have you fooled me?"

"I would let you shoot me," the writer answered.

"When could I do that?" the prisoner asked.

"At six a.m.," the writer said. The prisoner waited. "If it's just volts, and not . . ." The prisoner waited again. Then, "Will you know?" she asked.

"I . . . I . . . ," the writer could say nothing.

The prisoner gave a quiet signal to the guards. "I will ask for no hood," she said, and she turned and left.

31st Sunday, Ordinary Tme

Limbo States

Did not one God create us? Why, then,
do we break faith with one another,
profaning the covenant of our ancestors?
—Malachi 2:10

A man came back to his own country under amnesty. He had fled from service in his country's war. The war had been at least a mistake he heard now from many who ran it. At most? . . . a sin, he thought. Not a religious sin. Religion fought the war too. A human sin. But there had been no way of arguing that to a Court. A few years after his return he saw the reintegration of the veterans of that war into society. They were more and more accepted both for their suffering overseas and after, at home, humiliation by their own people. The moral issue was gone, the emotional issue took its place. Groups of veterans simply entered parades with Legionaires, and wore their berets, their fatigues, their medals, and the paraphernalia of the sixties and early seventies that proclaimed a whole genertion as differing from its elders. Then the memorial was built in Washington, a thing of soul, it took you into death itself and showed you the dead written across your own face, the way marble reflected whoever looked at it. And you went down into the earth. And you came back up out of the earth.

The man did this one day. There were hearings going on in Congress, about immigration, and he had become an immigration counselor for a church group. He wanted to lobby some congress people, ask them to be more open in policy toward Mediterraneans, particularly from North Africa, particularly from Christian groups who were caught between terrible forces, Palestinians, Copts, etc. "My name could be here," he thought, "I'm a Smith, there must be dozens." He was walking slowly down the pathway. And there were a cluster of Smiths, and there were three with his

227

name, but a different middle initial. So he put up his hand and traced all three as if they were braille.

"You know them?" a woman said, just off his shoulder. An older woman with her hair tied in a bun in back. She was wearing a trench coat, which she filled well.

"O, no," he said, "same name as mine. Different middle ones."

"This is mine," she said and she reached out and touched the third Smith. "I come here every month. From New York. Can I tell you about him?"

"Yes," the man said and stood back a bit to be beside her.

"He had to serve or go to jail. Small robberies but a lot of them. The judge was a hero from World War II so thought a taste of nobility would cure him. My son never had to steal. He had to have thrills, though. So he went. He was killed in an ambush. And now he's on that wall. He looks so noble there. But not so noble here."

"You loved him," the young man said.

"Yes," she said, "but he never knew what."

"There was something?" the young man asked.

"Yes, there was also a thrill about him, he was like a hunting dog for whom everything was a chase. Even his own tail. But he turned the thrill into . . . what? . . . a right?, a right to steal and screw and turn on. I tell this story every time I come here. To someone different each time. And there is no way out of the story. Like the rounds we sang in school." She paused for a minute. "You are a very peaceful man," she said. "You were not there. You seem to be free of all this."

"I am," he said. She knew enough not to intrude. "But I'm not," he added. "I should come back every month too, touch a different name, and hope someone comes up and tells me what the name means. Maybe that's what's missing here. A relative. This whole wall would become like a final judgment scene, but no judgment, just people, back in life, and . . ."

"Ready to do the same things," she finished for him. "It's what I'd be afraid of, that death teaches nothing."

"It doesn't teach us," he said, "why should it teach them?"

"So you can't help me?" she said.

"I just could not kill," he said. "Nor help to. Nor argue it. I went to Egypt and taught in a religious school. Ten years. And someone said come home and check in. So I did. And I have half a life back. Which I use for refugees. Half I leave dead. I leave it here or in places like it. You see me behind those names. That's where I really am. Reading them backwards. Limbo."

The woman was thinking. "His father was a detective. Surprised some robbers in a store one day. There was a gunfight. Those who saw it thought they were in a movie. He killed three and one killed him but didn't get away, too wounded, so he gave up. It was over a pitiful amount of money, five hundred dollars. O what a funeral! O what ceremony, sermons, volleys, New York's finest, New Jersey's. That's when my son went silly. It should have been hero worship. But he saw me. He saw my look of disgust. He saw it wasn't grief. He heard me tear the kitchen up one night, stupid! stupid! I said, print another five hundred! I'll give you another five hundred! And I grabbed all the souvenirs and I went out in the hallway to the trash chute and I threw the stuff down, the flags, the badges, the citations, O, that night! Then he went on a rampage of his own. Not much, really, a stolen car, a radio, just enough to ruin things. Then sex. Then drink. Then some judge saying you can make it all right if you go do the same things for Uncle Sam."

"Why would you have loved men like that?" the young man said.

"If they are not stupid, they are glorious, glorious fun," she said. "The father was exciting too. They could have been zoo keepers they were there so often. And they were at the Indian Museum every chance they got. He used to teach him how to gumshoe suspects as though the two were tracking Iroquois. Just to know where they were. The two of them found somebody one day off, they found a missing child now grown up. She had been on a milk carton. Then the OK Corral shootout and ugliness replaced the thrill."

"You didn't love the game," the young man said.

"No," she said, "I loved the life." She waited. Then said, "Just as you do."

"We are not left it to love," he said. He reached up and touched the name again. "It's little consolation to know we didn't put him here. We can't take him off."

"So what are we to do?" she said.

"Not shoot," he said, "but we don't do that anyway. Not play games, but we don't do that either. Maybe just love things, stupid or not. But we can't lie. Maybe some silence. Like this marble. With these names written across us. All across us. So they don't vanish. Unless we do. The same way they did."

"Stupidity!" the woman said. Then she stepped forward and put her head against her son's name. And the young man walked further down to the vee point, then back up the other side to go to the hearings. But he could see her facing herself. With her son between.

Tending Irises

*Wisdom herself walks about looking for those
who are worthy of her and graciously shows
herself to them as they go, in every thought
of theirs coming to meet them.*
        —Wisdom 6:16

An old man was tending his irises. An old woman from next door came down to see them. "They're great creatures," he said to her as she stood there looking. "The same since I was a kid, all ears and spilling over like a fountain of themselves." She nodded. "I'll cut you some. Have you got a tall vase?"

She said, "No, and don't cut them. It's a few steps down here and they look nice all together. Graduation."

"Been a long time," he said. "So long I couldn't prove it."

"I never got one," she said. "Never needed one."

"Why was that?" the old man said as he toed some earth around the base of a stalk.

"I matured early," she said. The man recognised the phrase. She meant she had grown breasts and hips long before her classmates and had maybe learned to use them. He looked up from the irises to her. She was as beat up looking as he was. Some patches of skin had been cut out of her face, her hair was still full, but her skin looked like slack sail. "We're a pair," she said.

"We are," he said as he came up beside her on the sidewalk and looked at the row of irises. "They wouldn't want to look at us. Might not want to come back," he concluded.

"My great granddaughter is fourteen. She has them shaking in their boots. Makes a fortune modeling already," the old woman said.

"She's like you?" the old man asked as he reached down to touch one of the flowers swaying toward him in the light breeze.

"Yes," the old woman said. "It's uncanny. Has to be proven with pictures, but that's easy enough."

"There are a lot of yours?" the old man asked.

"Too many," the old woman said.

"You look familiar," the old man said. "Since you moved here I've been trying to guess. Well, not every minute. Just crosses my mind occasionally."

"We don't come back like these," she said, "but wouldn't it be nice."

"They're dumb creatures too," the man said. "I wouldn't want to come back dumb. That's what I was the first time." And he started to laugh a bit. "I used to race anything that would fly. I even raced a guy off a cliff. We dove to see who'd hit first. Arms out, over the head the last second. God! He broke his neck! I had to bring him back to the States quick. Sneak him through in a truck. Underneath. Before they used mirrors. And I put him on his wife's door, rang the bell and ran. I don't know how she explained it. Never went back there. I been running from stuff all my life. This house is luck. Wrote a book about my running." He patted the iris on the head again. "And there were people dumb enough to buy it."

"You're the stunt man," she said. "You flew through those barn doors and under those bridges."

"Yes," he said. "For a few bucks and no insurance."

"I was there at the time," she said.

"Star?" he asked.

"No, stand in for one," she said.

He looked at her openly now. "Hedi?" he asked. "Good old drunken Hedi?"

"Yes," the woman said. "Thought they might see something more if they looked closer at me. But they didn't."

"She lasted a long time," the man said.

"Kept me working," the old woman said, "until . . ."

He waited. "Yes," he said, "that paternity suit. You won it. Ah, what a long time ago. And now you're to a great granddaughter."

"They don't come near me," the old woman said. "My daughter and my granddaughter were Puritan straight. Both had their noses bobbed to hide their faces. But the nose came back in the young one. And they're having a fit."

"You can't have been that bad!" the old man said.

"I was until my face was carved," she said. "Maybe twenty years ago. My skin turned into a time bomb. Still is. But let it. It's one way out. And one it'll have to be."

"Why the switch?" he asked.

"O," she said, "I was in the hospital. And my face was wrapped up like a mummy's. There were others and were we depressed! So we started to read fairy tales. About the ugly lady who married the prince to test his virtue. Then turned into a raving beauty by morning when he woke up doomed to a bitter life. Then we switched the stories and the beauty of the night turned into a beast of the morning. So I wrote a couple of them down. Made them like science fiction, though, not medieval. And they made a fortune. I do them all the time now. I can switch anything."

The old man was chuckling. "People were living off us. Now we're living off them."

"Maybe another day or so," the woman said. "Where are we going then? Into a bulb?"

"That's really what turned you," the old man said, "not the fairy tales."

"She was in the same hospital," the old woman said. "I found out by chance. Only my face was harmed. So when they took the bandages off and sanded me a bit, I went up to see her. She was in a detox room. They let me in. She saw me and she flipped, broke to pieces, like a hallucination, begging me not to take over her body and turn her ugly. Like I was Dorian Gray. And I saw if she did not stay beautiful she had to go crazy. Not die. Go crazy to keep the illusion. So I put my arms around her. And I made up a story. I said I had come in and taken the ugliness off her body and onto my own, and I would leave with it. And every time some blemish came she could call me and I would come and take it. She calmed and I left. She died ten years ago. She sent for me and asked me to take it from her. I said yes, now go to sleep. And she did and never woke."

"We're going to find out soon enough," the old man said. "It's not bulbs. I really never knew if I'd crash those barns right. And those bridges had funny air under them."

"I want to know," the old woman said. "If it's a blank screen . . . Or I come back with the same nose . . ." She didn't finish.

"I want something, if I could ever have it," the old man said. "That dive. I want to surface spitting water and see him spitting water. He was the only one I ever loved. She hated me. But she never turned me in. I kept looking over my shoulder. She let me live. I want to see her for what I can say. I want to say something. Not over a grave. A grave is like a bulb. It's dumb too." An iris head was moving against his hand under the wind, like something feeding, a bird.

"Well," the old woman said, "I will go back to my house now. I have some checks to send them. They don't return the checks anymore. Maybe that's a sign."

"It would be nice if it were," the old man said.

Bear Market

It is when people are saying, 'How quiet
and peaceful it is' that the worst sud-
denly happens . . . and there will be no
way for anybody to evade it.
—1 Thessalonians 5:3

A man lost a fortune on a day the stock market dropped like a rock. Lost it in the morning in fact. Half by eleven, half by one. It was like watching an egg roll off the other side of a table. Then hearing it splat. Actually comic. He was laughing by one. It was paper when he started, it was paper again.

"I'm hungry," he thought. So he went out and first time ever stopped at a hot dog cart. The hot dog guy was busy, but noticed everyone and let them know he'd get to them, a remark to this one, jerk of the head to that, finally came to the man and said, "Smoking? No smoking?"

"No," the man said.

"This side, with me," the guy said, "wind's that way, what'll it be?"

"Jumbo dog," the man said, "with everything and extra napkins."

"I got good buns," the guy said, "don't worry, I import them."

"Japan?" the man asked. "I'll buy stock."

"No, Jersey," the guy said. "Some Russians over there. They came up one day and said we got a leak-proof. Every day. On the spot. We wait for you. Look, mustard on, ketchup, relish, onions, now shake it, no, careful a bit, nothin's perfect, see!"

"Ah, but the bite's the test, the hole in the dike," the man said.

"Okay, so bite, I'll stand right here, run the risk too, my best workpants."

235

The man bit. Just right. Then he looked. No ooze. "How they do it?" he asked.

"Hard outside, soft inside. It soaks and it holds," the guy said.

"Like the old ball park roll for the dogs," the man said.

"Naw, naw, those old things used to split at the hinges," the guy said. "My wife had one go right down her blouse. Jesus I laughed. She was left holding the two halves. She pulled the dog out and we were roaring. She put it down my neck. So I pulled off my shirt right there and that damn thing bounced like a rubber ball. Good she didn't eat it. She smelled mustard for a week."

"Give me another one," the man said. "I may never eat again."

"Wait a sec," the guy said and served three or four others who had lined up meantime. "You want some drink?" he then said to the man.

"Yes, a beer," the man said, "you have one?"

"Grab one there and open it yourself," the guy said.

"No label on it," the man said.

"It's Russian too, same people, homemade, don't tell anybody, but see how good it is, black as a bear."

The man swigged out of the bottle. There was a little crowd around the stand so he had to be careful of his elbow. "It's a meal," he said to the guy who was serving.

"So what's next?" the guy said between shoveling out hot dogs, making change, and opening beers. "You go off a bridge?"

"Never," the man said, "these dogs are too good. And this beer. Cops know about it?"

"They love it, ride up on a horse and call it ginger juice. They say it's horse piss I owe them back."

"Give me just one more dog," the man said, "to go with the rest of this beer."

"Careful you don't get a belly," the guy said getting one ready. Other people were crowding around, but eating quickly and running. "Geez, what are you people doing in there? Maybe I should put up the umbrella. Break a few falls and save my cart."

"Nobody jumps," the man said through a mouthful. "The beach house goes, that's all. You move down to a Lincoln Continental. And you move in with your girl friend or your boy friend. Then you huff and puff another year and the balloon fills again."

"You do that?" the guy said, still busy and talking over his shoulder.

"Done it twice already," the man said.

"It's good for me," the guy said, "lookit business, and you meet people." There was more business.

The man had finished the dog and had a few more gulps of beer to go. He burped behind his hand.

"You're class," the guy said noticing him. "You couldn't live poor. You gotta go back." He wasn't being mean.

"Who eats more than three hot dogs?" the man answered. "Who sleeps in two beds?"

"Right," the guy said. Then, "All out, lady, sorry, all out fella." He slammed a few lids. "I better get more tomorrow. You think it'll be like this? I got some stock, you know. AT&T. They go up and down but not like a yoyo. Like my wife when she breathes at night. I can still smell that mustard."

"It won't be like this," the man said. "They'll be at MacDonald's tomorrow. Next day at Mama Leone's."

"You sure are cool," the guy said beginning to clean his cart top with a rag. The man reached a twenty dollar bill to the cart guy. "This enough?" he asked.

"Yup," said the guy, "owe you seven back."

"Keep it," the man said.

"Never take tips," the guy said, "but thanks. I got a box in front for something though, if you want."

"What for?" the man asked.

"For deaf people. My daughter's deaf. She's got these machines, though, and she owns the world."

"Love their hands," the man said as he put the finished beer bottle back in the cart. "Definitely horse piss," he said.

"So what do you do now, honest?" the guy asked, leaning like a bartender on the cleaned cart top.

"First I pay. That's absolute. Keep trust alive. Then I borrow against what I have left. Then I figure on slow fluctuations. Like watching heads bob at Coney Island in the water, figure the crest before it comes and buy, then sell at crest and watch who gets stuck in the trough. But it's no fun anymore. Not for myself anyway. When I get enough again I quit."

"Yeah?" said the guy with interest. "Then what?"

"Well," the man said, "you know I always liked the idea of digging things up. In Mexico out in the jungles there are some places lost. Loaded with great things. Great stories. Love to learn how to do it. Go back to school and learn."

"Nobody home so you can go?" the guy asked.

"Everybody home so I can't," the man said. "Almost made it this time, though. Hate to say it but family can be bought."

"Ah, it shouldn't be," the guy said. "Mine can't."

"So you can't come dig with me?" the man asked. He backed away a bit so the guy could unlock the back wheel on the cart and get ready to move.

"You gonna do it?" the guy said then. "You don't look tough enough."

"Takes brains, not brawn," the man said, "yes, I'm going to do it, have them bought off in a year. I'll come buy a hot dog and say hasta la vista."

"You work for this company here?" the guy said thumbing toward the building above them.

"It works for me," the man said.

The guy got a funny look on his face. "Don't believe it," he said.

"My card, sir," the man said, and showed him his driver's license.

"You must have lost a billion," the guy said.

"Have it back soon," the man said. "See you before I go."

"I'll wait," the guy said, "right here."

Feast of Christ the King

Just a Mosaic

. . . and the last of the enemies to be
destroyed is death.
— 1 Corinthians 15:26

"You're no judge," a woman said. "You're no jury either." She was talking to a mosaic above an altar, Jesus The All Ruler At The End Of Time. "And you're no help." She couldn't accept what had happened. She was as good looking as her. Every bit as alive. He just walked out. Got in her old car. And she drove off with him. This vacation would heal her some, her friends said, go away on your own and look at beauty, spend something on yourself, break the obsession. Here she was in Palermo. At Monreale outside. And there he was over the altar. With a lick of hair loose from the part down the center. With luscious brown eyes, luscious red mouth, luscious beard. "Oh, you hurt," she said, "you friend of my life."

Men were really staring at her. How could anybody be spiritual and that lovely. What's she doing in a place like this? "Praying for someone's soul," she said half aloud to a couple of men who kept circling her, eating her like a honeycomb. "Well, I have to decide," she said looking back up at Jesus The All Ruler. "He gets no divorce. So he gets no money. Not from me anyway. Why should I give up what I love?" She walked a bit, looked up at the jewel box ceiling, then at the back wall covered with scenes from Genesis. Adam and Eve and the tree and the snake. Then the Lord seated on a blue sphere raising a hand in judgment. Then Adam and Eve in animal skins hoeing the ground. "So I yank him back to Eden with me," she said. "O what? What? What's a love that goes off like fog? Why don't I? This is what you don't understand," she said. "He could walk back in. He'd know something, though."

239

She went back toward the altar. "What would he know? I think he'd know damnation. I think I'd damn him without saying a word. I think I would just love him and that would damn him." She stopped. "That's what you do, isn't it? It's what I do. Keep the pressure on. No divorce. I love you too much." She listened a minute. "Okay, so I should live the hell. To do him good. But you don't." Her old friend didn't move. "Okay, he gets the divorce, but you be sure you save him through it."

She left the church and went on a bus back down the mountain to Palermo and her hotel. At midnight, she called her lawyer in New York and told him not to block the divorce any further. Her lawyer's voice was strange, he let her speak without saying yes or no or why. She sensed it. "What is it?" she said.

"I've tried to reach you," he said. "You've been moving so much."

"What?" she said.

"He took his own life yesterday, at her place, and we can't find her, she called the Police, and she's gone."

"O love," the woman said and she fell back in the chair with the phone against her chest. He could hear her. It took a long time for her to speak again. "I'll come," she said, "he's still mine. Can you find her?"

"Police are looking," he said.

"I mean you, can you?" she asked again.

"I wouldn't know where to look," he said.

"I would," she said, "and I'll tell you. She knows how to live on the street. She did sidewalk drawings for money. People gave her canvas and she made money off some very raw stuff. He met her at a show and it was her raw stuff he wanted. So she's back on the street. She may be so dirty again she's invisible. You'll have to look in the Village."

"I'll tell the Police," the lawyer said. "You don't have to rush back, they'll hold his body for autopsy, three or four more days. And it's suicide, nobody faked this one."

"You have to rush," the woman said. He waited. "She's not raw," she said. He waited more. "She came out of an institution. Do you understand?"

"No," he said.

"She can take her own life also," the woman continued.

"Tell me how you know this," the lawyer said, "I'm not doubting you, but just tell me how you know."

"I had to find out," the woman said. "I had to know who could do this to me, who could just drive away with him. I saw her plate, I saw her number, I found her apartment, I watched out of windows and doors. I came close to killing her or killing myself."

"But not him?" the lawyer asked.

"No," the woman said and again said nothing while he heard her controlling her grief. "How could I? How could I her either? How could I myself? So find her and tell her not to. Tell her I told her don't, don't, I'll do something."

"Okay," the lawyer said, "I'll go out right now. You won't leave for another ten hours or so. Book your flight over the phone. I'll get you at this number. And rest. You're facing some hard days."

The woman hung up. And she stayed in that chair the remainder of the night, in and out of sleep and sorrow. Toward six, the phone rang her awake. She answered and it was the lawyer.

"We found her. She's nuts again. Makes no sense. She mimes the destruction of the world. Says some words from Bible then mimes them. This is not fake either."

"She did that before she was let out," the woman said. "Her paintings were the opposite. Like the beginning of the world."

"You saw them?" the lawyer asked.

"Yes, how could I not?" the woman answered.

"He left you for her?" the lawyer said before he thought not to say it. The breath went out of her. "I can't take that back," he said, "I wish I could."

"It's my question too," she said. "I think I was the end of something for him. I think she was the beginning. And I think she began to crack again before he shot himself. Yes, I think. And there was no way back to me. I was holding this against him. And he had no way to help her. Because she was his salvation." She was speaking between breaths.

The lawyer said, "It's too early for that kind of thinking."

"She's still alive," the woman said.

"Yes, but . . . ," he said.

She cut in gently, "Where is she?"

"At St. Vincent's," he said, "Police brought her there."

"Okay," the woman said, "you have the key to my house. Go in and down cellar, the stairs off the kitchen, and find the wine closet. In it are several of her canvases. Don't ask me where I got them. Show them to the staff there. Give them something early to work on. And you assume her bills. All my money is useless to me." She broke for a few minutes.

"Who's going to care for you?" he asked. She didn't answer. "You want me to come over and get you?" he asked further. "I could be there by tomorrow noon." She still didn't answer. "Just stay there, okay?" he said. "There's a day flight. Concorde. I'll get to you by tonight." Nothing from her. "Please say something," he said.

"Sorry," she said, "I was thinking about your question 'Who's going to care for me?' You know, I can't answer that. Yes, come today, I'll wait and have a room for you. I can spend the day with Jesus The All Ruler."

Now he said nothing but she could feel his worry over the phone. "Just a mosaic," she said. "I got to talking to one yesterday. A way of talking to myself."

"I don't know it, the one there, I know Ravenna," he said, "kind of cold, aren't they, those mosaics?"

"Yes, but not this one," she said, "this one looks like him."

"Don't go back," the lawyer said.

"He looks like me also," she said. "If he'd shave."

"Tell him not to," the lawyer said. "One of you may be enough."

And a Burning Match

My dear people, we are already children
of God but what we are to be in the
future has not yet been revealed;
    —1 John 3:2

A man was waiting for the elevator on the ground floor of his office building. He had just had lunch alone to think a case through. His client was to see him later in the afternoon. The elevator door opened and the Wicked Witch Of The West came out rattling a tin cup and screeching, "Give! Give!" The sign on the cup said Muscular Dystrophy. So the man fished in his coat pocket for the change from lunch, a few crumpled bills, and put them in the Wicked Witch's tin cup. "That's it, that's it," said the Wicked Witch, "money shouldn't make a sound, a sound!" The elevator door closed leaving the man to wait for another trip. And the Witch too. Who must have been a man because the two bumped shoulders as they reached to push the call button and the Witch was hard as a rock. Like a line-backer. Several people showed up to wait also and the Witch worked them for donations, but you could hear their money, quarters and dimes. They all got in for the ride up to floor thirty-nine and beyond. And the Witch kept humming in a scratchy voice, "Somewhere, under the rainbow, there's a pot of gold, hee, hee!"

So the man said, "Say, ol' buddy Witch, you get caught at this and you'll be pushing a broom not flying one."

"It's okay, pal," said the Witch, "I own the fortieth floor. Just over your head."

The man was surprised. "How come this?" he asked.

The Witch said, "I lost a bet. So I have to beg for charity. And do it so nobody knows who I really am."

"Who'd you lose the bet to?" asked the man.

"My daughter," said the Witch.

"Some bet," said the man.

"Right," said the Witch. "She bet I'd forget her birthday." The man laughed and so did the elevator which eased to a halt at thirty-nine to let the man out.

"She must be watching," he said to the Witch as the door started to close.

"And counting," said the Witch as the door clunked shut.

The man nearly bumped into one of his law partners in the corridor. "What's with the Wicked Witch?" she asked.

"Muscular Dystrophy," the man said. "Paying off a bet. His daughter's idea. Must be a little kid. He owns the floor above."

"Oh, that guy!" said the man's partner. "His daughter is twenty-five years old. She's in and out of an institution every six months."

"Wow," said the man. And the two of them didn't say anything for a space. They could feel the bruise of the guy. "And it's Halloween," the man said. "Perfect. That's the way to switch a Witch. Talk to you later."

"Not with lines like that," she said, and hit the down button on the elevator. Which opened as if by magic and there was the Wicked Witch again, shrugging his hard shoulders and waving the empty cup. "Couple of more times and I'm free," he said. The door closed and the Witch and the man's partner were gone.

"Free of what?" the man said to the closed door. "It's Halloween all the time." There was a note marked URGENT on his desk in the office. CALL YOUR WIFE. Which he did and she said he simply had to cut out early from work and pick up costumes for the children, her car wouldn't start, and pick up the children.

"Be sure to get the right wolf mask for Jimmy," she said, "the one with the extra long fangs or the world will stop. And get the right witch mask for Jeannie. The one with the extra long hook nose, or you can forget a friend forever."

"Don't worry," he said, "I know wolves, I have them in here every day. And I just had a long talk with the Wicked Witch of The West in the elevator. You can count on me." The phone was silent.

"You okay?" she asked.

"No," he answered. "I'm supposed to judge at four if a guy is crazy or not, responsable or not, and I'm supposed to inform the Court by seven, and in between I have to pick up a wolf mask and a witch mask so my two kids can trick or treat."

"I'll take a cab in and meet you," she said.

"I wish you would," he said. "I'll have two horns on my head and pointy earlobes and a forked beard and I'll be holding a burning match!"

"Oh, oh, emergency," she said. "Next siren you hear will be me. Just tie a tourniquet around your neck and don't breathe until I get there."

"It's done," he said, "but get here before four. I want you to see this client. He looks sweeter than wine, but I think he's a brute."

"Right," she said, "but all I have is intuition. Not very good for the Courts."

"Let me tell you something about the Courts," he said. "But see if you can get those masks on the way in. It'll save us time. Kids don't like to wait."

"I think I won't," she said, "I think I won't get any masks for anybody."

"Are *you* okay?" the man asked.

"No," she answered, "no. I think I'm also not. I think I don't want to let the kids do this."

"You'll be the monster," the man said. "Twenty years from now they'll keep psychiatry in business. Better to play the monster than be one."

"You really think so?" she asked.

"No, I don't," he answered. "What'll we do?"

"Whatever we do we'll pay for it," she said.

"Look," he said, "maybe we could dress them as Mickey and Minnie Mouse."

"That's last century," she said.

"How about E.T. and his sister Bessie?" he asked again.

"Hasn't got a sister," she answered.

"Isn't there anything loveable around that wears a mask?" he asked. She could hear the tears in his voice. So she said, "This is no good over the phone. I'll get a cab. And no masks for the kids. So get ready to do some explaining."

"Well," he said, "there's this guy on the floor above. He owns it. His daughter's disturbed. She has him riding elevators collecting for Muscular Dystrophy. And she waits at the elevator to count the take. He's the Wicked Witch Of The West. She's twenty-five and can maybe count to ten. And he does it, ride up and down. And he makes sense to me. But I wouldn't want to explain it to two kids." There was dead silence on the phone.

"You listening?" he asked.

"Yes," she answered. "That's too close to life."

"Exactly," he said. "And it's what we all do. I wonder what I look like going up and down on that elevator."

"You want me to tell you?" she asked.

"No, you're biased," he answered. "The Court does not accept your testimony. Instead the Court orders you to get in a cab right now and come down here. You will be held in contempt if you don't."

"Will you know what I look like?" she asked.

"Yes," he answered, "yes. You'll have horns on your head like mine and long earlobes and a burning match in your hand."

"But no beard," she said.

"I hope not," he said.

Nice Kisser

The Lord will wipe away the tears from
every cheek.
                    —Isaiah 25:8

"What a cold wake!" a woman said to her husband as they were leaving the funeral parlor.

"Like this snow," he said turning his face up to it.

"Didn't seem like death," she said, "more like an airport. Departures. Delayed. Brrr!"

"They've always been like that," he said. "Maybe not when they read the will. Snow's wet too. Nice kisses." He still had his face up.

"You've read it?" she asked.

"Had to," he said. "I have to check all sueable work we draw."

"What'll happen?" she asked.

"They'll try to break it. Left them nothing. We'll get wet. Come. You drive."

"Don't tease me," she said, "I can't imagine."

"Well," he said, "apparently she was disappointed in them. Wanted them to be movers and shakers. They all tried, ex-nun, ex-priest, ex-pol, one's a doctor but plays golf all the time, works for an insurance company."

"She have a lot?" the woman asked.

"A lot more than they know. She never told. About five million," he said.

"Wow," she said softly, "where'd she get that?"

"Promise you won't tell?" he asked.

"Not even you," she said.

"Prohibition. The husband ran liquor until scared off by the mob. He hid the money in a Swiss bank. It just grew there. She was ashamed of it, I guess, but kept it. So that's fifty years of interest."

"Government will get it," she said.

"Nope," he said. "It all goes to the Vatican. Propagation of the Faith. They'll have to sue the Vatican."

"Will the Vatican take it?" she asked.

"Not if it smells," he said.

"The children don't know it does," she said.

"So don't tell anybody," he said. They were at the car. She unlocked his side, opened the door, took him by the arm in mock help and said, "Now watch your head." He made some feeble sounds and said, "May God bless you."

They were moving out of the parking lot, blinker left, waiting for a stream to pass, when she said, "So she won't be dead when they find out."

"No," he said. "She'll be like a tatoo on a sailor's arm. She'll be alive with every move they make."

She turned into traffic. "She's awful."

Her husband looked at her.

"Maybe they won't contest," she continued.

"They will," he said, "but not for the money. To wipe her out for good, I guess. They might even give the money away if they win."

"Brrr," she said again. "It's all so dull."

"Your father was so different," he said. "I guess he spoiled you."

She saw a parking space through the wipers and pulled over with an easy motion. "I'm sorry," he said, "don't talk to the driver." He reached over and put his mouth right on her wet face. She started to laugh as well as cry.

"Right," she said, "this is what he did. I can't laugh but I cry, I can't cry but I laugh."

"Nice kisser," her husband said, "he was right."

"I thought he was gone," she said. "Mom did too and she just backed away. I think to catch him going out the door. I wanted to kiss him warm. So he says it after and scares us, then we all howled and he was gone in the howl, the crazy, crazy . . ."

"I'll drive," her husband said.

"No," she said, "just give me a wipe." She turned her face. "And he knew it was me. I think his last rumble was a laugh. Frig the phlegm. Okay, I drive."

She pulled out and headed off again. "He fooled around but you always knew he felt things. His words went one way but his body the other. My first prom I had this low cut gown and my breasts were right for it and I thought he might get mad, but he didn't, he came up and with the backs of his hands he pressed me on both and said, 'They're fine.' He waited a sec and said, 'Kisser's better,' and he gave me this one next to my eye so he wouldn't spoil the makeup. Then he said, 'Knockout!' Well, I was as free as a bird from then on. I remember I put on these jeans with a paint can later. My bottom was ready now. So I sassed by him. He was on the phone in the hallway and I was going out the door. 'Nice,' he said to me over the phone conversation. Then, 'No, my daughter's ass,' to someone, 'she's just leaving to wreck the world. You should see her face. No survivors.' O!" and she pulled over gently again. "He never said things to my mother. He could touch her, so it was always that, and never raw. He used to put his hands on her chest when they'd be figuring something out. Or he'd have her hand and hold it down on his shoulder like Michelangelo's David with the slingshot. Amazing! His body was all grace. His words were chunky. Where he grew up they had to be."

"Listen, let me drive," he said.

"No," she said, "I get us home. That's enough from me." She pulled out again. "Back there," she said, "I thought of those ice cube machines. The ones that rattle and bang out cubes every few minutes. In cafeterias. Generation unto generation."

"They're really good people," he said, "I hope they stay that way, though I think they may not."

"It's a dumb will," she said, "she doesn't really mean the Vatican. She means not them. That's a sin. Not the money. The motive."

"I've said we shouldn't put up much of a fight," he answered. "Vatican will hire someone. It'll all be overseas. My idea is to let the will stand, have the Vatican then give the money to the children, save years and millions."

"You'd have to get to the Pope," she said.

"They would," he said. "Embarrass him out of it."

"You mean the dirty money story," she said.

"Yes," he said, "we could leak it."

"What happened to the old man?" she asked.

"Died in dubious circumstances," he said.

"Like what?" she asked.

"He was fishing alone off Nahant. Thunder storm came up. Not a bad one. Boat was found upside down on some rocks when the tide went out. He was found later at the water line."

"That can happen," she said.

"You don't fish in pin stripe trousers," he said, "and in dress shoes and silk tie."

"How do you know this?" she asked.

"We had to trace the money. It turned up a lot else."

"What a sad night!" she said as she turned into their driveway. She switched off the wipers, then the lights, then the ignition. The snow began to fill in the arc left by the wipers. Wet snow, fat flakes. They watched. "Nice," she said, "nice. You remember the ending of Joyce's 'The Dead?'"

"Yes," he said.

"Snow is the dead coming back," she said.

"Is that Joyce or you?" he asked.

"Poor man's manure," she said.